Hugh MacDiarmid's Poetry and Politics of Place

Hugh MacDiarmid's Poetry and Politics of Place

Imagining a Scottish Republic

Scott Lyall

Edinburgh University Press

© Scott Lyall, 2006

Edinburgh University Press Ltd
22 George Square, Edinburgh

Typeset in 10.5/13 Adobe Sabon
by Servis Filmsetting Ltd, Manchester, and
printed and bound in Great Britain by
Biddles Ltd, King's Lynn, Norfolk

A CIP record for this book is available from the British Library

ISBN-10 0 7486 2334 5 (hardback)
ISBN-13 978 0 7486 2334 1 (hardback)

Contents

For my father
Daniel Ewan Cameron Lyall,
and
In memory of my mother
Elizabeth Thomson Lyall
(1944–2003)

Acknowledgements

Much of the research and writing for this book was done at the University of St Andrews, where for three years I benefited from scholarship funding from The Carnegie Trust for the Universities of Scotland. It was a pleasure to have Robert Crawford and Douglas Dunn oversee my doctoral research at the School of English there, and this book has gained much from their insight, ideas and suggestions, as it has, too, from being read in an earlier form by Christopher MacLachlan. Alan Riach also read this book at various stages, giving valuable counsel and much appreciated encouragement to seek publication; his own work in the field of MacDiarmid studies, particularly as the General Editor of Carcanet's MacDiarmid 2000 series, made that much more of a possibility. I thank Carcanet Press Ltd, on behalf of the poet's estate, for their kind permission to quote from this admirable collection, and the editors of *Scottish Studies Review* (Volume 5, Number 2) and *The International Review of Scottish Studies* (Volume 29), in which parts of Chapters 1 and 3 appear in a different guise. Material from the NLS archives is published with the generous assent of the Trustees of the National Library of Scotland. I am very grateful to Dorian Grieve for kindly providing the photographic frontispiece of his grandfather in Whalsay; my appreciation also goes to Graham Stephen for allowing me to use Edward Baird's remarkable *Unidentified Aircraft over Montrose* as a cover image.

A one-year Irish Higher Education Authority-funded postdoctoral research fellowship in English, in the Centre for Irish–Scottish Studies, Trinity College, Dublin gave me the opportunity to complete the writing of this book; I am grateful to the School of English at TCD, most particularly to Ian Campbell Ross, co-director of the Centre for Irish–Scottish Studies, for his assistance and advice. Many thanks also to George Davie for the privilege of discussing his friend, Chris Grieve, with me; to Brian Smith of Shetland Archives and Jacqueline Irvine of Whalsay History Group for their helpful guidance in Shetland, to Mamie

Morrison of the Langholm Library and to the librarians and archivists of Montrose Library and Angus Archives.

I am indebted to my family for generosity, help and kindness, and especially want to thank Christine Charles, Jenny Lyall and Maurice and Betty Lyall. For teaching me more than can be learnt from any book, this book is gratefully dedicated to those to whom I owe most: to my father, Danny, for his never failing support, and to the memory of my late mother, Liz. It grieves me deeply that she did not live to read this book; I hope something of her own republican spirit survives in its pages.

Abbreviations of Works by Hugh MacDiarmid

A   *Albyn: Shorter Books and Monographs*, ed. Alan Riach (Manchester: Carcanet, 1996).

Annals   *Annals of the Five Senses and Other Stories, Sketches and Plays*, eds Roderick Watson and Alan Riach (Manchester: Carcanet, 1999).

Company   *The Company I've Kept: Essays in Autobiography* (London: Hutchison, 1966).

CP1   *Complete Poems, Volume I*, eds Michael Grieve and W. R. Aitken (Manchester: Carcanet, 1993).

CP2   *Complete Poems, Volume II*, eds Michael Grieve and W. R. Aitken (Manchester: Carcanet, 1994).

CSS   *Contemporary Scottish Studies*, ed. Alan Riach ([1926] Manchester: Carcanet, 1995).

GT   *The Golden Treasury of Scottish Poetry*, ed. Hugh MacDiarmid ([1940] London: Macmillan, 1948).

Islands   *The Islands of Scotland: Hebrides, Orkneys, and Shetland* (London: Batsford, 1939).

L   *The Letters of Hugh MacDiarmid*, ed. Alan Bold (London: Hamish Hamilton, 1984).

LP   *Lucky Poet: A Self-Study in Literature and Political Ideas*, ed. Alan Riach ([1943] Manchester: Carcanet, 1994).

MR   *The Montrose Review* (reporter, 1919–20; editor–reporter, 1921–9).

NSL   *New Selected Letters*, eds Dorian Grieve, O. D. Edwards and Alan Riach (Manchester: Carcanet, 2001).

Revolutionary   *The Revolutionary Art of the Future: Rediscovered Poems*, eds John Manson, Dorian Grieve and Alan Riach (Manchester: Carcanet, in association with the Scottish Poetry Library, 2003).

RS   *Red Scotland* [1936], corrected typescript in the National Library of Scotland, Edinburgh, NLS MS27035.

RT1   *The Raucle Tongue: Hitherto Uncollected Prose, Volume I: 1911–1926*, eds Angus Calder, Glen Murray and Alan Riach (Manchester: Carcanet, 1996).

RT2   *The Raucle Tongue: Hitherto Uncollected Prose, Volume II: 1927–1936*, eds Angus Calder, Glen Murray and Alan Riach (Manchester: Carcanet, 1997).

RT3   *The Raucle Tongue: Hitherto Uncollected Prose, Volume III: 1937–1978*, eds Angus Calder, Glen Murray and Alan Riach (Manchester: Carcanet, 1998).

SE   *Scottish Eccentrics*, ed. Alan Riach ([1936] Manchester: Carcanet, 1993).

SS   *Scottish Scene; or The Intelligent Man's Guide to Albyn*, co-authored with Lewis Grassic Gibbon (Bath: Cedric Chivers, 1934).

A Note on the Text

Christopher Murray Grieve (1892–1978) was born in Langholm, but his main pseudonym, Hugh MacDiarmid, first appeared in Montrose in 1922. Throughout a long and varied writing career, Grieve adopted many pseudonymous masks under which he wrote poetry, plays, cultural criticism, two autobiographies, journalism, private and public letters along with political essays, speeches and propaganda. When quoting from his works, I am careful to pinpoint the specific identity of the author – whether Grieve, MacDiarmid or otherwise.

SHETLAND

Whalsay

Lerwick

Foula

Orkney

St Kilda

Kildermorie

Inverness

Aberdeen

Kirriemuir *Montrose*

Forfar

Dundee

Perth St Andrews

Cupar

Clydebank

Glasgow Edinburgh

Strathaven

Biggar Hawick

Langholm

SCOTLAND

MacDiarmid's Places

Imagining a Scottish Republic

I

> I once thought I would have done better in London, or Cape Canaveral, or Hollywood even. I had been taught that history was made in a few important places by a few important people who manufactured it for the good of the rest. But the Famous Few have no power now but the power to threaten and destroy and history is what we all make, everywhere, each moment of our lives, whether we notice it or not.[1]

Emerging from his emotional nadir, Jock McLeish reaches this understanding of the centrality of place to his personal growth close to the conclusion of Alasdair Gray's *1982 Janine*. By painfully gaining this ultimate acceptance of home, Jock, the Scottish Everyman, signals his willingness to proceed in a realistic yet hopeful manner with his life in actively local terms. Learning to refuse the self-hating escape clause of misogynistic fantasy, for Jock life is positively not elsewhere. The 'process' (as Marshall Walker puts it) of Jock's renewal also marks the beginning of the end for the Scottish cringe.[2]

Published in 1984, the anachronistic date of the title relates Gray's novel to the Falklands War of March–June 1982 – a British victory with echoes of imperial grandeur that paved the way for Margaret Thatcher's second-term General Election landslide of 9 June 1983. Jock is at war with himself at the same time as Britain is at war with Argentina for the Falkland Islands, a place he describes as a 'remote souvenir of the Great Britisher's Empire'.[3] But it is actually Scotland's state-sponsored failure to gain some measure of political independence from this crumbling imperial edifice that helps to ignite, and stands as a symbol of, Jock's suicidal battle with himself. The disappointment of the Devolution Referendum of 1 March 1979 followed on from Scottish Labour backbencher George Cunningham's 25 January 1978 amendment to the Scotland Act, which stated that 40 per cent of the registered electorate would have to vote Yes for devolution to be granted. In a 64 per cent turnout, 52 per cent voted Yes and 48 per cent No, meaning only 33 per cent of the electorate voted in favour of devolution. Carried through despite the opposition of the majority of Scottish MPs, Cunningham's jiggery-pokery with the democratic system not only denied Scotland devolutionary democracy but also, through the subsequent vote of no confidence of 28 March 1979 that would bring down the Labour government, helped usher Thatcher into power. The fantasy soaked repression of the Conservative-voting Jock McLeish is symptomatic of Scotland's self-repressed state.

In his Epilogue to *1982 Janine*, Gray cites the influence of Hugh MacDiarmid's *A Drunk Man Looks at the Thistle* – like Gray's novel, a poem that sees 'Scotland refracted through alcoholic reverie'.[4] Poem and novel have more in common than an inebriated narrator, however. While *1982 Janine* is set at the time of the Falklands War, its immediate historical background is the 1978–9 Winter of Discontent and the devolution referendum. Published in 1926, *A Drunk Man* deals with that year's General Strike and, while it grows in political impetus out of MacDiarmid's frustrated dissatisfaction with the first Labour government's failure to promote Home Rule for Scotland in 1924, the poem's modernism has its roots in the Great War.

International conflict (as the ultimate expression of imperialism), the inhibiting of Scottish self-determination and class discord – each of these lineaments of power relations informs MacDiarmid's poem and Gray's novel. Yet both artworks are more concerned with how these aspects of power manifest themselves internally, affecting the emotional innards of the individual Scot. Attentive, ultimately, to the personal politics of inner place, *A Drunk Man* and *1982 Janine* treat of the Scottish soul.

In this regard, a key connection is Thomas Carlyle (1795–1881). Epically modernist, *A Drunk Man* conducts an inner search for the metaphysical Scot who will save his people by heroically transcending his own commonality, while the clothes philosophy of *Sartor Resartus* (1833–4) is given pornographic postmodern resonance in *1982 Janine*.[5] As Jock's 'silly soul',[6] Janine contains the eternal possibilities of affirmation and negation – 'Ja/Nein', Yes/No – encountered by Professor Teufelsdröckh in *Sartor Resartus*. *1982 Janine* could be interpreted as a *Sartor Resartus* for the postindustrial era, seeking in the face of the deathly nexus of universal militarism to affirm, to say Yes, yet resisting the reinscription of Carlyle's masculinist, Victorian authoritarianism, as endorsed in *On Heroes, Hero-Worship, and the Heroic in History* (1841). *A Drunk Man* dissolves the reactionary element of Carlyle in the demotic of a specific locality, the spiky irony of Jean's Scottish humour deflating her drunken husband's individualistic flights of metaphysical fancy, so grounding him in loving relation to home. Both beginning in Dostoevskian (self) contempt, the Drunk Man and Jock McLeish learn to embrace the feminine principle of the soul, affirming the particularity of their lives and so accepting the multiple affiliations of authentic selfhood. As the Drunk Man realises, this entails the acknowledgement of spiralling responsibilities:

> I dinna say that bairns alane
> Are true love's task – a sairer task
> Is aiblins to create oorsels   [*perhaps*]
> As we can be – it's that I ask.
>
> (*CP1*, 113)

Finding the expression of our individuality in relation with others leads us outwards from the self: first we 'Create oorsels, syne [*then*] bairns, syne race' (*CP1*, 114). With a narrator who discovers the emotional resources to say Yes to the possibilities of a fuller self, *1982 Janine* follows *A Drunk Man* in the suggestion that such personal development can be the foundation of communal change. If the self-abuse of his soul committed by Jock once symbolised a national malaise, then the Yes/No options represented by Janine are also those appearing on a devolution referendum ballot paper. To create one's self anew is also to imagine the potential for a different nation.

Speaking in Dundee in 1994, the then Labour leader John Smith (1938–94) used legalistic language to formulate devolution as 'the settled will of the Scottish people'. None the less, democracy requires that the devolution achieved in 1997 remains a contested constitutional framework. MacDiarmid's idea of a Scottish Republic may seem to necessitate at least an element of wish fulfilment in order to have electoral plausibility in a nation that stubbornly adheres to the Union, and gives continued allegiance to the 'glamour of backwardness' that Tom Nairn describes as the most distinguishing feature of Ukanian royalism.[7] But the depressingly dreich sight of Scotland's newly elected representatives being ordered to rise for the Queen at the opening of the devolved Scottish Parliament at Edinburgh's Mound in 1999, some only taking the pledge to Her Majesty under protest that their real loyalty lay with the sovereign people of Scotland, then singing along with Sheena Wellington's rendition of Burns's egalitarian 'For a' that and a' that', indicates differences of political temper between Holyrood and Westminster that devolution may ultimately fail to placate. As Murdo Macdonald states, 'The assertion of the limited power of the monarch is a recurrent theme in Scottish history, finding its first expression in the Declaration of Arbroath in 1320.'[8] Summoning the spirit of the Declaration in a speech to the 1320 Club

Symposium at Glasgow University on 6 April 1968, MacDiarmid attacks 'those Anglo-Scots intellectuals who bleat of a false antithesis, internationalism, not nationalism, as if it were possible to have the one without the other. They sin against the universal law of life which invests life in individuals not conglomerations.' (*A*, 341).

Such ideas as to the importance of defending singularity, particularly in the face of varying forms of modern corporatism, may strike a chord with some contemporary anti-globalists. MacDiarmid's socialism, above all during his years in Montrose, had always at least one eye on the conditions of a specific community. Even his communism, disastrously totalitarian though it proved to be in effect, may be seen in the light of what he believed to be the perilous need to challenge the all-consuming global dominance of capitalism. But for MacDiarmid the crucial correspondence between the local and the universal was a relationship that could only be fully requited in national terms – in Scotland, this meant through complete political independence. 'True internationalism, and true nationalism go hand in hand' (*RT2*, 75), writes C. M. Grieve in the *Scots Independent* of February 1929, thus defining the crux of MacDiarmid's politics of place. Explaining his opposition to devolution, one that was to remain lifelong and that, had he lived to be able to do so, would have seen him vote No in the 1979 referendum,[9] 'Scottish Nationalism versus Socialism' is a deceptively titled article that seeks to promote the unity policy of the fledgling National Party of Scotland (NPS) as a means of defeating the divide and rule chicanery of (non-Tory) Unionism in Scotland, particularly that of the Labour Party:

> The devolutionary proposals of the Liberal and Socialist parties are hopelessly behind the times; and would, if put into effect, worsen rather than improve Scotland's position – by permanently provincialising us and preventing the emergence of a distinctive Scottish National idea, capable of contributing to the solution of the great problems of modern civilisation along its own lines, which is the aim and object of the National Party. We are not going to be confined within the mentality of English politics at all. We are out for something far bigger – the liberation of the dynamic soul of Scotland once again, without extraneous let or hindrance. Nothing else will regenerate Scotland or enable it to assume once again the place it ought to have in the comity of nations. (*RT2*, 75)

What MacDiarmid appears to mean by 'the great problems of modern civilisation' is imperialism's suppression of national difference. If the NPS offered a resolution by remaining within the problem's terms – 'along its own lines' – this was because it did not seek to break away from the British Empire, but wanted instead administrative equality with London in direct access to the riches of the Commonwealth. In Whalsay MacDiarmid would evolve an anti-British-imperialism, inspired by the markedly Scottish internationalism of the Marxist John Maclean, that would no longer contradict his belief in the political sovereignty of Scotland. So, in an unpublished letter of 7 April 1941 to Mary Ramsay, intercepted by the Security Services, Grieve claims to have been reading the work of Jawaharlal Nehru, who would become the first prime minister of independent India in 1947. Author of *Calvin and Art* (1938), Ramsay was Treasurer of the India League, an organisation joined by MacDiarmid, along with other Scottish nationalists such as George Campbell Hay, Oliver Brown and R. E. Muirhead.[10] When writing 'Scottish Arts and Letters' for the *National Weekly* of 5 March 1949, he can find a cultural connection between 'Rabindranath Tagore in regard to the Bengali language' and 'my own work in Lallans' (*RT3*, 176). By 1953, in his 'Author's Note to the Second Edition' of *A Drunk Man*, he would cite the example of the West Indies as a place more open to literary experimentation than Scotland.[11] 'Loathing all Imperialisms, colour-bars, and class-distinctions' (*CP2*, 782), *In Memoriam James Joyce* – published in 1955 but begun during his time in Shetland (1933–42) – locates a new cultural topography where 'All dreams of "imperialism" must be exorcised / Including linguistic imperialism, which sums up all the rest' (*CP2*, 790). Alive to its Eurocentric basis, the Scot is hopeful, none the less, that the postcolonial English of his macaronic poem, derived in part from the utopian spirit of Joyce's esoteric *lingua franca*, is the cultural signification of a universally progressive politics:

> The result would be neutral enough:
> For although purely 'Western'
> It would not be associated with any political power.
> This is where every man belongs
> Who is truly a philosopher and a world citizen,
> Not a chauvinist in 'orthological' clothing.[12]

(CP2, 790)

W. J. Mc Cormack may be sceptical of Yeats's postcolonial credentials, as espoused by Edward Said,[13] but it is surely time that greater critical consideration be given, particularly in Scotland, to the crucial role place plays in MacDiarmid's political evolution. Roaming around the 'post-colonial city' of Dublin with Ace de Horner, his poetic alter ego, Brendan Kennelly decides that 'feeling a bit lost in history and language is probably the first mark of post-colonialism'.[14] Impressed by Ireland's example, Grieve emerged from the Great War to sniff the first fresh breeze of postcolonialism, determined to find a distinctive poetic voice that would re-establish Scotland's place in history.

In 'National Literature and Cultural Capital in Scotland and Ireland' Cairns Craig describes the divergent contemporary routes each of these nations has taken in seeking to challenge the mixed legacy of imperialism and the attendant 'negative perception of their cultural past'.[15] Craig argues that, while the Republic has adopted postcolonial hybridity as a critical response to its relationship with Britishness, Scotland has aimed to establish a more traditional cultural identity, 'a continuity equivalent to that of France or England'.[16]

Ireland's intellectual embracing of hybridity not only signals identification with Third World decolonisation but has surely also been a tactical attempt to undermine the violent roots of nationalism – both Republican and Loyalist – in the north. Hybridity illustrates, in this latter regard, the Republic's desire to assimilate, transcend or simply forget the purificative sacrifice of its own origin in the 1916 Easter Rising – a Republican mythos all too potent in more recent decades in the sectarianism of Belfast, if not in Kennelly's postcolonial Dublin.[17]

If critics in the politically independent Republic of Ireland have endeavoured to move beyond the state's historical beginnings in nationalist culture, Scots intellectuals since the 1979 devolution referendum have striven to establish Scottish unity – or, at any rate, what Craig calls 'the internally coherent traditions of Scottish cultural development' – in terms of the nation's cultural history.[18] Citing, in particular, T. M. Devine's *The Scottish Nation 1700–2000* (1999) as a notable exemplar of this reformation of tradition, Craig declares that 'nowhere, perhaps, was this reconstitution of Scottish culture more clear than in the switch from the culture of Scots as a central cultural capital of Scotland to that of the Enlightenment'.[19]

Craig's observation has important implications in relation to MacDiarmid. The Enlightenment project of universalism, such a central part of Scotland's intellectual history, played a crucial role in building the Western idea of modernity's liberal nation-state, whilst concurrently occasioning the Self/Other dichotomy inherent in imperial design. Craig tells us that the Enlightenment was 'almost unacknowledged as in any real sense Scottish until the 1960s' – one reason, perhaps, why it is barely mentioned by MacDiarmid, whose best work was done by that decade.[20] But such scant reference in the work of the nationalist poet to a determining moment in the history of the national culture is more acutely explicable in that the origins of the Enlightenment appear, ostensibly at any rate, to be the fruit of the Union.[21] The self-declared universalism of the Scottish Enlightenment was grievously diluted in local terms to self-repression in North Britain. In 'Aesthetics in Scotland', first published in 1950, MacDiarmid points out that the majority of those Enlightenment writers on aesthetics in the eleventh edition of the *Encyclopaedia Britannica* listed as being English are actually Scots (*A*, 101). As Murray Pittock states, 'The paradox of the Scottish Enlightenment was that so many autonomous ideas rose from this paradigm of conformity.'[22]

In a lecture at Edinburgh University in April 1961, MacDiarmid cites David Hume (1711–76) as 'the greatest Scotsman who has ever lived' ('David Hume: Scotland's Greatest Son', *A*, 297). Attempting to excuse his own Anglophobia in an article for the *Free Man* on 4 June 1932, Grieve is 'delighted to find an earlier Scottish Anglophobe in no less a person than David Hume, the increasing concentration of learned attention upon whom is one of the signs of the times which ought not to be missed by Scottish Nationalists' ('An Earlier Anglophobe', *RT2*, 396). Lauding Hume's genius in *Lucky Poet*, MacDiarmid proceeds to decry the Common Sense school of Scottish philosophy:

> Any effort to grasp the nature of the live elements in the Scottish renaissance movement brings whoever makes it into conflict with the lingering common-sense outlook of [Thomas] Reid, [Dugald] Stewart, and [Sir William] Hamilton, whose disciples did not lose control in Scottish Philosophy until about 1900, and who have even yet several influential Scottish professors and lecturers among their numbers. Scotland's most pressing problem is undoubtedly the continued sway (in the head, if not on the lips) of the Common Sense Philosophy. (*LP*, 386–7)

Imagining it provides the philosophical rationale for the dour pragmaticism of the canny Scot, MacDiarmid wants to replace Common Sense, the doctrine advocated in attenuated form by Dugald Stewart (1753–1828), with Hume's sceptical brilliance.

MacDiarmid's *Scottish Eccentrics*, a book-length exemplification of G. Gregory Smith's 'Caledonian antisyzygy',[23] argues that 'almost every distinguished Scot' is made up of 'extraordinary contradictions of character, most dangerous antinomies and antithetical impulses' (*SE*, 284). This eminently variegated Scottish type in now an endangered species, however, having been largely supplanted by the monochromatically commonplace canny Scot. Writing as James Maclaren for the *Scottish Educational Journal* of 17 July 1931, in 'Whither Scotland?' he contends 'that the Union with England and other factors have favoured the wrong type of Scotland and promulgated on that basis – to the detriment and practical elimination of the finer elements of our race – a false and unworthy myth' (*RT2*, 269). For MacDiarmid, the myth of the canny Scot is politically disabling because it immobilises Scottish identity within the controllable confines of Britishness. Homi Bhabha describes such stereotyping as imperialism's 'dependence on the concept of "fixity" in the ideological construction of otherness'.[24] Looking for paradigms of Scottish exceptionality through which to shatter that 'fixity', MacDiarmid finds contemporary sustenance in Hume's philosophical radicalism.

Gordon Graham claims, however, that to his Scottish philosophical contemporaries, such as Thomas Reid (1710–96) and James Beattie (1735–1803), the empiricist, Lockean Hume was 'not properly regarded as an exponent of Scottish philosophy at all'.[25] Indeed Hume's anglocentric historiography, encapsulated by his *History of England*, encouraged the dualistic Scottish–British culture that MacDiarmid's politics of place seeks to make whole. Aiming to unify Scottish culture against such fissures of the past, MacDiarmid disputes the Enlightenment inheritance approvingly described by Samuel Johnson on his visit to Edinburgh in 1773:

> The conversation of the *Scots* grows every day less unpleasing to the *English*; their peculiarities wear fast away; their dialect is likely to become in half a century provincial and rustick, even to themselves. The great, the learned, the ambitious, and the vain, all cultivate the *English* phrase, and the *English* pronunciation, and in splendid companies *Scotch* is not much heard, except now and then from an old Lady.[26]

If the Scotophobic Dr Johnson's *Dictionary* (1755) impelled the process of British linguistic standardisation, then, in the historiography of the likes of Hume and William Robertson (1721–93), the Enlightenment ratified the Union's 'eclipse' of a distinctively Scottish culture and politics at a moment when, paradoxically, Edinburgh was the centre of the intellectual world.[27]

In *Devolving English Literature*, first published in 1992, Robert Crawford attempts to rescue the assimilationist Enlightenment from such charges of cultural self-suppression:

> The growing wish for a 'pure' English in eighteenth-century Scotland was not an anti-Scottish gesture, but a pro-British one. If Britain were to work as a political unit, then the Scots should rid themselves of any elements likely to impede their progress within it. Language, the most important of bonds, must not be allowed to hinder Scotland's intercourse with expanding economic and intellectual markets in the freshly defined British state.[28]

For Crawford, the result of the Scottish Enlightenment's 'pursuit of improving linguistic studies' was 'The Scottish Invention of English Literature'.[29] The anti-British gesture of recovering a Scottish voice – and subsequently a Scottish culture and politics – is the nationalist root of MacDiarmid's synthetic Scots, but it also informs his idiosyncratic Marxism, which sees the United Kingdom as a commercially motivated construct facilitating international capitalism (the extent of Marx's influence on MacDiarmid is debatable and I believe his credo to be idiosyncratic rather than doctrinaire, his economics more firmly influenced by Scotsman Major Douglas than by Marx). Reconciling the apparent antagonism of his positions, he finds a place for his politics in a radical tradition of Scottish Republicanism.

The surface incongruities of his politics derive from an opposition to what the poet believes to be Scotland's provincialisation. MacDiarmid wants a confidently internationalist nation undivided by what he sees as the ruptures of the past: the Reformation, the Unions of 1603 and 1707, and the anglophonic Scottish Enlightenment. Distrustful of imperial pretensions to universalism indulged in by the core culture, what Raymond Williams in his discussion of modernist politics calls 'the metropolitan interpretation of its own processes as universals',[30] MacDiarmid argues for the cultural significance and political independence of the peripheries, those places Tom Nairn terms the 'small battalions'.[31]

The idea of core and peripheral cultures has sociological roots in Michael Hechter's *Internal Colonialism: The Celtic Fringe in British National Development, 1536–1966* (1975). Hechter argues that 'there are two collectivities or objectively distinct cultural groups' that are central to an understanding of national development in the industrial era: '(1) the *core*, or dominant cultural group which occupies territory extending from the political center of the society (e.g. the locus of the central government) outward to those territories largely occupied by the subordinate, or (2) *peripheral* cultural group'.[32] While this influential analysis is useful in its definition of terms, it suffers somewhat from a tendency to see 'collectivities' as either black or white, being 'objectively distinct' and 'perfectly solidary', Hechter believing that 'oppressed minorities' have a straight choice of 'assimilationism *versus* nationalism'.[33]

More recently, postcolonial theory has emphasised the cultural fluidity between core and periphery. In this regard, MacDiarmid's excoriation and scornful anglophobic Othering of the English would seem to distort the heterogeneous potentialities of Scottishness to the essentialist shape of his own nationalist image. Writing for the *Scots Independent* of May 1929, in 'Towards a Scottish Renaissance: desirable lines of advance', MacDiarmid proposes to

> take a typical Anglo-Scot, opposed to Nationalism, ignorant of Scots and still more of Gaelic, and carefully catalogue all that he takes for granted as reasonable, natural, and inevitable in any connection – and repudiate the lot, and take up the very opposite positions. (*RT2*, 80)

Few, if any, Scottish writers use the term Anglo-Scot as frequently as MacDiarmid – his attempt, perhaps, to introduce to Scotland similarly pejorative connotations as those once disdainfully attached by Irish nationalists to what Julian Moynahan calls the 'hyphenated culture' of the Anglo-Irish.[34] In his absolutist search for the metaphysical Scot in Montrose, MacDiarmid denies the Anglo-Scottish element of Scottish identity through the organicist essentialism of a totalising project that attempts to uncover the 'real' Scotland. From a postcolonial perspective, such organicist repudiation of alterity, the striving after cultural and political unity, is the theoretical armoury for the very political and cultural imperialism that MacDiarmid is seeking to counter. By portraying Scottish identity, particularly since the Union, as dualistically fractured and failed; by accepting the essence of the true Scot as that delineated in Smith's contradistinctive Caledonian antisyzygy, a concept with uncomfortable echoes of Matthew Arnold's mercurial Celt,[35] MacDiarmid mirrors metropolitan culture's deliberately distorted vision of its Other, the peripheral or marginal culture. The organicist essentialism of nationalism helps keep the Enlightenment imperial dualism of centre and margin alive and is, in this reading, a self-defeating theory for the marginalised culture to embrace.

Postcolonial theory critiques the essentialist manoeuvres of colonial discourse, understanding them to be deterministic, perhaps mystical, and a rationalisation for racism. So Michael Gardiner, in *The Cultural Roots of British Devolution* (2004), regards what he terms 'The First Scottish Renaissance' as 'containing some of the seeds of a post-British culture',[36] but sees the movement as ethnocentric, with MacDiarmid's Enlightenment individualism and synthetic Scots being conducive to an elitist concept of national anteriority. Yet postcolonialism, along with other theories that have an interest in political and social emancipation, such as feminism, may need to rely on what Gayatri Spivak has termed 'operational essentialism' precisely in order to resist the essentialist procedures of power; this tactic can be deployed even if no 'ontological integrity' can be ascribed to liberation's objective – womanhood or a particular national culture, for instance.[37] An understanding of identity that apprehends the (psychological and cultural) alterity of the subject is a useful theoretical tool that allows us to perceive the hybridism of cultural construction. However, by challenging the essential wholeness of subject formation, it also undermines the possibility of political action arising from a sense that the subject position of the colonised, as seen and constructed by the coloniser, is subordinate. This is important in Scotland where, according to James Kelman, 'there is simply no question that by the criteria of the ruling elite of Great Britain so-called Scottish culture, for example, is inferior, just as *ipso facto* the Scottish people are also inferior'; as such, 'Scotland is oppressed'.[38] Kelman understands essences such as 'Scotsman' and 'Scottish culture' to be 'material absurdities'.[39]

Nevertheless, as Ania Loomba says, 'decentring the subject allows for a social reading of language and representations, but it can also make it impossible to think about a subject capable of acting and challenging the *status quo*'.[40]

MacDiarmid's insistence that the Scots are more internationalist in comparison with what he believed, or wanted to believe, to be the insularity of the English certainly smacks of over-compensatory and self-deluding chauvinism, but also arises from the provincial's (Other-induced) understanding of the provinciality of metropolitanism, the parochialism of the core cultural. He eschews what Gerry Smyth points to as the aspiration of 'liberal decolonisation', that is, a replication of the political mechanisms of the coloniser under the new regime, aiming instead for a more 'radical decolonisation' that repudiates the core's values, reinstating in their place native traditions.[41]

MacDiarmid deplores Scotland as a stateless nation subsumed in a multinational state governed by London's metropolitan monetarism and addicted to pledging political allegiance to monarchical British Labour Unionism. In this binary province Scotland and the Scots are damagingly double, international when British, parochial as Scots. The nation can at once be the self-styled 'backbone of the British Empire' and consigned to the neo-colonial Celtic fringe. Industrially advanced in Lowland reality, it is also romantically retrogressive in Highland myth; a place folk pragmatically leave to build a more prosperous future elsewhere but sentimentally return to in order to trace their Scottish roots. Scotland's true republican self as MacDiarmid envisions it – internationalist, politically radical and culturally modernist – is dwarfed by a political Union that is actually an extension of English nationalism, 'or', as Grieve says in the *Pictish Review* of May 1928, 'that variant and projection of it, British Imperialism' ('Backward *Forward*', *RT2*, 50). This political state is fostered by canny Anglo-Scots who are the civic weeds of a cultural Kailyard that, according to a despondent Drunk Man, consists merely 'o' bagpipes, haggis, and sheep's heids' (*CP1*, 106). Through the Scottish Renaissance movement, MacDiarmid envisions the radical transformation of a retrograde national culture blinded to its international potential by the false, imperialistic universalism of the cultural and political centre.

According to Christopher Harvie, however, MacDiarmid's movement towards a new Scotland is no modernist vision:

> Intellectually the Renaissance was archaic. Its ambitions were democratic, internationalist, scientific, and socialist, but at a time when urbanization and mass culture – housing, industrial change, cinema, and radio – was determining a new politics, it was actually less urban than Hume, Smith, Ferguson,

and the literati had been; its ambitions utopian and remote from modern Scotland.[42]

Significantly, in listing the 'ambitions' of the Scottish Renaissance, Harvie omits one pivotal idea – that it was also nationalist. Even if certain major figures of the period, such as Lewis Grassic Gibbon, were not politically nationalist, most shared what we might now translate – even in a Scotland neither truly 'post' colonial nor 'post' imperial – as MacDiarmid's apprehension of the cultural importance of place.

In this the Renaissance movement is, in fact, crucially modern. In what Cairns Craig calls our 'post-age', the grand narratives of universal progress piloting the transcendent flight of Hegel's world spirit of historical consciousness, such as the Enlightenment and doctrinaire Marxism, are challenged by 'a value which does not conform to the stages of historical development, a value which is grounded outside of the historical trajectory as it has been defined by Western ideology'.[43] The totalitarian ubiquity of historical time is defied in a postcolonial era by the stubbornly immovable autochthony of place. This is what MacDiarmid means when he writes of Culloden and the Highland Clearances:

> 'Incompatible with British civilization' may well mean vital to the new order about to supplant that civilization. The chief of these hitherto vanquished ideas perhaps is just the denial of the present general assumption that 'History had to happen', and, with it, of the idea of Progress. (*LP*, 210)

In Scotland the progress of Enlightenment universalism suppressed those differences between Highland and Lowland standing in the way of Great Britishness. Aware of its ideological role in the internal colonisation of Scotland, MacDiarmid was, none the less, stimulated by Enlightenment universalism, which foretokens the materialism of Marx. His own idea of progress synthesises a Marxian evolutionism that seeks the emancipation of the masses from the promiscuous culture of global capitalism with a nationalist covenant to exorcise Scotland's ambiguous imperial patrimony.

Harvie is correct, however, to point to the small town, rural localism of the Scottish Renaissance. Inspired by Langholm, MacDiarmid's best creative work was written in Montrose and Whalsay. It is by living and working in these peripheral places that MacDiarmid developed a political strategy through which to resist the symbiotic assault of anglification and capitalism, and so suggest a radically nationalist Scotland. Rejecting the Enlightenment metropolitanism favoured by Harvie, in 'Talking with Five Thousand People in Edinburgh' MacDiarmid believes that

All the big centres of mankind are like thunder-clouds to-day
Forming part of the horrific structure of a storm
That fills the whole sky – but ere long
Will disappear like the fabric of a dream.

(*CP2*, 1156)

His vision of the moral bankruptcy of metropolitan centres, compounded by Edinburgh's 'terrible inability to speak out' (*CP2*, 1156) as a world capital, doesn't lessen the impact of the internationalism central to the poet's political image of a radical Scotland. Speaking to the 1320 Club in 1968, he argues that if 'one of the great problems of the modern world is the search for identity' then the Scots must reinvent their nation, not only so they can regain political autonomy and cultural distinction, but in order also that Scotland continues to assist in the universal invention of modernity's identity:

> We are too apt to be dismissed by the believers in big units as a small people of no particular consequence in relation to the major problems of modern times; but I think the historian James Anthony Froude, was right when he said that no small people in the history of the world had so profoundly affected the whole of mankind as the Scots people had done. (*A*, 340)

If Scotland is to carry on contemporaneously shaping the world in the same impressive measure as in the past, the nation must bid farewell to the defeated Celticism of its own past and find a different political idea, a tradition of radical Scottish Republicanism that combines the universalism of the Enlightenment with a liberating refusal to hush a distinctly local voice. MacDiarmid predicts in 'Good-bye Twilight' that

> The day is not far distant when the Scottish people
> Will enter into this heritage, and in so doing
> Enrich the heritage of all mankind again.

(*CP2*, 1126)

Terry Eagleton believes that 'if a political end is not to make men and women desire uselessly, and so to fall ill of longing, it must be possible to point in the present to what might prefigure its realization'.[44] Working towards a Scottish Renaissance whilst in Montrose, in 1925 Grieve predicted, 'it may be that effective cultural devolution will precede rather than follow political devolution' ('Frederick Niven; J. J. Bell', *CSS*, 68). Scotland may not be the politically independent radical republic that MacDiarmid desired, but the years since his death in 1978 have seen a renewed literary vitality. The cultural hope in spite of the political facts of, for instance, Alasdair Gray's Scottish Cooperative Wholesale Republic: 'Work as if you live in the early days of a better nation', Robert

Alan Jamieson following Cairns Craig in 'A Formal Declaration of Cultural Independence' and Angus Calder writing 'Notes from the Scottish Republic' in a pluralistically *Revolving Culture* owes much to the vivifying spirit of MacDiarmid's poetry and politics.[45]

Hugh MacDiarmid's Poetry and Politics of Place does not seek to theoretically circumscribe the manifold, inventive abundance of MacDiarmid's poetic imagination. Instead, it aims to make clear the political vision of a poet whose creative multiplicity has undermined understanding of his politics in the minds of those who conclude that everything must have an answer in the present tense – as if imagining a collective future could ever possibly be achieved in the singular. Estimating the critical outlook for MacDiarmid's work, Seamus Heaney recognises this unresolved, prospective element – a factor with manifestly political bearings – when he speculates that 'MacDiarmid's poetry is kind of like Irish history; it is moving towards its fulfillment. It will be perceived as ancestral when, say, Caribbean literature and Nigerian literature and Irish literature come into their strength in the twenty-first century.'[46] Alan Riach pinpoints the cultural and political framework in which the poet's work can now be judged: 'MacDiarmid's aesthetics may be prophetic of the post-colonial literatures of the modern world.'[47] By using culture as a crucial weapon in the fight for a new political identity, MacDiarmid's influence is not only discernable in those Scottish writers and intellectuals, such as Gray, who sought cultural means to counteract the political disorder of 1979 and the Thatcherite 'no such thing as society' '80s, but is also recognisable in continuing international resistance to the cultural politics of the metropolitan core.

II

That MacDiarmid's ideological influence still powerfully – if subliminally – resounds in Scottish cultural politics means it is important to try to fathom the poet's political imagination, his vision of a Scottish Republic. Declaring the centrality of nationality and cultural identity to the formation of his creative work, I will trace the fundamental bond between MacDiarmid's poetry and his drive to create a modern, internationalist Scotland – a politics of place that evolves from an often refractory but always actively radical relationship with home.

This connection may seem obvious in examination of a poet who so strongly identifies himself with Scotland. There is little danger, after all, of MacDiarmid's work being easily assimilated into the canonical realms of 'English Literature', an academic area from which this Scottish nationalist is still largely excluded. As Scottish political self-determination remains a live issue, a distinct Scottish cultural identity and Scottish literature's contribution to cultural movements such as international modernism remains generally unacknowledged by metropolitan critics, disinclined to attribute the importance of a Scottish accent to the powerful constitution of their own cultural and political domain. Appalled by the parochialism of vision issuing from his country's attachment to English metropolitanism, MacDiarmid sometimes also neglects to admit the influence of Scottish cultural and political traditions on his work. However, it is his ideological and actual interaction with Scotland that enables his formulation of a radically *inter*nationalist politics.

Considering MacDiarmid's legacy, Kenneth Buthlay believes, 'The inter-relationship between his work and the rise of Scottish Nationalism, an altogether deeper matter than the recorded history of political parties, will always be beyond calculation.'[48] Despite his critical importance to modern Scottish culture, analysis of MacDiarmid's work in relation to his political ideas has been scarce – even in Scotland. Examination of his politics has tended to emphasise a supposedly crippling irreconcilability in his positions, particularly with regard to his Scottish nationalism and internationalist communism. Andrew Marr instances a standard response: 'MacDiarmid's politics were extreme, often contradictory and almost entirely devoid of common sense.'[49] Marr epitomises other commentators in being deliberately offhand as a means of dismissing MacDiarmid's political aims for Scotland as utterly daft, the unworkable daydreams of an idealistic poet. If MacDiarmid's politics do not make sense then, by implication, the idea of a radical Scottish Republic can also be rubbished.

Writing of 'The Marxist Poet', David Craig considers MacDiarmid's communism to be illustrative of 'the inconsistencies typical of his thinking'.[50] Craig believes, however, that the 1930s poetry has a 'truly Marxist intellectual content'.[51] He understands that MacDiarmid's radicalism in the 1930s has greater depth than that illustrated by the 'clever-clever style' of 'MacSpauden' (Louis MacNeice, Stephen Spender, W. H. Auden), but through adherence to a materialist analysis Craig fails to discern the spirituality of MacDiarmid's communism.[52] Douglas Young's 'The Nationalism of Hugh MacDiarmid' recognises the 'twofold principle of Nationalism and Internationalism' central to MacDiarmid's politics.[53] But the essays of Craig and Young, appearing back to back in the 1962 festschrift, illustrate the unhelpful ideological rupturing of MacDiarmid's nationalism and socialism.

'A Scottish nationalist, international communist, social creditor would appear to be a description of MacDiarmid's political affinities'; for

Duncan Glen, in *Hugh MacDiarmid (Christopher Murray Grieve) and the Scottish Renaissance* (1964), this represents 'a strange conglomeration of political beliefs'.[54] Ann Edwards Boutelle's *Thistle and Rose: A Study of Hugh MacDiarmid's Poetry* (1980) also emphasises MacDiarmid's idiosyncratic political vision: 'His political career has been as consistently paradoxical as his poetic career.'[55] Stephen Maxwell, in 'The Nationalism of Hugh MacDiarmid', looks at MacDiarmid's nationalism from the early 1920s in Montrose to the evolution of the John Maclean-line in Whalsay. Maxwell sees the poet's Scotland as a 'mental construct', a place of the mind designed to be 'an exemplar of universal intellectual and aesthetic qualities'.[56] As such, Maxwell thinks that 'MacDiarmid's impact on Scottish political opinion has been slight.'[57] Catherine Kerrigan's *Whaur Extremes Meet: The Poetry of Hugh MacDiarmid 1920–1934* (1983) provides a useful historical perspective but splits the poet's politics chronologically, analysing MacDiarmid's 'Scottish Nationalism' and 'Dialectical Materialism' in separate chapters.[58] Even Hamish Henderson, in 'To Hugh MacDiarmid', perpetuates the view of MacDiarmid's ideological capriciousness: 'Just what *do* you stand for, MacDiarmid? I'm still not certain.'[59]

While most critics, then, have somewhat neutered the poet's politics by stressing what they believe to be his contradictory thinking, I want to argue for the essential relatedness of MacDiarmid's political ideas. His nationalism and socialism should not be thought of as separate, clashing political entities; rather, in MacDiarmid's political imagination, they find a symbiotic union in a Scottish Republicanism that develops from his concerted engagement with Scotland, especially those places most important to his poetry: Langholm, Montrose and Shetland.

MacDiarmid understood his political importance to Scotland. Writing to Neil Gunn from Whalsay on 25 November 1933, he considers himself, even at this distance from the mainland, 'by far the most powerful non-Conservative personal force in Scotland today' (*L*, 254). After leaving school in Langholm, at the age of sixteen MacDiarmid became a member of the Independent Labour Party; he helped to found the NPS in 1928 while in Montrose; and the nationalist poet, convinced while in Shetland of the synchronous relationship between the local and the universal, the national and the international, joined the Communist Party of Great Britain in 1934, and also gave fresh ideological voice to a radical Scottish tradition of republicanism. Yet for all this political group activity, the use of the adjective 'personal' in his letter to Gunn suggests that MacDiarmid understood himself to be something of a rebelliously lone voice. As he says in a letter of 5 November 1928 to R. E. Muirhead, he conceived that in Scotland his poetry would have 'a powerful influence because it springs from the deeps of the destined' (*L*, 298). Such egotism, encouraged by his elect Calvinist sense of self, helps explain the lapses into solipsism of MacDiarmid's more extremist political positions; it also illustrates an artistic commitment to the nation of an exceptionally intimate, ultimately spiritual, nature.

This book examines MacDiarmid as a political activist and cultural theorist of continuing importance, particularly for Scotland. As Tom Leonard points out, this prioritisation of MacDiarmid's politics can be used as a 'reason not to see poetry as expression from one individual universally to another, but as some kind of "contribution to Modern Scottish literature" '.[60] While aware of the philistine pitfalls of such a position, MacDiarmid's political ideas are given critical precedence here in concordance with Leonard's belief that 'the aesthetic experience [should] be left private to the individual',[61] not through any complacent conviction that individual artistic vision is somehow of less consequence than the practicalities of workaday politics. But as he emphasises to Muirhead, clear in his refusal of the bourgeois division between art and action, MacDiarmid combatively combined the poetical and political as a means to imagine a modern nation: 'all my work hangs together – my poetry and my general propaganda are parts of each other: and I am unquestionably doing far more for Scotland when my activity issues in poetry rather than in any other form' (*L*, 297).

Structurally confirming its argument, the book's architectonics are grounded in MacDiarmid's oft-repeated maxim that the universal, far from being simply the preserve of imperial 'normality', is in fact to be found in all places. He confirms this dictum of decolonisation in *Forward* on 16 October 1948. 'Memorial to William Stewart' (1856–1947; author of a Keir Hardie biography and a study of the insurrectionary radicals of 1820), issues the ascetic republican precept 'that those who fail to discharge the duties that lie closest to their hands, no matter how relatively small they may be, are not fit to be charged with greater responsibilities', before crucially declaring: 'This, after all, is the tie between nationalism and internationalism. There is nothing more universal than the local' (*RT3*, 135). So Chapter 1 establishes the historical basis of MacDiarmid's *nationalism* in the First World War, before examining how the Scottish modernism of the Renaissance he envisaged attempted to culturally institute a new, inclusive Scotland in political, religious and educational terms. The next three chapters study those *local* Scottish places – Langholm, Montrose, Whalsay – central to the creation of MacDiarmid's poetry and politics. His radical republicanism comes from Langholm and is then put into practice and theoretically elaborated in Montrose and Whalsay. In Montrose his engagement in local self-government acts as a personal example of the republican virtue he wants Scots to realise nationally. As noted by Iseult Honohan in *Civic Republicanism*, 'the good of citizenship lies in active participation in collective self-determination'.[62] Councillor Grieve's resolve to be involved in civil decision-making in Montrose is commensurate with his Scottish nationalism, which in turn internationally authenticates Scotland. Chapter 5 concludes by interpreting the *internationalism* of the poet's vernacular modernism as a challenge to capitalism's global marketing of mass culture.

Explicit in its Scottish Republicanism, this book posits MacDiarmid's politics of place as a major component of what James D. Young calls 'Scotland's hidden cultural history'.[63] Republicanism, in my understanding, not only means (to cite *Chambers Dictionary*) 'a form of government without a monarch, in which supreme power is vested in the people and their elected representatives',[64] but also implies a concern with the commonwealth, from the Latin definition of *respublica*, adapted by Edwin Morgan in his aptly titled 'The Coin' from *Sonnet from Scotland*: '*Respublica Scotorum*'.[65] MacDiarmid's imagined Scottish Republic would appear to be a dauntingly masculine community; whether Scots or otherwise, his heroes – Dunbar, Dostoevsky, Lenin, Christ – are all male. But as Alan Riach suggests, 'No editor of Scottish poetry before or since has done as much as Grieve/MacDiarmid to insist that the voices of women should be heard to represent the nation.'[66] Riach's contention is corroborated by *Contemporary Scottish Studies*, Grieve's key critical undertaking to reshape Scotland as a modernist culture. Here he accounts Violet Jacob (1863–1946), Marion Angus (1866–1946), Rachel Annand Taylor (1876–1960) and the Englishwoman Muriel Stuart (1889–1967) as being among the foremost contributors to the Scottish Renaissance. Further, in 'Various Poets (IV) Ladies' Choir' (*CSS*, 336–41), he considers a number of other female poets – Jessie Annie Anderson, Muriel E. Graham, Agnes Falconer, Isobel W. Hutchison, to name only four of several – who, as Riach points out, have mostly disappeared from the contemporary critical radar. The editor of *Gendering the Nation*, Christopher Whyte, introduces this volume with the thought (of an unnamed, female, 'English-identified' academic) that nationalism is not conducive to the liberation of women.[67] Grieve reverses these terms, suggesting in 'Violet Jacob', from the *Scottish Educational Journal* of 17 July 1925, that 'the present position of Scotland as a nation has deprived us of all but a shadow of the Mrs Jacob whom in less over-Anglicised circumstances we might have had' (*CSS*, 34). The progressive gender representation of the devolved Scottish Parliament may indicate the beginnings of a radical Scottish politics intimated in MacDiarmid's cultural praxis.[68]

That the nation, once fully realised on its own terms, is central to the international community is a concept peopling MacDiarmid's political landscape, a place where, however marginal national particularity seems to be, the universal *is* the particular. Ostensibly writing to the journalist and literary critic William Power (1873–1951), in 'The Kulturkampf' MacDiarmid imagines an 'ideal figure', an individual reminiscent of himself, who is 'an inveterate foe / Of bigness, jingoism, and regimentation' (*CP1*, 704) and who uncovers the tradition of radical Scottish Republicanism, a hidden casualty of the injurious dualities of Scottish history and the conceptual contestation that is the cultural politics of modern capitalism:

> and out of the past
> He brought to life again all those
> Who had lived through that developing history
> And yet asserted life – George Buchanan, Arthur Johnstone,
> Thomas Muir (*Thomas* Muir – not *Edwin* Muir),
> William Livingston, John Murdoch, John Maclean – and showed how
>   these
> Create for us a tradition, inspire us with faith,
> Help us to find new gods
> To replace the old we cannot worship.
>
> (*CP1*, 699)

Notes

1. Alasdair Gray, *1982 Janine* (Harmondsworth: Penguin, 1985), p. 340.
2. See Marshall Walker, 'The Process of Jock McLeish and the Fiction of Alasdair Gray', in Robert Crawford and Thom Nairn (eds), *The Arts of Alasdair Gray* (Edinburgh: Edinburgh University Press, 1991), pp. 37–47.
3. Gray, *1982 Janine*, p. 334.
4. Ibid., p. 343.
5. See Christopher Harvie, 'Alasdair Gray and the Condition of Scotland Question', in *The Arts of Alasdair Gray*, p. 87.
6. Gray, *1982 Janine*, p. 341.
7. See Tom Nairn, *The Enchanted Glass: Britain and its Monarchy* (London: Vintage, 1994).
8. Murdo Macdonald, *Scottish Art* (London: Thames & Hudson, 2000), p. 51.
9. See Stephen Maxwell, 'The Nationalism of Hugh MacDiarmid', in P. H. Scott and A. C. Davis (eds), *The Age of MacDiarmid: Essays on Hugh MacDiarmid and his Influence on Contemporary Scotland* (Edinburgh: Mainstream, 1980), p. 221.
10. A copy of Grieve's letter to Ramsay, made by Military Intelligence, is held in the National Archives, Kew, KV2/ 2010 2S1020. In the same collection a letter of 17 April 1941 from Scottish Regional Security Officer Major P. Perfect addressed to R. Brooman-White at a P.O. Box in Oxford discusses

the connections between Scottish nationalism and the India League. Significantly, on a trip to Dublin, Nehru had approved of Sinn Féin Ireland; see Niall Ferguson, *Empire: How Britain Made the Modern World* (London: Penguin, 2004), p. 333.

11. Appendix B, Kenneth Buthlay (ed.), *A Drunk Man Looks at the Thistle* (Edinburgh: Scottish Academic Press, 1987), p. 197.

12. In August 1929, James Joyce went to the Orthological Institute at 10 King's Parade, Cambridge, to give a reading of 'Anna Livia Plurabelle' for Charles Kay Ogden, the founder of Basic English. The 12-inch discs are part of the Joyce Collection at the State University of New York, University at Buffalo. See the University of Tulsa, 'In Good Company: James Joyce & Publishers, Readers, Friends' <http://www.lib.utulsa.edu/speccoll/JJoyce/readers_and_critics.htm> [accessed 23 August 2005].

13. W. J. Mc Cormack, *Blood Kindred: W. B. Yeats: The Life, The Death, The Politics* (London: Pimlico, 2005); Edward W. Said, *Nationalism, Colonialism and Literature: Yeats and Decolonization* (Derry: Field Day, 1988).

14. Brendan Kennelly, *Poetry My Arse: A Riotous Epic Poem* (Newcastle upon Tyne: Bloodaxe, 1996), p. 13.

15. Cairns Craig, 'National Literature and Cultural Capital in Scotland and Ireland', in Liam McIllvanney and Ray Ryan (eds), *Ireland and Scotland: Culture and Society, 1700–2000* (Dublin: Four Courts, 2005), p. 62.

16. Ibid., p. 63.

17. For a critique of revisionist attitudes to Easter 1916 see Declan Kiberd, 'The Elephant of Revolutionary Forgetfulness', in *The Irish Writer and the World* (Cambridge: Cambridge University Press, 2005), pp. 191–207.

18. Craig, in *Ireland and Scotland: Culture and Society, 1700–2000*, p. 62.

19. Ibid., p. 62.

20. Ibid., p. 62.

21. Arthur Herman's *The Scottish Enlightenment: The Scots' Invention of the Modern World* (London: Fourth Estate, 2002) sustains such congruence between the Enlightenment and the Union. However, Alexander Broadie demonstrates how the Scottish Enlightenment issues from a pre-Union tradition of Scottish philosophy in *The Scottish Enlightenment: The Historical Age of the Historical Nation* (Edinburgh: Birlinn, 2001) and *Why Scottish Philosophy Matters* (Edinburgh: Saltire Society, 2000).

22. Murray G. H. Pittock, 'Historiography', in Alexander Broadie (ed.), *The Cambridge Companion to the Scottish Enlightenment* (Cambridge: Cambridge University Press, 2003), p. 260.

23. G. Gregory Smith, *Scottish Literature: Character and Influence* (London: Macmillan, 1919), p. 4.

24. Homi K. Bhabha, *The Location of Culture* (London & New York: Routledge, 1995), p. 66.

25. Gordon Graham, 'The Nineteenth-century Aftermath', in *The Cambridge Companion to the Scottish Enlightenment*, p. 341.

26. Samuel Johnson, *A Journey to the Western Islands of Scotland* (1775), in Johnson and Boswell, *Journey to the Hebrides*, ed. Ian McGowan (Edinburgh: Canongate Classics, 2001), p. 143.

27. See Craig Beveridge and Ronald Turnbull, *The Eclipse of Scottish Culture:*

Inferiorism and the Intellectuals (Edinburgh: Polygon, 1989) and their *Scotland After Enlightenment: Image and Tradition in Modern Scottish Culture* (Edinburgh: Polygon, 1997).

28. Robert Crawford, *Devolving English Literature* (Oxford: Clarendon Press, 1992) p. 18.
29. Ibid., p. 18; see also Robert Crawford (ed.), *The Scottish Invention of English Literature* (Cambridge: Cambridge University Press, 1998).
30. Raymond Williams, 'Metropolitan Perceptions and the Emergence of Modernism', *The Politics of Modernism: Against the New Conformists*, ed. Tony Pinkey (London & New York: Verso, 1999), p. 47.
31. See Tom Nairn, *Faces of Nationalism: Janus Revisited* (London & New York: Verso, 1997), Part III.
32. Michael Hechter, *Internal Colonialism: The Celtic Fringe in British National Development, 1536–1966* (London: Routledge & Kegan Paul, 1975), p. 18.
33. Ibid., pp. 18, xvii.
34. Julian Moynahan, *Anglo-Irish: The Literary Imagination of a Hyphenated Culture* (Princeton: Princeton University Press, 1995).
35. Matthew Arnold, *On the Study of Celtic Literature* ([1867] London & Port Washington, NY: Kennikat, 1970).
36. Michael Gardiner, *The Cultural Roots of British Devolution* (Edinburgh: Edinburgh University Press, 2004), p. 29.
37. Gayatri Spivak, 'Remarks, Center for the Humanities, Wesleyan University, Spring 1985', cited in Judith Butler, 'Gender Trouble, Feminist Theory, and Psychoanalytic Discourse', in Linda J. Nicholson (ed.), *Feminism/Postmodernism* (London & New York: Routledge, 1990), p. 325; Butler also refers here to Julia Kristeva's recommendation that 'feminists use the category of women as a political tool without attributing ontological integrity to the term'.
38. James Kelman, *Some Recent Attacks: Essays Cultural and Political* (Stirling: AK Press, 1992), pp. 71, 72.
39. Ibid., p. 72.
40. Ania Loomba, *Colonialism / Postcolonialism* (London & New York: Routledge, 1998), pp. 42–3.
41. Gerry Smyth, *Decolonisation and Criticism: The Construction of Irish Literature* (London: Pluto Press, 1998), (pp. 15–19) p. 17.
42. Christopher Harvie, *Scotland: A Short History* (Oxford: Oxford University Press, 2002), p. 193.
43. Cairns Craig, *Out of History: Narrative Paradigms in Scottish and British Culture* (Edinburgh: Polygon, 1996), pp. 207, 224.
44. Terry Eagleton, *Heathcliff and the Great Hunger: Studies in Irish Culture* (London: Verso, 1995), p. 242.
45. Gray is quoting Dennis Lee; Robert Alan Jamieson, 'MacDiarmid's Spirit Burns On', *Chapman* 69–70, MacDiarmid Centenary Issue (Edinburgh: Autumn 1992), p. 7; Angus Calder, *Revolving Culture: Notes from the Scottish Republic* (London & New York: I.B. Tauris, 1994).
46. Seamus Heaney, interviewed by Nancy Gish (1980), in Nancy K. Gish (ed.), *Hugh MacDiarmid: Man and Poet* (Edinburgh: Edinburgh University Press, 1992), pp. 69–70.

47. Alan Riach, 'Demolition Man', Introduction to *CSS*, p. xxx.
48. Kenneth Buthlay, *Hugh MacDiarmid (C. M. Grieve)* (Edinburgh: Scottish Academic Press, 1982), p. 134.
49. Andrew Marr, *The Battle for Scotland* (London: Penguin, 1995), p. 75.
50. David Craig, 'The Marxist Poet', in K. D. Duval and Sydney Goodsir Smith (ed.), *Hugh MacDiarmid: A Festschrift* (Edinburgh: K. D. Duval, 1962), p. 97.
51. Ibid., p. 87.
52. Ibid., p. 87.
53. Douglas Young, 'The Nationalism of Hugh MacDiarmid', in *Hugh MacDiarmid: A Festschrift*, p. 107.
54. Duncan Glen, *Hugh MacDiarmid (Christopher Murray Grieve) and the Scottish Renaissance* (Edinburgh & London: Chambers, 1964), p. 124.
55. Ann Edwards Boutelle, *Thistle and Rose: A Study of Hugh MacDiarmid's Poetry* (Loanhead: MacDonald, 1980), p. 196.
56. Maxwell, 'The Nationalism of Hugh MacDiarmid', in *The Age of MacDiarmid*, p. 202.
57. Ibid., p. 222.
58. Catherine Kerrigan, *Whaur Extremes Meet: The Poetry of Hugh MacDiarmid 1920–1934* (Edinburgh: The Mercat Press, 1983), chs 10 and 11.
59. Hamish Henderson, 'To Hugh MacDiarmid', *Collected Poems and Songs*, ed. Raymond Ross (Edinburgh: Curly Snake Publishing, 2000), p. 120.
60. Tom Leonard, *Reports from the Present: Selected Work 1982–94* (London: Cape, 1995), p. 235.
61. Ibid., p. 26.
62. Iseult Honohan, *Civic Republicanism* (London & New York: Routledge, 2002), p. 155.
63. James D. Young, *The Very Bastards of Creation: Scottish-International Radicalism: A Biographical Study, 1707–1995* (Glasgow: Clydeside Press, [1996]), p. 21.
64. Ian Brookes et al. (eds), *The Chambers Dictionary* (Edinburgh: Chambers, 2003), p. 1286. See Aladair Gray and Adam Tomkins, *How We Should Rule Ourselves* (Edinburgh: Canongate, 2005) for a *précis* of their republican vision; also Willie Hamilton, *My Queen and I* (London: Quartet, 1975).
65. Edwin Morgan, 'The Coin', *Collected Poems 1949–1987* (Manchester: Carcanet, 1996), p. 455.
66. Alan Riach, *Representing Scotland in Literature, Popular Culture and Iconography: The Masks of the Modern Nation* (Basingstoke & New York: Palgrave Macmillan, 2005), pp. 128–9.
67. Christopher Whyte, 'Introduction', in Christopher Whyte (ed.), *Gendering the Nation: Studies in Modern Scottish Literature* (Edinburgh: Edinburgh University Press, 1995), p. ix.
68. According to the Women and Equality Unit, as of June 2005, female representation in the devolved Scottish Parliament was 39.5 per cent, fourth in the world behind the Welsh Assembly, Rwanda and Sweden, and well ahead of Westminster's 19.7 per cent <http://www.womenandequalityunit. gov.uk/public_life/parliament.htm> [accessed 1 September 2005].

Chapter 1

'Towards a New Scotland': Selfhood, History and the Scottish Renaissance

Hugh MacDiarmid's writing career was a committed act of engagement and identification with the land of his birth, a poetics of place striving to reveal the essential totality of the nation:

> So I have gathered unto myself
> All the loose ends of Scotland,
> And by naming them and accepting them,
> Loving them and identifying myself with them,
> Attempt to express the whole.
>
> ('Scotland', *CP1*, 652)

In *A Drunk Man Looks at the Thistle* he claims that 'a' that's Scottish is in me' (*CP1*, 145). The Drunk Man's self is compiled of 'a composite diagram o' / Cross-sections o' my forbears' organs' and although he attempts in self-disgust to exorcise this haunting by his ancestors he finds that 'like bindweed through my clay it's run' (*CP1*, 93). On examination of himself, the Drunk Man understands that his innermost spiritual identity is irredeemably connected to a metaphysical Scotland:

> My ain soul looks me in the face, as 'twere,
> And mair than my ain soul – my nation's soul!
>
> (*CP1*, 93)

In 'Dìreadh I' MacDiarmid names the nation as his Muse, 'the very object of my song / – This marvellous land of Scotland' (*CP2*, 1168), while 'Conception', one of a number of poems to paintings by fellow Borderer William Johnstone (1897–1981), gives birth to a new idea of Scotland that is at one with the poet's identity:

> So that indeed I could not be myself
> Without this strange, mysterious, awful finding
> Of my people's very life within my own

– This terrible blinding discovery
Of Scotland in me, and I in Scotland

(*CP2*, 1070)

Suggestive of MacDiarmid's nationalist-impelled Christ complex, such intimate and consciously chosen creative connection with nationality illustrates what Robert Crawford terms the identifying poet, those artists who 'construct for themselves an identity which allows them to identify with or to be identified with a particular territory'.[1]

MacDiarmid's self-identification with Scotland, and his desire to culturally and politically free the nation from what in *Lucky Poet* he calls 'the mystery of Scotland's self-suppression' (*LP*, 381), was ignited during the First World War. 'By the rule of well-established associations,' writes Vincent Sherry, 'the Great War of 1914–18 locates the moment in which the new sensibility of English – and international – modernism comes fully into existence.'[2] Despite the war's significance in the shaping of modernism, Paul Fussell points out that none of 'the masters of the modern movement' – amongst whom he includes Yeats, Woolf, Pound, Eliot, Lawrence and Joyce – were actually involved in the conflict.[3] In his influential 1975 study *The Great War and Modern Memory*, Fussell argues that the war 'was a hideous embarrassment to the prevailing Meliorist myth which had dominated the public consciousness for a century. It reversed the Idea of Progress.'[4] Through participation in the war MacDiarmid experienced for and in himself the foundering of history's forward trajectory as a European campaign of imperial advancement and improvement. If the inception of modernity is posited as the Enlightenment period, modernism as a cultural phenomenon can be seen as the disintegration of Enlightenment reason. But for MacDiarmid the political ruins other modernists sought to shore with the fragments of classical literary texts were not necessarily worth saving. His modernism attempted to hasten the collapse of imperialism in the realisation that such cultural and political precedence is a construct manufactured largely by and through metropolitan economic might.

From a historical crisis, a crisis of History, Grieve returned home armed from the war to challenge the idea of history as an imperial project of capitalist expansion. Strategically essentialising his (pseudonymous) identity in national terms, Grieve became MacDiarmid in order to unravel at a personal level and in the national culture the inscriptive influence of Scottish history's imperial direction. Having undertaken an autodidactic course of educational self-reformation during the war, Grieve came back to Scotland determined to cast himself as MacDiarmid the makar – maker of a new identity for himself and his country. Such national re-creation entailed a radical reassessment of the ideologically key Scottish institutions that moulded Chris Grieve: religion and education.

MacDiarmid may have believed the lineaments of modern Scottish experience to be hopelessly compromised by anglicisation, the culture an Eliotian wasteland in the Drunk Man's vision of 'sic a Blottie O' (*CP1*, 115), but even in his denunciation he expresses his linguistic debt to the national past. Despite claiming in 1922, in the first issue of the *Scottish Chapbook*, that he desired 'Not Traditions – Precedents',[5] he found in Scottish history a means to imagine the Scottish future, challenging the cultural legacy of the Reformation and a Calvinistic educational system geared to the dictates of British capital. Galvanised by the knowledge he gained in the Great War to wage his own war for Scotland, MacDiarmid adapted the generalist tools of the Scottish democratic intellect to stimulate a modern Scottish Renaissance and write the Scottish Republic.

Prelude – 'A Voice from Macedonia': Sergeant Grieve's War

Duthie, a character in MacDiarmid's playlet 'Nisbet, an Interlude in Post War Glasgow', diagnoses Nisbet's writer's block as a modernist aboulia resulting from the psychic traumas of the First World War: 'You haven't even written your war book, I suppose? That's fatal. Like internal bleeding. The only cure for modern war experiences is to write a book about them. An inexpressible emotion must be Hell . . .' (*Annals*, 107). It is not only the hellishness of the war that prevents Nisbet from expressing his experience of it to others; his artistic problem entails finding a form that will communicate the incommunicable horrors he has seen. With his populist materialism, Duthie cynically recommends that Nisbet 'toddle right off home and do a love story the *People's Friend* could accept' (*Annals*, 107). As a poet, though, Nisbet has higher ambitions, and is 'trying to invent a new insubmersible sort of song' – a difficult matter in a national culture drowned by anglicisation, where 'modern Scottish acoustics are so bad that it isn't worth while trying to make himself heard' (*Annals*, 108).

Published in 1922, when Grieve became MacDiarmid, the two leading characters of 'Nisbet' illustrate aspects of the Grieve/MacDiarmid identity: Duthie the socialist propagandist, politically engaged in the big city, bringing the war home by reversing its class terms in his battle for the future, and Nisbet, the young modernist Christ foretokening a new civilisation, who Duthie believes might 'have been all right if he'd stayed in Nazareth or Auchtermuchty or whatever his native village was' (*Annals*,

109), but now, crucified by the spiritual hopelessness and poverty of postwar Glasgow, he is 'quite unfit for civilised life' (108). In 1977 Tom Nairn cast Grieve/MacDiarmid as the psychologically split symbol of Scotland's identity crisis in a national culture ruptured by history; for the author of *The Break-Up of Britain*, modern Scotland is psychically sick, 'a sort of lunatic or deviant'.[6] The writer of 'Nisbet' had, however, suggested his own solution to this dualistically defective inheritance in the unseen figure of Moira, proponent of Dostoevsky and Sinn Féin Ireland. Sexually patronised by Duthie and the Communist Young for having 'No balance', as her 'Brain's like quicksilver' (*Annals*, 112), the stereotypically irrational Moira can actually cure Nisbet (and Scotland) of an identity crisis derived from the fractures of history. Moira does in fact display balance – that of the East–West synthesis of MacDiarmid's Gaelic Idea, in which Dostoevsky's Russia finds a complement and corrective in a radical Celtic Scotland. If 'Pearse and Plunkett and MacDonagh were only minor poets' (*Annals*, 112) of the 1916 Easter Rising in Ireland, then Nisbet's destiny is to give high modernist form to Scotland's historical awakening. Moira may remain offstage, but her ideas were to be central to MacDiarmid's conceptual liberation of his still passive motherland.

The dislocation of Nisbet may indicate something of Grieve's feelings on returning to Scotland from the war, but he did at least return. Of the 690,235 Scots who served, officially 74,000 did not come home – the real tally of the dead reckoned unofficially at nearer 100,000.[7] One such was 23-year-old John Brogue Nisbet, killed in the 1st Battle of Loos on 13 April 1915.[8] While training to be a teacher at Broughton Junior Student Centre in Edinburgh, Grieve was good friends with John Nisbet, describing the dead Royal Scots' 2nd Lieutenant in a letter to his former teacher George Ogilvie as 'infinitely more than a brother, a very spiritual familiar' (*L*, 10). Fellow socialists and lovers of German poets such as Rilke and Spitteler, Grieve and Nisbet had much in common, but when writing to Ogilvie Grieve suggests a deeper alignment:

> One of the many contrasting personalities in me was essentially Nisbet, thinking in me with his brain, working in me with his splendid sensuous vitality, reflecting upon the other personalities, part and parcel of the debating society which is my mental life. He must not go indedicate – I have the very poem (for poem it must be without saying). It trembles on my tongue – at times in semi-sleep I can read it in the volumes of my sub-consciousness as from a printed page – perfect, adequate. But I have not yet contrived to write it. Must I forever plan what I shall never execute? I am tortured worse than any Tantalus. (*L*, 10)

The first sentence here exhibits the multiple selves of modernism, but from the archaic 'indedicate' onwards contrivance increases until we arrive at the classical allusion of Greek myth. Grieve may have remembered 'indedicate' from Ernest Dowson's 'In Preface: For Adelaide' (1896): 'So for once you shall go indedicate, if not quite anonymous.'[9] Dated 20 August 1916, this important letter illustrates two things: firstly, hovering on the edge of a new era, Grieve has not quite found a settled modernist form yet, still fluctuating in the realms of the neo-Georgian, and, secondly, despite the immature, artificial language, Grieve genuinely seems to associate his developing creativity, the striving of his subconscious to find poetic expression, with the death of Nisbet, a friend he intimately equates with his own self. As Sarah Cole suggests in her study of male friendship and the First World War, 'the story of lost friendship will be most compellingly imagined as a site for the heightened and unmediated experience of modernity'.[10] Grieve's dedication to Nisbet came in the form of a play, not poetry: appearing in the *Scottish Chapbook*, August and September 1922, 'Nisbet' was the first work attributed to Hugh M'Diarmid. If Grieve authored 'Nisbet', Nisbet inspired MacDiarmid. From the theatre of war Grieve returns to adopt a battling persona. Impelled by the sacrificial death of his alter ego fighting for a British Empire that was jingoistically reduced in Churchillian rhetoric to 'dear England',[11] Grieve is reborn as MacDiarmid, radical saviour of modern Scotland. As he says in a letter to Ogilvie, in relation to his future political outlook, 'Nisbet's death finally settled matters' (20 August 1916, *L*, 13). Nisbet did not come home to write the war book his eponymous character subconsciously discerns in flux within him; with *Annals of the Five Senses*, written mainly in Salonika in 1917, but published in 1923, Grieve did this for him.

In *Annals* and his letters home to George Ogilvie we catch Grieve in the act of an autodidactic intellectual awakening that will lead to the union of his new identity with his vision of a new Scotland. Born in Glasgow in 1871, Ogilvie became the recipient of some of Grieve's most personal letters after establishing a friendship with the fledging writer while teaching him at Broughton. Writing to him on 9 December 1926 from Montrose, just after the publication of *A Drunk Man*, he calls Ogilvie 'my English master. I never had a Scots master' (*L*, 91). From Catherine Kerrigan we learn that Ogilvie had a similar evangelical background to MacDiarmid, and that he also 'had distinct socialist leanings'.[12] MacDiarmid's father died while he was at Broughton, one of the reasons for his departure. MacDiarmid says in *Lucky Poet* that the abandonment of his teacher training was 'one thing which I have never, for one moment, regretted', imagining teaching to 'be an utterly soul-destroying job'; Ogilvie, however, 'was a man in ten thousand, who meant a very great deal to me' (*LP*, 228). For Kerrigan, this goes as far as being 'a replacement for his dead father'.[13] Grieve's early letters to

Ogilvie certainly have the immature, overly earnest tone of a young man still seeking direction. There is a formality of address – Ogilvie always preceded by Mr – combined with a disingenuous nod to the discrepancy of talent between the professional English teacher and the self-styled poetic genius, 'Your Old Pupil' (4 December 1917, *L*, 19). Grieve writes his early manifestos to Ogilvie, what he hopes to achieve and believes himself to have already accomplished.

In a letter to Ogilvie from Macedonia, Grieve boasts of his 'ceaseless reading, wide as the world of books, in every conceivable subject' (20 August 1916, *L*, 14). Battling with 'the monotony of existence' in Salonika's 42nd General Hospital, he finds intellectual invigoration in Turgenev, Henry James and J. M. Synge, along with Georgian poetry, John Galsworthy's *Fraternity* (1909) and the Greek translations of Gilbert Murray (4 December 1917, *L*, 19). Such reading exacerbated Grieve's growing apartness from others, his elect solipsism. 'It is a terrible thought,' he writes Ogilvie on the 13 February 1918, 'shutting me in most horribly on myself, that of a list of say twelve people in whom I am for the moment pre-eminently interested, not one of them is known to any other member of the mess' (*L*, 21–2). Like the narrator of 'Cerebral', who worries that he has 'paralysed his creative faculties by over-reading' (*Annals*, 13), the people Grieve is interested in are authors, and include the Sitwells, Rebecca West (pseudonym of the Edinburgh-educated Cicily Isabel Fairfield), Remy de Gourmont and Theodore Maynard's poetic tribute to Pádraic Pearse from the *Dublin Leader*, a Sinn Féin periodical. Serving with the Royal Army Medical Corps in Greece, the proverbial cradle of European civilisation, Grieve is busy acquiring his own civilisation, enabling MacDiarmid's searing blast at the cultural paltriness of a broken modern world in 'Ode to All Rebels': '*Keep ga'en to your wars, you fools, as o' yore; / I'm the civilisation you're fechtin' for.*' (*CP1*, 501).

Fussell claims, 'The idea of endless war as an inevitable condition of modern life would seem to have become seriously available to the imagination around 1916.'[14] Primarily he means that, after two years of horrific conflict, at what would prove to be its midpoint, a resolution to the war must have seemed unimaginable. Fussell's use of 'imagination' can be interpreted more subtly, however. In *Ulysses*, Stephen Dedalus fears those big words, and the heroic ideas behind them, which make us so unhappy. Writing to F. G. Scott from Whalsay on 23 September 1940, MacDiarmid claims that 'all the Big Words died in the *last* war' (*NSL*, 187). But if the big words were killed in the First World War, a language of conflict, the terms of engagement of battle, helped define modernity's historically fractured psyche. In *Lucky Poet*, written during the Second World War, MacDiarmid contends that there can be no end to war, to mutual mass-extermination, so long as most people remain such morons. Their condition – their attitude to life – is in fact a species of cancer, entirely similar to the way in which cancer cells develop in the body of the host, by the failure of his own tissues to abandon their embryonic form and assume adult status and responsibility. (*LP*, 406–7)

If Joyce's contribution to the Great War effort was to write the hugely learned, pacifist *Ulysses*, by the next war, and with Joyce in mind, MacDiarmid is dreaming 'of a literary equipment which may bring immense erudition' (*LP*, 407) to the task of curing such general insanity, combating the deadening cancer of the universal mind. MacDiarmid's poetry, from the thirties in particular, wages intellectual war on a capitalist society that ceaselessly creates the conditions for war and limits the educational opportunities of those who will fight and be killed in them as so much proletarian cannon fodder. The Grieve who wrote the unpublished *A Voice From Macedonia*, also known as *Salonika Poems*, could never have been counted amongst the war poets, not only because he did not find a mature voice in Greece through which to adequately express war's emotions, but because the expression of such was never amongst his primary aims. If the poetry of the Great War is largely a lament for the death of comrades, it also marks the passing of the Victorian era and the decline of an Empire. MacDiarmid's *métier* is never death but a modern life more abundant – for the masses and his nation.

Grieve's war book, *Annals of the Five Senses*, illustrates his gladness at being alive in such life-threatening circumstances. The title, taken from G. Gregory Smith's *Scottish Literature: Character and Influence* (1919), conceives a chronicle or history of the war as it was written on the body, filtered through the five senses, of a survivor. 'Spanish Girl' records the 'disembodied memory' (*Annals*, 69) of a sexual encounter, as does 'Consummation' and 'A Moment in Eternity', dedicated to Ogilvie – a gesture surely intimating the quasi-sexual nature of the love this brainy boy of the class had for his teacher father figure. Each poem employs images of infinity as a means to fix in precious permanence the ephemerality of life, raising the nature of sexual love in wartime to that of a religious experience. In the midst of the jostling, sensual richness of Edinburgh's Princes Street, 'Sartoria' finds a male gaze 'discriminating countless shades where the common eye sees but gloom or glare; pursuing countless distinct movements where the common eye sees only a whirling perplexity' (*Annals*, 63). The somewhat Paterian narrator 'overflowed with sudden appreciations', understanding the sad momentariness of all those solitary lives lying beneath the exquisite externals of normality that so delight him: 'He "lived in the flicker" and darkness was all about. Souls glided in the human river, small green souls, red souls, white souls, pursuing, overtaking, joining, crossing each other, then separating slowly or hastily. So he seemed to see life' (*Annals*, 63).

Perhaps because of the influence of the recurrent malarial infection Grieve suffered three times in as many years between 1916 and 1918, the intellectuality, or tenor of mind, of *Annals* seems also to have a basis in the senses. Writing to Ogilvie from Marseilles on 12 June 1919, Grieve describes an excess of creative energy that 'tottered on the verge of cerebral vertigo' (*L*, 36). Alan Bold, Alan Riach and Roderick Watson all discern the influence of *Notes from Underground* (1864) on *Annals*, Riach noting that 'the twisted intensity of Dostoevsky's Underground Man infests their psychopathology' (*Annals*, xi–xii). Despite the constant background presence of the 'pathological element' ('A Four Years' Harvest', *Annals*, 36) in *Annals*, and in the letters to Ogilvie, the surrealistic conjunctions and collapse of enlightened reason occurring in many stories suggest a largely optimistic mind exercising its mental muscles rather than the obsessive misery of Dostoevsky's character.

Stimulated by the internationalism of his experiences in Salonika, 'where Russian, Frenchman, Italian, Greek pro-ally revolutionary, Serb and Britisher meet and make friends', Grieve excitedly tells Ogilvie that 'a curious polyglottery is the current medium of expression' (20 August 1916, *L*, 14). *Annals* exhibits a form of mental polyglottery, Grieve attempting different genres, styles and moods, but seeking always to find 'an essential and most excellent harmony in all this' ('Cerebral', *Annals*, 8). The narrator of 'Cerebral' makes an unconvincing attempt to maintain equilibrium of mind, but his loss of balance is controlled and deliberate, a mechanism designed to prompt creativity rather than a desperate fall into sterile insanity. Mapping the 'cranial geography and anatomical activities' (*Annals*, 6) of someone who describes himself as 'the Ibsen of Edinburgh' (9), 'Cerebral' is written by a man 'athrill with the miracle of sentience, quivering in every filament of his perceptions with an amazing aliveness' (7). For Fussell, 'the essence of the Great War', during which the psyche of the soldier split between that of actor and spectator, is found in 'its multitudinousness'.[15] The narrator of 'Cerebral' displays such many-sidedness. 'Constantly a new ego of his nature came in out of the multitudinous darkness and lit to a flame' (*Annals*, 7), he writes of himself in the third person, an onlooker to the various parts of his personality parading within his malarial brain:

> The Cynic, the Poet, the Prig, the Working Journalist, the Mere Human Being, his Father's Son, his Mother's Son, the Social Man, the Beardless Boy, the Seeker, Lazybones, the Innermost Critic, the Impersonal Factor, and an ever-increasing host more of them, all had fair play and carried on their separate activities with the mingled and protean materials of his mental life with the

fair effect of social commonwealth in being. His internal economy realised the dreams of the Socialist idealists . . . (*Annals*, 10)

Grieve's identity was to proliferate and take on many guises, with Hugh MacDiarmid being only the most renowned. The pseudonyms under which he operated include Gillechriosd Moraidh Mac a' Ghreidhir, A. K. Laidlaw, A. L., James Maclaren, Stentor and Pteleon, as well as Isobel Guthrie, Arthur Leslie and Mountboy. The procreative parental dualism of Grieve/MacDiarmid and their multiplicity of offspring is a device familiar to the fragmented identity of literary modernism; witness the disquietingly heteronomous Portuguese poet Fernando Pessoa, writer of another latterly peripheral, once imperial nation: 'My God, my God, who am I watching? How many am I? Who is I? What is this gap between me and me?'[16] The mind of 'Cerebral' communicates Grieve's 'vague distrusts of certitude' (*Annals*, 10). Unsure of his real self, the undetermined nature of personal identity in *Annals* issues from the crisis of national identity suffered by Grieve during the war. Fighting to discover his identity in a newly post-colonial terrain in which identity itself becomes a debatable land, the multiplying of self is both a form of cultural self-defence and a route to political liberation. From Ossian Macpherson to Scott the Great Unknown, 'Fiona MacLeod' and Leslie Mitchell's cousin Lewis Grassic Gibbon, the propagation of personae, what Hamish Henderson terms 'Alias MacAlias',[17] signifies a diminished modern Scottish identity that impels Scottish artists to adopt some sort of pseudonymous disguise or literary contrivance, so circumventing an inherited national inferiority complex that may otherwise have muted personal expression. Such troubling of individual identity as experienced during the war by Grieve is nationally externalised by MacDiarmid, used in political combat for the self-determination of Scotland. The canny Scots of Britain can never truly express themselves, silenced by their Calvinist complicity in Scotland's self-repression. Only able in these circumstances to give authentic voice to the nation through wearing a mask, an inverted form of the Yeatsian anti-self that allows him to damningly speak the truth about the nation, Grieve creates an immoderately expressive Scot in his invention MacDiarmid.

'A Four Years' Harvest' focuses specifically on the war and helps chart the progress from Grieve's personal uncertainties to the appearance of MacDiarmid the Scottish saviour. Again we find a multi-layered mind brimming over with ideas from books, full of projects to write his own, a self-consciously cracked actor watching himself watch the world fall apart and attempting to find among the ruins some internal order 'in that teeming brain of his' (*Annals*, 31). In such grievous external circumstances the narrator must believe 'that his own thought was part of the consciousness which sustained the world', and he hopes to 'find a rational quality in its final outlines as well as in human history' (*Annals*, 33). Believing that 'times of great human calamity had always thrown men back on first principles' (*Annals*, 45), he is searching for an almost mystical inner coherence that can also heal a fractured history. The Neo-Catholic character of 'A Limelight from a Solitary Wing' is drawn 'always to the whole, to the totality, to the general balance of things' (*Annals*, 90), but understands that the remedying of social ills must precede the attainment of spiritual liberation. Similarly, in 'A Four Years' Harvest' recourse to first principles demands curing 'the sickness of acquisitive society' (*Annals*, 52) before a transcendent vision can be achieved. The radical republican narrator attacks the Royals – 'a little German family and their vast crowd of German relatives and dependants' (*Annals*, 53) – and the class-based society of which they are the rotten crown. Reaching the end of his narrative, 'he saw in the dark lineaments of the man he was to become some such resemblance as Stephen Graham saw in a portrait of Robert Louis Stevenson to a painting of Christ in a Russian Monastery' (*Annals*, 59–60). Reminding us of the diseased body of Stevenson, the universal pathology of modernity's body politic is reflected in the disordered mind and senses of Grieve, who will return home from the sickness that is the war to become another Scottish Christ, saving the nation from its historical sins through art.

Writing to Ogilvie from 'Somewhere in France' on 24 November 1918, Grieve claimed that 'we have lost this war – in everything but actuality!' (*L*, 27). The pointlessness of mass slaughter, and the passivity with which he believed the war's victims were led to their death, saw him question the meaning, particularly in Scottish terms, of patriotism, democracy and the imperial purpose of history. Like the autobiographical narrator of 'A Four Years' Harvest', Grieve 'brought back to civilisation an ardour of revolt' (*Annals*, 43). Such radical zeal was not only stirred by the war, but also by national revolutions around the world. As far back as 1911, Grieve writes to Ogilvie from Wales on 24 October in admiration of 'the present Chinese revolution' (*L*, 5), which saw the establishment of a Republic through the toppling of the Manchu (Qing) dynasty. Fundamental to Grieve's developing nationalism was the 1916 Easter Rising in Ireland, described by Charles Duff as marking the 'dissolution of the British Empire'.[18] In barracks in Sheffield when the Rising took place between 24 and 29 April, MacDiarmid recalled, 'If it had been possible at all I would have deserted at that time from the British Army and joined the Irish.'[19] Claiming to have been a gunrunner for the Irish, he relates his notorious anglophobia to disgust at the killing of the 1916 leaders: 'The picture of [Roger] Casement hanged, and [James] Connolly taken out on a stretcher and executed, are two of the great rallying points of my spirit in its eternal and immeasurable hatred of everything English.'[20] In Russia the overthrow of the Romanovs in February 1917 and the subsequent Bolshevik Revolution in October of that year inspired Grieve to plan a short work on 'The Soviet State', a project that, according to his letter to Ogilvie of 23 March 1919, 'entailed a fearful amount of reading' (L, 33). Interpreting these national revolutions as republican interruptions of imperial history, Grieve plans the writing of a similar historical redirection in Scotland.

Grieve's programme for a new Scotland is not immediately obvious from either *Annals* or his letters home to Ogilvie. Except in one important letter of 20 August 1916, from neither source do we get a sense that his reading matter, always so integral to his work, has as yet a specifically Scottish dimension. Grieve does mention, in two letters to Ogilvie,[21] the poet and playwright George Reston Malloch (1875–1953), who published *Poems and Lyrics* in 1917. Focusing on Malloch's work as a Scottish poet, in the *Scottish Educational Journal* for 18 September 1925, Grieve thought him 'unquestionably one of our greatest twenty' ('George Reston Malloch', *CSS*, 119). In discussion with a character called Malloch, the narrator of 'A Four Years' Harvest' agrees with him 'that the real literature of the war could not possibly be written for a few years – possibly for a good few years – if ever' (*Annals*, 31). This 'real literature of the war' would not have as its subject the war itself, but rather the mechanisms of civilisation that generate war:

> Old ideas, old standards were inevitably judged with an acrid bitterness which sought to destroy and to cast into oblivion the oldest and most respected of human institutions – anything, if war be made impossible. He came back with an *idée fixe* – never again must men be made to suffer as in these years of war . . . Book after book was coming out now on this theme, each in its own way, according to the temperament of the author, formulating an indictment of modern society . . . (*Annals*, 44)

Eschewing depictions of the war, real war literature questions the direction of history and the nature of modernity. In the definition of Grieve's character, modernism maps radical societal change.

When writing to Ogilvie, Grieve was incapable of communicating his modernist desire for change in Scotland due to 'the strictness of the Censorship', but in this letter from Macedonia, dated 28 April 1918, he hints at his intentions:

> However loyal I may be to certain ideals bound up in the Allied Cause I was never to say the least of it an Anglophile – and when I am free of his majesty's uniform again I shall have a very great deal indeed to say and to write that I have not nearly enough desire for premature and secret martyrdom to say or write until then. (L, 25)

Unable to voice his political and cultural aims for Scotland during the war, Grieve imagines that publicising his radical republicanism when back home will invite persecution. Censored whilst involved in an imperial war, on his return he plans to be Scotland's saviour by resurrecting a censored Scottish tradition of anti-imperialism. In a letter to Ogilvie of 11 November 1918, he states that his 'plans for after the war are all cut and dried – I am ready and eager for a time of systematic production' (*L*, 26). Thirteen days later he writes, 'What I meant was that my life-work is really done – that various books exist complete and unchangeable in my mind – what remains is only to do the actual writing' (*L*, 28). From 'Somewhere in Macedonia' (20 August 1916, *L*, 7), Grieve will 'come back and start a new Neo-Catholic movement. I shall enter heart and body and soul into a new Scots Nationalist propaganda' (*L*, 14).

'The Scottish Vortex': or The Scottish Renaissance and Back to the Future

Grieve's thinking during the war had turned to Neo-Catholicism as a means to save Scotland's soul, which he identifies with his own, from historical oblivion. In the letter of 20 August 1916 to Ogilvie he claims to have 'completed' essays on 'Neo-Catholicism's debt to Sir Walter Scott' and 'The Indisseverable Association' (*L*, 8) between Catholicism and Scotland. Grieve is positing a relationship between Catholicism and the nation that is akin to the indisseverable Aristotelian link between the body and the soul.[22] Scotland's Catholic past could play a unifying role in healing the historical ruptures MacDiarmid believed the nation to be suffering from in the present: the Reformation and the Acts of Union, followed by the massive material developments of the Industrial Revolution, tore Scotland's soul – language, culture and art – from the body politic of the nation.

In his letter to Ogilvie from Macedonia we see Grieve begin the process of acquiring Scottish cultural omnipotence, something connected, even at this early stage in his development, with his idea of a failed national culture:

> I have my *The Scottish Vortex* (as per system exemplified in *Blast*), *Caricature in Scotland – and lost opportunities*, *A Copy of Burns I want* (suggestions to illustrators on a personal visualization of the national pictures evoked in the poems), *Scottish Colour-Thought* (a study of the aesthetic condition of Scottish nationality in the last three centuries) and *The Alienation of Our Artistic Ability* (the factors which prevent the formation of a 'national' school and drive our artists to other lands and to 'foreign portrayal'). (*L*, 9)

This small snippet, taken from Grieve's notebook and sent to Ogilvie as part of a longer manifesto-like letter, encapsulates MacDiarmid's programme in Montrose for a Scottish Renaissance. Ostensibly concerned with the visual arts, in his five planned studies Grieve is actually attempting the visualisation of a new Scotland. He wants to:

1. Rebut the burlesque stereotyping of Scotland (characterised by such as Harry Lauder), and the lost political and cultural opportunities such caricature entails.
2. Present a personalised vision of the Burns he wants to see, one related to the Scottish landscape.
3. Investigate the ways in which Scotland has been coloured aesthetically by and since the Reformation.
4. Find out why there has been no national movement in Scotland when Scots have played such a prominent role in recreating other nations.
5. Link Scotland with European, avant-gardist modernity, in the shape of specific movements such as Vorticism and, more generally, international modernism.

Although its influence continued to be felt in the modernist aesthetic, as a movement, interested in the reality of the machine age, Vorticism was weakened by the Great War – the ultimate negative expression of industrial power. Born in Nova Scotia of an American father and English mother, Wyndham Lewis, the prime practitioner and theorist of Vorticism alongside Ezra Pound, may have wished to 'Kill John Bull with Art!' but the concerns of his journal *BLAST* were avowedly metropolitan.[23] Issued on 20 June 1914, the first edition of this 'Review of the Great English Vortex' – the second and final *BLAST* was the war edition of July 1915 – sees Lewis picturing England as an 'Industrial Island machine, pyramidal workshop, its apex at Scotland, discharging itself on the sea'.[24] Lewis recognises Scotland as the pinnacle of industrial development, but he views the British pyramid from an English angle with London as the economic, political and artistic base. On settling in Montrose after the war MacDiarmid began to implement his planned Scottish Vortex as the Scottish Renaissance, a movement with designs to generate a whirlpool of creative activity that will fill the cultural cavity at the centre of Scottish experience and wash away the exploitative pyramidal structure of Britain.

If Vorticism, by adapting Cubism, German Expressionism and the Italian Futurism of Marinetti, looked to the future as decidedly urban and industrial, then the Scottish Renaissance movement that MacDiarmid helped instigate from the provincial setting of Montrose looked back in order to posit a modernist future for the nation. By no means, however, does this imply that MacDiarmid was blind to the industrial realities of modernity. Writing a serialised essay for the *New Age* in the first three months of 1925, Grieve aims in 'The Third Factor' 'to deal with the effects and potential effects of current scientific discoveries on Arts and Letters and Human Culture generally' (*RT1*, 241). Humanity and nature may formerly have been the two main factors in culture, but for Grieve modern conditions propose the necessity that artist and audience assimilate a third factor: machinery. With this new third factor in mind, Grieve decides that 'the Italian Futurists were undoubtedly on the right lines when they sought (in 1915) to establish their Synthetic Futurist Theatre', the irrationalism of this venture – considering the fascist affiliations of Italian Futurism – mirroring that of the war, which was itself 'to them a species of intensified Futurism' (*RT1*, 245). He goes on to claim that the immense popularity of theatre over other literary forms in Italy influenced the Futurists in the choice of medium through which to express their manifesto. MacDiarmid adapted his synthetic Scots poetry with a similar insight into the cultural specificities of his own nation as that displayed by the Futurists in Italy. *The Criterion*, launched by T. S. Eliot in 1922, published MacDiarmid's 'English Ascendancy in British Literature' (1931) which contends that 'there is not the divorce between poetry and popularity in Scotland that is to be found elsewhere. This is a vital matter and one of the real foundations for hoping for a great Scottish literary revival' (*SP*, 75).

Such a revival required its manifesto. Launched in August 1922, the *Scottish Chapbook* declared its six 'principal aims and objects', which included bringing 'Scottish Literature into closer touch with current European tendencies in technique and ideation', and developing 'the distinctively Scottish range of values'.[25] The targets set by Grieve as founding editor of the *Scottish Chapbook* were largely literary, and MacDiarmid may have felt he had met many of these in 1925 with *Sangschaw*, followed a year later by *Penny Wheep* and *A Drunk Man*. As such, he broadened his concerns in 1927 with *Albyn: or Scotland and the Future*. *Albyn* does, however, offer a 'theory of Scots letters' (*A*, 13), one that endorses his own work in Montrose. The famous literary keynote of the MacDiarmidian Renaissance is 'Not Burns – Dunbar!' (*A*, 14). Grieve wants to go back beyond the linguistic compromises of the Enlightenment to rediscover 'the full canon of Scots used by the Auld Makars and readapt it to the full requirements of modern self-expression' (*A*, 14). By trading the broken tongue of different dialects for a whole national language, MacDiarmid hopes modern Scottish poets will avoid the concessions to metropolitan taste that he believes dislocates Burns's oeuvre. 'His poetry in English is wholly negligible,' Grieve argues of Burns, 'and of his work as a whole it may be said that it rises in poetic value the further away from English it is, and the stronger the infusion of Scots he employs' (*A*, 15). For MacDiarmid, writing in Scots achieves a depth and seriousness lacking in English because it facilitates access to the artistic, and hence national, psyche. Recourse to the language of William Dunbar (c.1460–c.1520) will solve an artistic problem in the contemporary national culture, saving it from the sentimentalities of Kailyard Scots – a linguistic half-breed. However, if he is heroically attempting to recover some 'of the future that was foregone at Flodden' (1513) by going back to Dunbar, and so suffering from and perpetuating a Scottish lost-historical-cause syndrome that the movement wishes to finally defeat, Grieve also wants the Scottish Literary Revival to be 'aligned with contemporary tendencies in European thought and expression' (*A*, 17). He discerns 'that there is a tendency in world-literature today which is driving writers of all countries back to obsolete vocabularies and local variants and specialized usages of language of all kinds' (*A*, 14).

A manifesto of the Scottish Renaissance as the movement was conceived by MacDiarmid, *Albyn* benefited from the five years of experience he had already acquired in Montrose working towards a new Scotland. This important state of the nation essay could be broadly characterised as postcolonial, but perhaps, in the light of Scottish centrality to the British Empire, it should tentatively be termed post-imperial or, more surely, post-British. Grieve points out that the birth of the Scottish Renaissance 'synchronized with the end of the War', arguing that the aims of the movement 'will be seen to have had a genesis in kin with other post-war phenomena of recrudescent nationalism all over Europe' (*A*, 1). Such postwar nationalism was coincident with a 'wave of Catholic revivalism' (*A*, 1). Although the renaissance of a native literature was initially its main ambition, by 1927 MacDiarmid understands that the concerns of the movement must broaden to include the realms of politics and religion. This interest in religion is in itself, however, primarily political. Grieve may claim that in Scotland 'materialism is giving way to new spiritual ideals' (*A*, 5), but it is precisely because this is not true of the political ethos of the nation's electorate that the Scottish Renaissance is necessarily idealist and ostensibly elitist. *Albyn* actually uses religion as a strategic device through which to attack the historical foundations of the British state.

C. M. Grieve's *Albyn: or Scotland and the Future* was written in response to *Caledonia: or The Future of the Scots* by the journalist and author George Malcolm Thomson (1899–1996). Both were published in 1927 in Kegan Paul's 'To-day and To-morrow' series. Stimulated by response to contemporary conditions, the title of each uses an ancient historical term for Scotland to posit self-determining yet markedly different futures for the nation. Whereas Thomson's book uses Imperial Rome's name for the country (derived from the Pictish Caledonii) and his subtitle is specifically concerned with the future of the Scots as a people or race, Grieve's title has older Celtic connotations and its inquiry into modern Scotland is more broadly adapted to ideas of national inclusiveness. *Scottish Scene*, coauthored by MacDiarmid and Lewis Grassic Gibbon (1901–35) and published in 1934, is subtitled *or The Intelligent Man's Guide to Albyn*. Here, in sarcastic vein in 'Glasgow', Gibbon claims to 'like the thoughts of the Scottish Fascists evicting all those of Irish blood from Scotland, and so leaving Albyn entirely deserted but for some half-dozen pro-Irish Picts like myself' (*SS*, 140). None the less, Gibbon thought highly enough of Thomson to have made him the dedicatee of *Cloud Howe* in 1933. This despite the fact that for Thomson, a combination of Scottish emigration and Irish immigration – the former partly prompted by the latter – means that 'the Scots are a dying people. They are being replaced in their own country by a people alien in race, temperament, and religion, at a speed which is without parallel in history outside the era of the barbarian invasions.'[26] Scotland is, in fact, experiencing 'the gravest race problem confronting any nation in Europe today'.[27] Thomson imagined that, coupled with the Scottish diaspora, the so-called Irish invasion would spell the end of Scotland by 2027.

In the main, MacDiarmid reacted positively to the anti-anglicisation of *Caledonia* and Thomson's explicit portrayal of Scotland's social and economic plight. However, believing sectarianism to be largely caused by such material problems rather than by seemingly insurmountable religious differences, with *Albyn* he seeks to counteract the racialised and divisive factionalism of Thomson's book, in which the Irish are nearly always identified as Catholic and essentially foreign to the Scottish character. In 'The Truth About Scotland', a review of *Caledonia* appearing in the *New Age* on 10 November 1927, Grieve thought that a 'weakness of Mr Thomson's book is its failure to realise the recent great growth and new tendencies in Scottish Nationalism' (*RT2*, 27). When 'Irish Lessons for Scottish Nationalists' appeared in the *Modern Scot* in April 1931, Grieve, strategically adopting the Gaelic pseudonym Gillechriosd Moraidh Mac a' Ghreidhir, grouped Thomson with the Duke of Montrose and Andrew Dewar Gibb for 'political ineptitude and the egregiousness of their so-called constructive proposals' for Scotland (*RT2*, 377).

Born in 1888, Andrew Dewar Gibb MBE was Regius Professor of Law at the University of Glasgow when he was appointed leader of the Scottish National Party (1936–40). In *Scotland in Eclipse* (1930), extolling what he imagines to be the characteristic imperialism of 'Aryan peoples', he argues that 'viewed in any light the great Irish trek to Scotland is a national problem and a national evil of the first importance'.[28] James Graham, 6th Duke of Montrose (1878–1954), was a founding member of the National Party of Scotland (NPS) with Grieve in 1928. In 1930, disaffected by the ca' canny Home Rule constitutionalism of the NPS, and the sectarianism of some of its leading members, MacDiarmid sought to develop Clann Albainn, a nationalist organisation along the lines of Sinn Féin in Ireland. Criticised as a militant extremist by the Duke of Montrose, he was also attacked by Lewis Spence (1874–1955), poet and mythographer, historian of Atlantis and fellow founder of the NPS. MacDiarmid countered in the *Modern Scot* by denouncing the illiberality of their nationalism:

> His Grace [the Duke of Montrose] contends that Scottish people can look after their own interests without the help of Irish, Poles, English, and other aliens. The answer is – then why haven't they done so? Even His Grace's efforts over many years have failed to stir them up, and Scottish interests have been sacrificed all along the line. In any case, these aliens are citizens of Scotland and their interests are bound up with its condition. Does His Grace propose to disfranchise them – or, like Mr Spence, to evict them? Why can't he face the practical political situation, recognize them for the important, permanent, and increasing factors they are in our electorate, and be ready to welcome any signs they show of identifying themselves with Scottish interests and becoming true citizens of our country? They cannot be worse Scots than the majority of our own people have been, and are. ('Clann Albainn', *SP*, 56)

The Scottish National Party was born in 1934 from the amalgamation of the NPS with the right-wing Scottish Party, a group of Conservative and Liberal professionals established in 1932 by Dewar Gibb and the Duke of Montrose, amongst others. Richard Finlay points out that 'the Scottish Party was driven as much by a desire to keep a lid on Scottish nationalism as by a wish to promote it'.[29] Thomson, with the novelist Neil M. Gunn (1891–1973), acted as intermediary in the merger. MacDiarmid was ostracised for his radical nationalism and expelled from the NPS in 1933. Grieve argues in *Albyn* that 'Scotland is unique among European nations in its failure to develop a nationalist sentiment strong enough to be a vital factor in its affairs' (*A*, 19). As such, a contemporary nationalist movement can only hope to recreate the conditions for political autonomy by undermining the historical factors through which Scottish nationalism was extinguished.

For MacDiarmid, the great historical movement responsible for initiating Scotland's loss of political autonomy was the Reformation. Not only was the Reformation disastrous for the cultural life of the nation, Grieve also claims that it 'subverted the whole national psychology' (*A*, 12). The Reformation, in fact, 'progressively severed the Scottish people from their past' (*A*, 12), undermining the use of Scots and facilitating the Acts of Union. The Scottish Renaissance seeks a cultural Counter-Reformation that will secure an independent political future, achievable in part through the 're-Catholicization' (*A*, 12) of Scotland. MacDiarmid welcomed Irish-Catholic immigration to Scotland, hoping it would help to reverse what he perceived as the negative effects of the Reformation. Similarly, just as many of the cultural leaders of the Irish Revival were Protestant in a largely Catholic country, MacDiarmid thought the Scottish Renaissance would be politically more potent if several of its prime cultural practitioners were Catholic.

Some were Catholic converts; many who did not become so remained anti-Calvinist. Tom MacDonald (1906–75), born in Montrose and Grieve's Links Avenue neighbour in the town for a spell in the 1920s, became Fionn Mac Colla. He joined the NPS in 1928 and converted in 1935. *The Albannach* (1932) and *And the Cock Crew* (1945) castigate the cultural blight of Scotland's Knoxian heritage. Cofounder of the NPS, Compton Mackenzie (1883–1972) converted to Catholicism in 1914. *Sinister Street* (1913), his early autobiographical *Bildungsroman*, climaxes with the hero Charles Michael Saxby Fane coming to the faith. Attending St James's Preparatory School before going up to Oxford, Michael is obsessed with the Jacobite cause and 'longed to hear that in some way he was connected with Jacobite heroes and the romantic Stuarts'.[30] In *Catholicism and Scotland*, published in 1936 as part of Routledge's important 'The Voice of Scotland' series that also included Edwin Muir's *Scott and Scotland* and MacDiarmid's suppressed *Red Scotland*, Mackenzie compares the Reformation's imposition with the totalitarianism of Russian Bolshevism and Hitler's Fascism. Instigating the continuing 'downward movement' of Scottish spiritual fortunes, the Reformation was 'a spectacular attempt at self-destruction in the year 1560'.[31] Mackenzie mentions the Jesuit John Ogilvie in *Catholicism and Scotland*, Scotland's only post-Reformation saint since his canonisation in 1976. Born near Keith to a Calvinist family in 1579, Ogilvie converted in 1596 and was hanged in Glasgow in 1615, the only official Catholic martyr of the Scottish Counter-Reformation. Significantly, Mackenzie's multi-volume epic *The Four Winds of Love* (1937–45) charts the peripatetic life of the autobiographical character John Ogilvie, from *The East Wind of Love*, exploring Ogilvie's youthful sympathy with Irish self-determination, through the war to the concluding *The North Wind of Love*, which sees the mature Ogilvie finally settle in Scotland and commit himself to working for the nation's independent future.

Posted to Rome in 1949 as Director of the British Council, Edwin Muir (1887–1959) was deeply struck by how Christ seemed everywhere incarnate in the Eternal City, something that 'would have shocked the congregations of the north'.[32] Muir didn't convert to Catholicism, but anti-Calvinism is evident in, for instance, 'Scotland 1941' and his 1929 biography *John Knox*. Dedicated to MacDiarmid, Muir's 'Portrait of a Calvinist' argues that the Knoxian revolution deprived 'Scotland of all the benefits of the Renaissance'.[33] Continuing to indulge his own brand of Calvinist revisionism in *Scott and Scotland*, Muir notoriously claims that the Enlightenment Edinburgh inherited by Sir Walter was nothing but 'a blank'.[34] In her contribution to 'The Voice of Scotland' series, *Mrs Grundy in Scotland* (1936), Willa Muir (1890–1970) confirms that 'the Reformation was a kind of spiritual strychnine of which Scotland took an overdose'.[35] Calderwick, a fictionalisation of Muir's Montrose birthplace, suffers the icy patriarchal grip of Calvinist repression in her novels *Imagined Corners* (1931) and *Mrs Ritchie* (1933).

With *Virtue, Learning and the Scottish Enlightenment* (1993), David Allan has endeavoured to undermine the still pervasive view, inherited from Scottish modernism, of the Reformation as a kind of cultural blitzkrieg that crushed the flower of Renaissance humanism in the north, pointing particularly to the work of George Buchanan (1506–82) as 'tapping into some form of Renaissance thought'.[36] MacDiarmid admired Buchanan for the radical republicanism of the reformist political essay *De Iure Regni apud Scotos Dialogus* (1579),[37] but also for the Latin poetry of 'Epithalamium for Mary Stuart and the Dauphin of France' (1558). As a self-proclaimed atheist MacDiarmid never became a Catholic, despite his wartime interest. Like other Scottish Renaissance writers, however, his ideas seem often to accord with what William Storrar calls 'the parrot cries of the Scottish *literati* about the continuing blight of Calvinism on the nation's psyche' and culture.[38] The Drunk Man laments the cultural influence of Calvinism in almost pathological terms, suggesting a disease particular to the artist that has communal side effects:

> O fitly frae oor cancerous soil
> May this heraldic horror rise!
> The Presbyterian thistle flourishes,
> And its ain roses crucifies . . .

> (CP1, 152)

Writing in the *Pictish Review* of June 1928, Grieve claims in 'The Conventional Scot and the Creative Spirit' that

> the general type of consciousness which exists in Scotland today – call it Calvinistic or what you will (it has, at any rate, been very largely coloured and determined by the unique and peculiarly unfortunate form the Reformation took in Scotland) – is anti-aesthetic to an appalling degree, and none the less so because it is, *ipso facto*, constitutionally unconscious of its disability, and naïvely disposed to set up its own gross limitations as indispensable criteria. (RT2, 55)

Despite his negativity, in attacking the spiritual essence of British Scotland MacDiarmid's anti-Calvinist, Catholic Scotland of the modernist Renaissance is a polemical construct with a radical political purpose. 'It will not do to identify Scottish nationality and traditions wholly with Protestantism', Grieve contends in *Albyn*, mapping a theoretical route back to the future; 'there has always been a considerable native Catholic population, and most of the finest elements in our traditions, in our literature, in our national history, come down from the days when Scotland was wholly Catholic' (*A*, 29). When Linda Colley asks, 'Who were the British, and did they even exist?' her answer is categorical: 'Protestantism was the foundation that made the invention of Great Britain possible.'[39] Irishness may be critically absent from Colley's historical definition of Britishness but it is decidedly present in MacDiarmid's sense of contemporary Scottishness. By emphasising the cultural bountifulness of Scotland's pre-Reformation past, MacDiarmid is seeking to counter the influence of Protestantism in unifying the nations of the United Kingdom and undermine its continuing power to do so in the present. If monarchical Britain is constitutionally anti-Catholic then his proposition is a new republican Scotland emerging from a modern nationalist movement, each being inclusive and catholic rather than sectarian.[40] Mirroring the multiplicity of MacDiarmid, Grieve advocates 'Scotland as a diversity-in-unity' (*A*, 4).

'The Reformation was in a key sense a revolutionary Year Zero', according to Murray Pittock, who continues: 'To contrast the Church of England's adoption, even usurpation, of the Catholic past with the iconoclasm of Scotland is to see the beginnings of Enlightenment attitudes towards Scotland as barbarous and backward.'[41] Pittock's point can help us understand MacDiarmid's hostility to the Renaissance proper, the humanist antecedent of Enlightenment universalism. Grieve wants to 'go back behind Burns to Dunbar', retrieving for use by his modernist descendants the techniques and language of Scotland's Renaissance makar, 'and the Old Makars – great Catholic poets using the Vernacular' (*A*, 4). In spite of his laudation of Dunbar, Grieve believes that 'today there is a general reaction against the Renaissance' (*A*, 9) of the late medieval, early modern period. In Scotland this reaction took the form of the Scottish Renaissance movement, clearly definable as culturally nationalist, even if not wholly politically so. Grieve the cultural and political nationalist states that 'the future of the Scots spirit may depend upon the issue of the great struggle going on in all the arts between the dying spirit of the Renaissance and the rediscovered spirit of nationality' (*A*, 9). He believes that the revival of dialect, 'entering into the stuff of modern literature in every country' (*A*, 9), signals the exhaustion of the imperialistic universalism characteristic of the Renaissance. The annexation of autochthonous culture by the Greek and Roman classicism of the Renaissance was problematical in Scotland. The application of such universalistic criteria rendered Gaelic barbarian and Scots embarrassingly irrelevant in acts of Othering judiciously confirmed by the anglophonic and largely Presbyterian Enlightenment. But in a postwar climate in which Enlightenment universals of self-suppressing rationality and imperial internationalisation have disintegrated, MacDiarmid promotes a modern Scottish Renaissance that speaks with the historically silenced voice of the uniquely local. To Grieve, 'Dialect is the language of the common people; in literature it denotes an almost overweening attempt to express the here-and-now. That, in its principle, is anti-Renaissance' (A, 9).

The Renaissance defines the birth of modern Western European civilisation, history and competitive individualism in the mapping of previously uncharted terrain. 'English Ascendancy in British Literature' repeats the desire 'to get back behind the Renaissance!' (SP, 80). In MacDiarmid's Defence of the West, elaborated in Whalsay, he wishes to reverse history's terms precisely in order to protect peripheral European cultures such as Gaelic from the obliteration of difference constituted by imperial expansion. In Albyn Grieve recognises Scotland as 'one of the great founder nations of the Empire' (A, 25). But, strategically seeking common ground with moderate nationalists and those of other political creeds, he is disingenuous in his claims that Scottish autonomy will not threaten the Empire. With the Scottish Renaissance Grieve advances a movement that will 'reverse the existing order' of politics established by the imperial project of history, so rediscovering the suppressed tradition of 'old Scottish radicalism and republicanism' (A, 2). The recovery of this tradition contemporaneously establishes a historical basis for the 'closer inter-relationship of the Scottish Socialist and Nationalist Movements' (A, 38). If this tradition is to find contemporary scope, however, the metropolitan historiographical operation as it is administered in Scotland must be reoriented by the educational programme of the Scottish Renaissance movement.

Writing the Scottish Republic: learning from history in the new Scotland

MacDiarmid understands that education has been central to the politically designed anglicisation of Scottish experience and the continuance of Scotland as British. In 'After George Robey', from the Scottish Nation, 15 May 1923, he argues, 'The Scottish educational system, once the finest in Europe, has been poisoned by English influences' (*RT1*, 65). By exerting metropolitan pedagogical control over Scottish education, the British state seeks to secure the political conformity of its potentially unruly northern province. MacDiarmid believes that an anglocentric educational policy ensures that 'Scottish interests are systematically subordinated to English' (*RT1*, 65). Even Scottish intellectuals 'belong to England rather than Scotland. London is their "spiritual home" – in so far as they have any' (*RT1*, 65). Crucially, the denationalisation of those who should be formulating the politics of this place, the nation's educators, signals that 'the Scottish *Intelligentsia* is dead' (*RT1*, 65).

Like Edwin Muir, MacDiarmid was responsible for his own higher education. This may partly explain each man's tendency to make personalistic generalisations regarding Scottish cultural history, such as those underpinning Muir's *Scott and Scotland* or, indeed, what may be viewed as MacDiarmid's pridefully tendentious premise that, excepting himself, Scottish intellectuals do not exist. Mindful of Muir and MacDiarmid, Cairns Craig characterises this tendency of certain Scottish writers to commit a national form of historical suicide as 'Scottish culture as erasure'.[42] Craig's theoretical attempt to maintain contemporary cultural health ignores, however, the dismal historical reality as witnessed by MacDiarmid on return from the war. In a postwar era that saw Scottish identity shaken by the loss of imperial certitudes, Richard Finlay claims, 'it was thought that Scotland would soon cease to exist as an identifiable nation', his questioning subtitle, 'The End of Scotland?', illustrating the historical acuity of the crisis.[43]

Despite MacDiarmid's grim assessment of the culture before its modernist Renaissance, Scottish academia had shown signs of regaining a more distinctly national approach at the turn of the twentieth century. MacDiarmid exploited such historical glimmers in imagining a Scottish Republic, whilst also seeking radical educative outsiders through which to censure the Scottish education system and attack political consensus. In the midst of the Highland Crofters' Revolt, led by John Murdoch (1818–1903), Gaelic finally won academic acceptance in the capital of Enlightenment as the University of Edinburgh was granted a Chair of Celtic Languages in 1883. MacDiarmid found Murdoch late, which he attributed to historical obfuscation of the radical tradition. In his Foreword to *The Scottish Insurrection of 1820*, MacDiarmid protests in 1970 that due to the political bias of the Scottish 'educational system scarcely anything of value in relation to our literature, history, national biography, or economic facts gets through the filter'; this is especially true with regard to 'Scottish Radical and Republican thinkers' such as the executed radicals of 1820, not to mention the likes of John Maclean,

John Swinton (1829–1901), the reforming journalist and correspondent of Marx, and Murdoch.[44] In 'A Brief Survey of Modern Scottish Politics', from the *National Weekly* of 4 October 1952, he connects Murdoch with 'a Scottish revolutionary Republican Movement', calling the Crofters' Revolt 'the greatest agrarian worker's victory in modern Scots history' (*RT3*, 292).

In the 1890s, Patrick Geddes (1854–1932), Professor of Botany at University College Dundee (1889–1914), instigated his own 'Scots Renascence', establishing the Outlook Tower in Edinburgh in 1892 and, with William Sharp (1855–1905), the *Evergreen: A Northern Seasonal* in four editions (1895–7). In the *Scottish Nation*, 27 November 1923, MacDiarmid describes the generalist project of the Tower as enabling 'the fullest understanding of the place by its people' ('The Outlook Tower', *RT1*, 131). Geddes is valuable to MacDiarmid as a Scottish rebel within the specialised educational establishment, his career illustrative of the traditional generalist approach of the democratic intellect. 'Geddes "practiced synthesis in an age of specialism" ', he writes in 1966, quoting Lewis Mumford, 'the very practice that has been the theme of all my later poetry and work as a teacher and publicist' (*Company*, 79).

The *Scottish Historical Review* was established in 1903 and the 1911 Scottish National Exhibition in Glasgow endowed a Chair of Scottish History and Literature at the University. The teaching union the Educational Institute of Scotland (EIS) was founded in 1847. In 1876 the EIS began publishing its own journal, the *Educational News*, which in 1918 became the *Scottish Educational Journal*, scene of much of Grieve's Geddes-like project to teach teachers to modernise Scottish education. Robert Anderson tells us that the *Educational News* (which he cites from 7 November 1885) was a trenchantly Unionist publication:

> Parochialism and sentimentality were always the main charges against those who argued for a distinctive Scottish identity, along with the brisk historical view put by the *Educational News* that 'until Scotland was united to England it was one of the poorest and most wretched countries in Europe. Since the Union it has flourished, and become rich and prosperous.' Such views were not imposed from London by the SED [Scottish Education Department], or from Edinburgh by Anglicized university professors, but were to be found at the heart of Scottish educational culture.[45]

Anderson confirms 'that for the Scottish élite in the years before 1914 nationalism was not the opposite of unionism but fused with it'.[46] Having served in what he came to regard as an imperial war, such politics could only be dismissed as inferiorism by MacDiarmid. In 'Towards a New Scotland' he angrily asks, 'Was it for little Belgium's sake / Sae mony thoosand Scotsmen dee'd?' (*CP1*, 451). The establishment of a new

Scotland will require the radical reconstruction of a national education that has 'been utterly de-Scoticized and adapted in the most shocking fashion to suit the exigencies of English Imperialism and the Capitalist system' (*LP*, 229).

With no direct professional investment in the Scottish educational system, MacDiarmid's analysis of the role education should play in reviving the nation at this critical period can certainly make him appear something of a maverick; but it is precisely this lack of tenure, his freedom to investigate the business of education from the perspective of his own individual needs as a creative writer in Scotland, that sharpens his critique. MacDiarmid had no narrowly specialised interest in education, but a life-long and committed engagement to changing the fundamental tenets of teaching in Scotland as a means to unlock the nation's historical self-suppression. This 'Scottish republican and revolutionary Socialist' says in *Lucky Poet*, 'I have devoted a great deal of my life to Scottish education' (*LP*, 341). MacDiarmid believes that education should be a general preparation for life that will 'enable the child to develop his personality to the full and to realize all that he has it in him to be' (*LP*, 140). He hopes that such successful self-realisation of the students in the nation's schools and universities will in turn institute a free Scottish identity. If 'the absence of Scottish nationalism' that Grieve laments in *Albyn* is 'a form of Scottish self-determination' (*A*, 19), then MacDiarmid proposes to radicalise Scottish education in order to facilitate the self-determination of individual Scots, understanding that such personal autonomy is a necessary prelude to the creation of a Scottish Republic. As he points out in *Albyn*, this local proposition has universally anti-imperial implications:

> The type of international education which is everywhere gaining ground today is that which seeks to perfect, and even to intensify, different cultures already existent among different peoples, and sets for its ideal that each people has, first, the right to its own interpretation of life; and, second, the duty of understanding, and sympathizing with, the different interpretations given by its neighbours as fully as possible. Back of this type of international education lies the belief that differentiation in matters of culture is more valuable to life than a stereotyped homogeneity. (*A*, 12)

As a first step towards the institutional sanctioning of difference, the commercial and philistine agenda of the teaching profession must give way to 'the place where reality, properly speaking, begins' (*LP*, 342): the imagination.

Aiming to provoke a radically creative approach to teaching in Scotland, Grieve wrote a series of articles for the *Scottish Educational Journal*, collected in 1926 as *Contemporary Scottish Studies*. In 'Creative Art and the Scottish Education System (II)', appearing on

19 November 1926, he confronts the suppression of the child's personality by a capitalist system of education 'that propagates this vicious and anti-human Gospel of Work' (*CSS*, 406). By discouraging the free play of imagination in school, the state confines the child to the passive role of economic functionary. This standardisation is exacerbated in a stateless nation that neglects its own past to teach its children the history of a ruling foreign power. In his 1916 essay on education, Pádraic Pearse characterised the effects on the individual and national imagination of a capitalist–colonial education in Ireland as 'The Murder Machine'. For MacDiarmid, if the personal imagination is to be murdered by the state then education should not be in state control. Welcoming the 'growth of free, private and experimental schools' as harbingers of personal freedom, Grieve believes this must be preceded by 'the autonomy of the teacher' (*CSS*, 408).

In this regard, Alexander Sutherland Neill (1883–1973) was a Scottish teacher of whom MacDiarmid could certainly approve. Born in the Angus town of Forfar, where MacDiarmid worked briefly as a journalist for the *Forfar Review* in 1913, Neill's small-town childhood must have borne similarities to MacDiarmid's in Langholm. Neill's parents were both teachers and in Forfar the teacher was a central part of the life of the town, a figure to be respected, even feared. As Neill says in his autobiography, 'the village dominie was the oracle, for, apart from the minister, he was the only educated man in the village'.[47] Neill made it to Edinburgh University where, taught by Saintsbury, he gained a degree in English literature. He was later to express disillusionment with his higher education saying that 'a specialised university education is no education at all'.[48] On becoming a teacher, Neill experienced all the restrictions and frustrations of teaching in a small Scottish school that the one-time trainee-teacher MacDiarmid was so glad to have escaped:

> If I had gone on and qualified and become a teacher, my sojourn in the profession would have been of short duration in any event, and I would have been dismissed as Thomas Davidson and John Maclean and my friend, A. S. Neill, were dismissed. (*LP*, 229)

MacDiarmid believes most Scottish teachers to be 'hopeless Safety-Firsters' (*LP*, 229). In 'The Teaching Profession', dedicated to Neill, he attacks them as a type who are 'lucky to earn a livin'' / Wi' what they'd learnt at twelve' (*CP2*, 1261). Neill also objects to the limited nature of teachers and teaching in a specialised system:

> I want to teach my bairns how to live; the Popular Educator wants to teach them how to make a living. There is a distinction between the two ideals.

> The Scotch Education Department would seem to have some of the Educator's aspirations. It demands Gardening, Woodwork, Cookery; in short, it is aiming at turning out practical men and women.
>
> My objection to men and women is that they are too practical.[49]

MacDiarmid similarly opposes the educational aim of training 'the child specifically for a vocation' (LP, 140). Coming at the problem of educational, cultural and political sterility from different angles as they do, one a poet the other an educationalist, the two men still share a deep desire to change the nature of the educational system, each seeing this as the key to changing Scottish and international society. Both are socialists with a disdain for democracy, small-town boys who should have been that apotheosis of Scottish education, the lad o' pairts, but instead turned rebel poet and educational heretic. Frustrated in a Scotland that isn't listening to their modernist message, outsiders in a nation they think is almost irremediably provincial, MacDiarmid and Neill exile themselves geographically, the poet to Shetland and the educationalist to Hellerau and then, more famously, to Summerhill, where he established a school based on his own principles of individual freedom and choice in learning. From these small places, believing themselves to be prophets without honour in their own country, they spread an internationalist gospel.

Neill must be counted as part of the Scottish Renaissance movement when he writes in 1922 that 'we cannot be international unless we are first national',[50] but also due to the anti-Calvinism of Is Scotland Educated?, another in the 1936 'Voice of Scotland' series. Approved by MacDiarmid as a 'useful little exposé of our much-boosted Scottish education' (LP, 143), Neill would later say that Is Scotland Educated? was 'full of pudding to hide my gross ignorance of Scotland',[51] thus supplying his own answer to the book's inquiry. A product of the educational system that has left him in ignorance of his country's history, he claims that the present marriage of commercialism and Calvinism is responsible for eroding the basis of Scottish higher education:

> Our Scots universities are conservative of the right (Tory) or of the left (Liberal). Psychologically there is no difference between a Tory and a Liberal: both support capitalism and the Old Men of Life. Our professional classes, university trained, show much less originality than our Clydeside workers show. That is mainly because a university training does not deal in fundamentals.[52]

Having attended university, Neill was not self-taught in the strictest sense, however, he shares with MacDiarmid and other Scottish Renaissance writers an autodidactic urge to get back to first principles. If the national education system has been de-nationalised it will tell us nothing about ourselves – at least, not in any enriching sense. As such, those who stand outside the system – workers, self-teachers, dropouts – are best placed to change it. The desire of MacDiarmid and Neill to rediscover the vital elements of creative selfhood ultimately relates to their discontent with the contemporary system of Scottish education and its persistent myth of superiority in the midst of pervasive inferiorism. Indeed, for MacDiarmid, the idea that Scottish education is still the best in the world is complacent compensation for a lack of direct rule in a post-Union, stateless nation:

> Tell me o' love o' country
> Content to see't decay,
> And ony ither paradox
> Ye think o' by the way.
> I doot it needs a Hegel
> Sic opposites to fuse;
> Oor education's failin'
> And canna gie's the views
>   That were peculiar to us
>   Afore oor vision narrowed
>   And gar'd us think it time
>   The claith was owre the parrot!
>
> (*To Circumjack Cencrastus*, *CP1*, 193)

On 5 March 1926, in 'A. S. Neill and our Educational System', Grieve named Neill as 'the only Scottish educationist to-day of the slightest significance from the point of view of real education' (*CSS*, 294). He elucidates what he means by a 'real education' in opposition to the ideas of James Maxton (1885–1946) as well as in concurrence with those of Neill. According to Grieve, Maxton wants the education system in Scotland to be based on a rediscovery of the 'national characteristics' of 'independence, thrift, courage and so forth' (*CSS*, 290), but the poet thinks it 'the sorriest Chauvinism to imply that there is anything distinctively Scottish about' (*CSS*, 292) such features. Grieve believes that the 'national spirit is something apart from any such qualities' (*CSS*, 292). If given free reign, it could be manifested in a direction rather different from the utilitarian thinking of a socialist such as Maxton, so challenging the idea of a canny Scotland fostered by a capitalist education system grounded in Calvinist self-repression. Wishing to create an educational approach that individualises Scots, MacDiarmid wants a return to 'first principles' (*CSS*, 291), a concept once central to the traditional generalism of Scotland's universities. In the context of Neill's educational ideas, however, his description of what a return to first principles means essentially relates to inner, individual freedom:

> The present educational system in Scotland – like every other educational *system* – is concerned with the superficial self. Real education – upon which

everything that is vital in life depends – is concerned solely with the funda-mental self; it is in direct opposition to everything that tends to create the superficial self, beyond the working minimum of sanity, and especially, to any-thing that tends to so harden that crust as to inhibit or handicap the funda-mental self, or give a direction to life from without rather than purely from within. (*CSS*, 294)

MacDiarmid values Neill's educational experimentalism for its attempt to allow children to find a path without external imposition, to determine their self without being told what that self should be. The poet suggests that this may have beneficial consequences for the emergence of Scottish nationalism: if individuals should be allowed to discover for themselves, and in their own way, their potentialities and the imagina-tive possibilities of self-creation, then why not the community of indi-viduals that is the nation? In the current educational schema, Scottish education does not produce free-thinking individuals, but colonial administrators and 'heids o' depairtments', leaving Scotland a place of 'comparative cultural backwardness and creative sterility' (*CSS*, 409). Only an education that is not a system, one that allows individuals to invent themselves, has the potential to free Scotland from its political and cultural provinciality through the creation of artists and thinkers: 'The educational objective should be the polarisation of personalities' (*CSS*, 409). MacDiarmid's thinking on Scottish education is in keeping with his politics of place in that it encourages the propagation of differ-ence. In the face of metropolitan capitalist conformity, MacDiarmid seeks provincial places such as Montrose and Whalsay and a dissident like Neill as sparks of creative hope.

The absence of an operational Scottish Republican tradition forces MacDiarmid to theoretically deploy the work of individuals whose values he can use in his battle against anglocentric and capitalist ortho-doxy in Scottish education and experience. He promotes the genera-lism of rebels such as Neill, Geddes and Maclean (who will be examined more closely in Chapter 4) because the poet sees himself as them in a different guise, a radically idealistic troublemaker expelled for disrupt-ing the English class. Seeking an interdisciplinary approach that compiles an understanding of Scottish affairs, MacDiarmid believes 'it is the ability not to think of one thing alone for a long time, but of one thing in relation to many others' (*Company*, 253) that characterises and gives worth to the Scottish generalist tradition of philosophical education. Adducing his generalism in *Lucky Poet*, an autobiographical arche-type of anti-specialisation, he perceives 'the intellectual complement of Scottish Republicanism in my work' to be 'the drawing of subtle dis-tinctions' (*LP*, 348).

Undermining the generalist tradition by abandoning the philosophical basis of the teaching of Scottish students is, according to George Davie, a means by which 'to prepare the way for the cultural subordination of Scotland to England parallel to its political subordination'.[53] By dissolving the sense of 'diversity in what may be called social ethics',[54] the future elite produced by the Scottish university will bear a remarkable similarity to their English counterparts. Scotland will no longer have a national intelligentsia with any historical understanding of its distinctive traditions, facilitating rule by a unified British elite. MacDiarmid understands that the long-term acceptance of such a position would be sufficient to eradicate the national culture:

Oor four Universities
Are Scots but in name;
They wadna be here
If ither folk did the same
– Paid heed tae a' lear
Exceptin' their ain,
For they'd cancel oot syne
And leave us wi' nane.

(To Circumjack Cencrastus, CP1, 203)

If Scotland cannot find the political will to develop an educational policy that prioritises its own national culture then the nation will disappear from the map of history.

MacDiarmid despairs of Scotland as a place that has 'a general determination to dispense with all the national roots' (*LP*, 84). He passionately insists, when writing 'Scots and the Schools' for the *Dominie* in 1958, that 'Scottish children ought to be put into full possession of the national heritage' (*RT3*, 401). Only a Scottish education that allows a distinctive Scottish accent to be heard, adhering to what in *Albyn* he calls 'the axis of our own mentality' (*A*, 30), will see this aim fulfilled. This entails a radical reorientation in the writing and teaching of Scottish history. Grieve argues in 'The New Movement in Scottish Historiography: George Pratt Insh', appearing in the *Scottish Educational Journal* on 18 December 1925, that, like Scottish education generally, Scottish historical research has been 'inadequate to the conception of "Scotland – a Nation" ' and subsequently is 'lagging far behind contemporary European scholarship' (*CSS*, 220). MacDiarmid adjudged M. V. Hay's *A Chain of Error in Scottish History* (1927) to be 'an important book in the initiation of the Scottish Renaissance Movement' (*LP*, 294) for re-establishing the foundations of ecclesiastical history in Celtic Scotland as Roman Catholic. Considering Scottish history to be written from a largely Presbyterian perspective, he wants Catholicism and Episcopalianism to be represented also; aiming to unify

Scotland in the present, he urges a reading of Scotland's whole past. To achieve this, what is needed is an understanding that there is a notable history of Scottish history, a 'great tradition', including 'Knox and Bishop Lesley, Calderwood and Archbishop Spottiswoode, Woodrow [*sic*] and Father Innes, Hume and Robertson, and so on' (*CSS*, 222),[55] that scholars can draw on, follow and surpass. 'Scottish history is only now in the process of being rediscovered', writes Grieve in *Albyn*, and this means that much of the work previously understood to be written from a distinctly Scottish perspective, such as that by Peter Hume Brown (1849–1918),[56] will be seen on reassessment to be 'little more than a mass of English propaganda' (*A*, 12–13). The present anglicised condition of Scottish education should not give us 'the idea that history in Scotland was a negligible thing before the advent of English professors in our midst about the end of the nineteenth century' (*CSS*, 222). Thirty-six years before Davie's *The Democratic Intellect* (1961) appeared telling of the changes in direction in Scotland's universities in the nineteenth century due to the Anglo-driven assault on the generalist tradition of a metaphysical Scotland, MacDiarmid the autodidact shows his awareness of the history of Scottish education.

His own education, and the history of his refashioning of self and Scotland, began at home, in the Langholm Library.

Notes

1. Robert Crawford, *Identifying Poets: Self and Territory in Twentieth-Century Poetry* (Edinburgh: Edinburgh University Press, 1993), p. 1.
2. Vincent Sherry, *The Great War and the Language of Modernism* (Oxford: Oxford University Press, 2003), p. 6.
3. Paul Fussell, *The Great War and Modern Memory* (London: Oxford University Press, 1979), p. 314.
4. Ibid., p. 8.
5. Cited in Alan Riach, *Representing Scotland in Literature, Popular Culture and Iconography: The Masks of the Modern Nation* (Basingstoke & New York: Palgrave Macmillan, 2005), p. 21.
6. Tom Nairn, *The Break-Up of Britain: Crisis and Neo-Nationalism* (London: New Left, 1977), p. 164.
7. See Richard J. Finlay, *Modern Scotland 1914–2000* (London: Profile, 2004), pp. 7, 35, 37.
8. See Alan Bold, *MacDiarmid: Christopher Murray Grieve: A Critical Biography* (London: John Murray, 1988), p. 77.
9. Mark Longaker (ed.), *The Poems of Ernest Dowson* (Philadelphia: University of Pennsylvania Press, 1962), p. 39.
10. Sarah Cole, *Modernism, Male Friendship, and the First World War* (Cambridge: Cambridge University Press, 2003), p. 6.

11. See Bold, *MacDiarmid*, p. 77.
12. Catherine Kerrigan (ed.), *The Hugh MacDiarmid – George Ogilvie Letters* (Aberdeen: Aberdeen University Press, 1988), p. xvii.
13. Ibid., p. xvii.
14. Fussell, *The Great War and Modern Memory*, p. 74.
15. Ibid., p. 183.
16. Fernando Pessoa, from *The Book of Disquietude*, in Eugénio Lisboa with L. C. Taylor (eds), *A Centenary Pessoa* (Manchester: Carcanet, 1995), p. 176.
17. See Hamish Henderson, *Alias MacAlias: Writings on Songs, Folk and Literature* (Edinburgh: Polygon, 1993), pp. 304–7 for Henderson's analysis of Grieve–MacDiarmid, 'the two-headed bard', (p. 305).
18. Charles Duff, *Six Days to Shake an Empire* (London: J. M. Dent, 1966), p. iii.
19. 'Valedictory', MacDiarmid interviewed on BBC Radio 4, 15 September 1977, in Alan Bold (ed.), *The Thistle Rises: An Anthology of Poetry and Prose by Hugh MacDiarmid* (London: Hamish Hamilton, 1984), p. 289.
20. NLS MS27142 f.27v, quoted in 'Introduction', *Revolutionary*, p. xv.
21. See *L*, 13 February 1918 and 28 April 1918.
22. See J. A. Smith's translation of Aristotle's *De Anima: On the Soul*, Book 1, Chapter 5, in W. D. Ross (ed.), *The Works of Aristotle*, Vol. 3 (Oxford: Clarendon Press, 1931).
23. Wyndham Lewis, *Blasting and Bombardiering: Autobiography (1914–1926)* (London: Eyre and Spottiswoode, 1937), p. 36.
24. Wyndham Lewis, *BLAST 1* (June 1914), reprint (Santa Barbara: Black Sparrow Press, 1981), p. 24.
25. *The Chapbook Programme*, cited in Margery Palmer McCulloch (ed.), *Modernism and Nationalism: Literature and Society in Scotland 1918–1939, Source Documents for the Scottish Renaissance* (Glasgow: ASLS, 2004), p xii.
26. George Malcolm Thomson, *Caledonia: or The Future of the Scots* (London: Kegan Paul, 1927), p. 10.
27. Ibid., p. 16.
28. Andrew Dewar Gibb, *Scotland in Eclipse* (London: Humphrey Toulmin, 1930), pp. 187, 53.
29. Finlay, *Modern Scotland*, p. 112.
30. Compton Mackenzie, *Sinister Street* (Harmondsworth: Penguin, 1960), p. 180.
31. Compton Mackenzie, *Catholicism and Scotland* (London: Routledge, 1936), p. 73.
32. Edwin Muir, *An Autobiography* ([1954] Edinburgh: Canongate, 1993), p. 274.
33. Edwin Muir, *John Knox: Portrait of a Calvinist* (London: Jonathan Cape, 1930), p. 309.
34. Edwin Muir, *Scott and Scotland: The Predicament of the Scottish Writer*, introduction by Allan Massie (Edinburgh: Polygon, 1982), p. 2.
35. Willa Muir, *Mrs Grundy in Scotland*, in Kirsty Allen (ed.), *Imagined Selves* (Edinburgh: Canongate, 1996), pp. 75–6.
36. David Allan, *Virtue, Learning and the Scottish Enlightenment: Ideas of*

Scholarship in Early Modern Scotland (Edinburgh: Edinburgh University Press, 1993), p. 33.

37. Buchanan 'held to a doctrine of truly popular sovereignty in which the people as a whole exercised continuous authority that was never surrendered or delegated to any representative body of inferior magistrates'; Roger A. Mason and Martin S. Smith, *A Dialogue on the Law of Kingship among the Scots: A Critical Edition and Translation of George Buchanan's De Iure Regni apud Scotos Dialogus* (Aldershot: Ashgate, 2004), p. lvii; see *RT2*, p. 538 for MacDiarmid on *De Iure*.

38. William Storrar, *Scottish Identity: A Christian Vision* (Edinburgh: The Handsell Press, 1990), pp. 53–4.

39. Linda Colley, *Britons: Forging the Nation 1707–1837* (London: Vintage, 1996), p. 58.

40. See T. M. Devine (ed.), *Scotland's Shame? Bigotry and Sectarianism in Modern Scotland* (Edinburgh: Mainstream, 2000) for a recent analysis of sectarianism in Scotland.

41. Murray G. H. Pittock, *A New History of Scotland* (Stroud: Sutton, 2003), p. 150.

42. Cairns Craig, *The Modern Scottish Novel: Narrative and the National Imagination* (Edinburgh: Edinburgh University Press, 1999), p. 33.

43. Finlay, *Modern Scotland*, p. 90.

44. MacDiarmid, 'Foreword', to P. Berresford Ellis and Seumas Mac a' Ghobhainn, *The Scottish Insurrection of 1820* (London: Victor Gollancz, 1970), pp. 14, 15.

45. R. D. Anderson, *Education and the Scottish People 1750–1918* (Oxford: Clarendon Press, 1995), p. 213.

46. Ibid., p. 212.

47. A. S. Neill, *Neill! Neill! Orange Peel!: A Personal View of Ninety Years* (London: Weidenfeld and Nicholson, 1973), p. 16.

48. Ibid., p. 117.

49. A. S. Neill, *A Dominie's Log* (London: Herbert Jenkins, 1915), p. 46.

50. A. S. Neill, *A Dominie Abroad* (London: Herbert Jenkins, 1922), p. 67.

51. A. S. Neill, cited in Jonathan Croall, *Neill of Summerhill: The Permanent Rebel* (London: Routledge & Kegan Paul, 1983), p. 228.

52. A. S. Neill, *Is Scotland Educated?* (London: Routledge, 1936), p. 33.

53. George Davie, *The Democratic Intellect: Scotland and her Universities in the Nineteenth Century* (Edinburgh: Edinburgh University Press, 1999), p. 58.

54. Ibid., p. xi.

55. John Knox (c.1513–72), *History of the Reformation of Religion within the Realm of Scotland* (completed 1586); Bishop John Lesley (or Leslie) (c.1527–96), *Historie of Scotland* (completed 1571); David Calderwood (1575–1651), *True History of the Church of Scotland* (1678); Archbishop John Spottiswoode (1565–1639), *The History of the Church of Scotland* (1655); Robert Wodrow (1679–1734), *History of the Sufferings of the Church of Scotland from the Restoration to the Revolution* (1721–2); Father Thomas Innes (1662–1744), *A Critical Essay on the Ancient Inhabitants of the Northern Parts of Britain or Scotland* (1729); David Hume (1711–76), *History of England from the Invasion of Julius Caesar to the Revolution of*

1688 (1754–62); William Robertson (1721–93), *The History of Scotland during the Reigns of Queen Mary and James VI till his Accession to the Crown of England* (1759).

56. In MacDiarmid's personal book collection, held in the Langholm Library, Hume Brown's two-volume biography, *John Knox* (1895), finds shelfroom beside Franco Cordero's *Against the Catholic System* (1972), presented to MacDiarmid by its translator from the Italian, Anthony Johnson.

Chapter 2

Debatable Land

The Autodidact

When James and Elizabeth Grieve moved their young family to Parliament Square in the centre of Langholm in 1899 they unwittingly introduced Christopher, their eldest son, to a realm that was to dominate his adult life, one through which he would both challenge the power of metropolitan English rule and conform to the dictates of native national mythology. MacDiarmid's book learning – never systematic, or systematised by a university education, always driven by his own idiosyncratic needs as a poet – began with his omnivorous trawling through the library that occupied the upper storey of the building in which the family lived. MacDiarmid claims it was access to this library 'that was the great determining factor' (*LP*, 8) in his becoming a poet, boasting somewhat fantastically in *Lucky Poet* of having read every book in the library before the age of fourteen – some twelve thousand volumes.

Such exaggerations in the cause of self-styling are common throughout MacDiarmid's career and are hardly unknown amongst poets. Robert Crawford describes MacDiarmid and Ezra Pound as 'man-myths'.[1] Fellow modernist, political extremist and autobiographical fabulist, Pound was one of MacDiarmid's heroes, also preferring a poetics of lengthy, generalist displays of learning. In *Lucky Poet*, once more in braggart mode, MacDiarmid claims, 'I could go up into that library in the dark and find any book I wanted' – a library that was, however, 'strangely deficient in Scottish books' (*LP*, 8). It took this Scottish autodidact until the age of twenty-seven to find his way out of the darkness into which Scottish culture had allowed itself to fall as 'an inevitable consequence of the relation of Scotland to England' (*LP*, 15). Referred to here as an autodidact because he did not attend university, MacDiarmid believed that a Scottish university education of the time would not have remedied the gap in his knowledge of the native culture more successfully than he could through his own scholarship.

His self-imposed intellectual task began in the Langholm Library. The importance to MacDiarmid of his hometown library, of which his poetry-writing mother was the caretaker, is expressed in his inscription to his personal copy of *Scottish Eccentrics*, presented to the library on his death by Valda Grieve: 'For the Langholm Library to which I owe so much.' In *Lucky Poet*, MacDiarmid professes to 'have never met anyone who has read anything like as much as I have, though I have known most of our great bookmen' (*LP*, 13). Such intellectual swaggering characterises his 1943 autobiography, illustrating the self-taught MacDiarmid's pugnacious pride as to the extent of his learning, but also camouflaging his insecurity as to the absence of an institutional basis for such learning.

We could speculate that as he grew older MacDiarmid became more comfortable with his lack of formal higher education, accustomed to his self-appointed role as the Carlylean poet-prophet with a purported knowledge of all things specifically Scottish, and *welt-literatur* in general, superior to that of any professor. According to Walter Perrie, however, MacDiarmid retained the educational anxieties of a working-class autodidact his whole life, and was 'habitually deferential towards academics with little of his intellect and nothing of his creative powers merely because they represented a world he found esoteric, in which he was never at ease, but which he continued to admire'.[2] MacDiarmid revenges his insecurities by creating a fictional autodidact epitomising the generalism of the foregone academic tradition of a metaphysical Scotland. This 'common workin' man' (*CP1*, 368) with 'neist to nae lear' (369) explores the mystery of existence overlooked by the career intellectuals in their specialised professional roles:

> Tam was a Scotsman o' a splendid type
> O' which our puir country is near bereft.
> We're a' owre weel-educated noo I doot
> To ha'e ony real knowledge – or love o't – left
> > ('Tam o' the Wilds and the Many-Faced Mystery', *CP1*, 377)

Perrie believes MacDiarmid's ambiguous attitude to academia, particularly the native intelligentsia, can be traced to the disorienting disjunction between the 'rural, still semi-peasant ethos deeply imbued with presbyterianism' of his Langholm upbringing, and his experience of Edinburgh where he went to train as a teacher at Broughton:

> Like many a scion of the working classes, then and since, he must have found the transition painful and disturbing, for the loss of identity involved in the

business of gaining an education – all but inevitable for a Scot from a working-class family – cannot be made good by a simple adoption of the values and mores of a new environment.[3]

On his arrival in Edinburgh, George Ogilvie noted that some of the other students found amusement in Grieve's provincial appearance and thick Border accent.[4] This may help explain MacDiarmid's anti-metropolitanism: 'I do not like Edinburgh (or any city very much)' (*LP*, 105). Perrie points out that the 'pattern' of a rural, small-town boy moving to the city to be educated 'was common enough in Scotland', and that 'Grieve displays many of its predictable characteristics'.[5]

The phenomenon Perrie describes is the lad o' pairts. Chris Grieve failed to follow the successful path expected of a talented and respectable ex-pupil of Langholm Academy, however: his progress to Edinburgh and training to become a teacher miscarried on his removal from Broughton in January 1911 for stealing books. Like his 'Essays in Autobiography' from 1966, *The Company I've Kept*, *Lucky Poet* charts the intellectual rather than material development of a writer who preferred to live in 'out-of-the-way and little-known places' (*LP*, 309). Written in Whalsay, where MacDiarmid was far from libraries and had to rely on friends such as Bill Aitken and George Davie to send him books and articles, the sheer sweaty bravura of *Lucky Poet* – brimful of frantic facts, off-hand details and kaleidoscopic variety – means that the book reads like a library all of its own, one that is almost wholly uncategorised. When transcribing a life lived in literature and ideas without sundry books to refer to, many of his own collection having been left behind on leaving Montrose, or kept by his first wife, MacDiarmid must have been almost solely reliant on memory and, in particular, his recollection of those books he read as a boy in the Langholm Library.

The Langholm Library was founded in 1800. Originally a subscription library serving a wealthy local elite of around forty Langholmites, in 1852 it expanded its membership by amalgamating with the Langholm Trades Library (founded in 1813). On his death, Thomas Telford (1757–1834), born at Westerkirk near Langholm, left an initial £1,000 to the library, a sum that rose to £3,000 on the settlement of his will. The posthumous son of a shepherd, Telford became the civil engineer, road-, canal-, bridge-builder and architect who laid the communications ground plan facilitating the British Industrial Revolution. In Scotland alone, to give only a few examples, he opened up the Highlands with over 920 miles of road and 120 bridges, built the Caledonian Canal and developed harbours at Dundee, Aberdeen, Peterhead, Wick and Banff. His achievement is such that Robert Southey, his Poet Laureate friend, called him in pun the

'Colossus of Roads'. Telford's bequest to the Langholm Library may have led to more modest accomplishments, but it allowed a book fund to be set up and, with the overall growth in the library's fortunes, a new building was built in 1878.

What books would Christie have been able to read in Telford's new library where he was, quite literally, at home? Nowadays, the library consists of a little over five thousand volumes. Most of the books are humanities oriented, something that 'is entirely typical of Scottish community libraries',[6] and this would also have been the case in MacDiarmid's day. Of the total number of books, almost half can be classed as geography, history and biography, roughly a further thousand as popular fiction, with half as many again as literary classics.

MacDiarmid claims in *Lucky Poet* to have read in the Langholm Library all of the same books that Compton Mackenzie had access to in London and at Oxford University. Indeed, he describes his first piece of luck, the good fortune that inextricably shaped his poetic vocation, as being born in Langholm and having such intimate connection with the town library. Despite this, MacDiarmid complains twice in *Lucky Poet* of the lack of Scottish books in the library, partly because at this point he was still 'in the dark' about the extent of Scottish literature, but also so that later he could be seen as the poet-saviour who, through autodidactic self-sacrifice, had brought a culture to light. He could, however, have read Ramsay, Burns and Scott, as well as the anthology *Scottish Poetry of the Eighteenth Century* (1896). Jamieson's *Etymological Dictionary* would help him navigate the vernacular of the past and John Davidson's *Selected Poems*, published by John Lane in 1904, certainly provided pre-modernist inspiration. In 'Of John Davidson', which concludes *Scots Unbound* (1932), MacDiarmid claims to 'remember one death in my boyhood / That next to my father's, and darker, endures', the hellish image of Davidson's suicide in 1909, aged fifty-two, being analogous to a vision of 'God through the wrong end of a telescope' (*CP1*, 362). MacDiarmid probably also began reading the work of the popular novelist, poet and journalist Neil Munro (1863–1930) in the Langholm Library. Having 'read and re-read almost all that he has written, and brooded long hours over it', in 'Neil Munro', appearing in the *Scottish Educational Journal* on 3 July 1925, Grieve was to conclude that, despite 'having been in some ways the greatest of his contemporaries amongst our countrymen' (*CSS*, 22), Munro is critically negligible in international terms, his rather dated work having merely historical interest. As such, 'Neil Munro is the lost leader of Scottish Nationalism' (*CSS*, 21). In MacDiarmid's new Scotland, Davidson, among the first of the moderns, would replace the cultural old guard such as Munro.

Continuing his imaginative journey in the Langholm Library, the young Grieve must surely have delved into *Wilson's Tales of the Borders and of Scotland* for local lore, and as a teen he may have read Henrietta Elizabeth Marshall's *Scotland's Story: A Child's History of Scotland* (1906). An 1867 edition of *The Scottish Nation; or the Surnames, Families, Literature, Honours and Biographical History of the People of Scotland* by William Anderson (1805–66) was available to provide a sense of the nation's past. His Laidlaw cousins, John and Robert, themselves locally published poets, also aided his intellectual development. Robert was particularly influential, MacDiarmid recollecting that he 'gave a definite Scottish twist to my already well-developed tastes as a reader' (*LP*, 8). In spite of this approbation in *Lucky Poet*, Robert Laidlaw disowned MacDiarmid in anger at his autobiography's treatment of local minister T. S. Cairncross. Robert's daughter, Nan Walty, remembers her family having little to do with the Grieves.[7] But for all Laidlaw's early help, Christopher is likely to have gained the rudiments of his Scottish history from the fiction of Walter Scott (1771–1832). In *Lucky Poet*, MacDiarmid states 'that for a subject nation the firm literary bulwark against the encroaching Imperialism is concentration on the national language and re-interpretation of the national history' and, reading against the grain of Sir Walter's Unionism, he argues that 'Scott's work has real value where a stand is being made against Imperialism' (*LP*, 203).

The apparent paucity of Scottish books did not dampen MacDiarmid's anti-British-imperialism, which was partly fired by his youthful interest in American history and literature, subjects he discovered in abundance in the Langholm Library. MacDiarmid looked 'forward eagerly and confidently to the United States supplanting England in the leadership of the English-speaking world' (*LP*, 11), a wish articulated in *Lucky Poet* at least a decade or so before the Cold War dance of death between American capitalism and Soviet communism saw the USA emerge as the world's only twenty-first-century superpower. In purely political terms, MacDiarmid wants English imperial domination globally usurped by the United States in order that Scotland win free from London's metropolitan control and the politically paralysing unity of the British Empire. If the Empire is in decline, its world pre-eminence supplanted by its anglophone cousin across the Atlantic, then its British component parts may break up – or be more susceptible to being broken – and go their separate and sovereign national ways.

The contemporary practice of American imperial power may seem to undermine MacDiarmid's sense of the liberatory promise of the United States – as well, perhaps, as making mock of the academic idea that we live in a postcolonial era. But MacDiarmid's concern is categorically with

Scotland and how, as in the case of Scott, even those apparently on the reactionary side of the political tracks can be used to oppose imperialism at home. From America, particularly early American literature, he heard a republican voice of equalitarianism that freed him – in a library where he found few Scottish books – from too great a reliance on English literature and what he believed to be the English ethos of snobbish social division and cultural superiorism. Whitman's democratic, epical multiplicity was central in this regard. But he also points in *Lucky Poet* to the modernist work of William Carlos Williams, Upton Sinclair and Gertrude Stein, as well as literary founding fathers such as Emerson, Hawthorne and Twain, as being important to him – alongside the lively and amoral popular wit of Mae West.

In 'On American Literature', appearing in the *New Age* in May 1924, Grieve relates his current enthusiasm for American literature, noting that twenty years previously – in his twelfth year, and just going into secondary school in Langholm – he had proposed to write a book on the subject, endorsing the work of 'Sidney Lanier, "H. H." (Helen Jackson), Emma Lazarus, Emily Dickinson, Ambrose Bierce and George Sterling' (*RT1*, 158). Written while he was in Montrose promoting the Scottish movement, in the same article he also refers appreciatively to Carl Eric Bechhöfer's *The Literary Renaissance in America* (1923). When writing anonymously for the *Stewartry Observer* on 11 August 1927, this approval of America modernism relates directly to his aims for a Scottish Renaissance:

> All the best American writers today are out to create – not a mere form of English literature, but a native American literature, expressed not so much in English as in a specialised American kind of English which has rhythms and effects peculiarly its own, and little save derivation to relate it to the English used in England. ('Canada and Scottish Literature', *RT2*, 100)

American culture was an abiding interest: his personal library included *The Penguin Book of American Verse*, published in 1977, the year before he died. In the Langholm Library, the boy may have read *Life and Liberty in America; or, Sketches of a tour in the United States and Canada, in 1857–8* (1859) by the Scotsman Charles Mackay (1814–89). Perhaps he dipped precociously into *The Works of Benjamin Franklin* (1806). In *Lucky Poet* he identifies himself in class terms with Franklin, apprentice printer and son of a soap maker, and cites Thomas Jefferson and Abraham Lincoln as being 'among the early companions of my spirit' (*LP*, 10).

We can only speculate as to specific texts but, according to MacDiarmid, 'it was certainly this early American reading that helped me to resist the refining influence of English education' (*LP*, 10) being taught in the local

Scottish classroom. As 'one of the few Scots who learned anything at all in his boyhood about American history' (*LP*, 12), MacDiarmid understands that the absence of American history and literature in British universities seriously undermines British comprehension not only of America but also of Britain and the British past. That American topics figure more frequently nowadays on British university curricula may point, in part, to an acceptance of the loss of British imperial precedence and a concomitant postcolonial willingness to comprehend the relatedness of culture – something history's 'losers' may be better placed to achieve than those currently in the economic and political ascendant. Ahead of the game in 1943, MacDiarmid was among the first to 'welcome the entrée American history is at last securing here and there, and the vogue American literature is now enjoying' (*LP*, 12–13), believing that this signalled a historical renegotiation of imperial power that could also have beneficial cultural and political side-effects for Scotland.

Reading of America in the Langholm Library the child would have been excited by the sense of adventure and promise held by a young land, a place foreign yet familiar. As an adult, this may have retrospectively transmuted into MacDiarmid's desire to create ancient Scotland anew in a republican spirit. His exploration of America's revolutionary history, particularly Scotland's central role in defining the new nation – the 1320 Letter of Barons of Scotland to Pope John XXII, better known as the Declaration of Arbroath, echoing in the Unanimous Declaration of the Thirteen United States of America of 1776 – must surely have helped to harness MacDiarmid's dream of an independent Scottish future; unlike thousands of Scottish emigrants to the United States, however, he would not leave Scotland to try to build it. Situated as it is in the Debatable Land of the border between Scotland and England, it is significant, given his familiarity with American history, that in both *Lucky Poet* and 'Kinsfolk' MacDiarmid should describe Langholm as possessing a 'frontier spirit' (*LP*, 16; *CP2*, 1150). If Scotland is also, in political terms, a debatable land, what in 2000 Andrew O'Hagan called 'the world's best hypothetical nation',[8] then from the Debatable Land of the Borders grew MacDiarmid's wish to put beyond debate the nation's independent political state.

What is most striking about the Langholm Library, particularly in its somewhat reduced modern form, is the extent to which books about foreign countries (classified as geography) fill the shelves. As a boy, MacDiarmid could not only have read about the United States, but Central and Latin America, Spain, Russia, Italy, even the North Pole – the list of places could go on. In our mass-communications, televisual age, in which the internet and jet travel enable a speedy and far-reaching knowledge of much that the globe has to offer, complacency may tempt the assumption that this embryonic lad o' pairts sought his only possible escape from the narrow milieu of a small provincial town through the exploration of books. However, attributing to himself a 'universal curiosity' (*LP*, 14), from MacDiarmid's autobiography we get an over-riding sense of gratitude that such an enlargement of his intellectual vistas is what he gained precisely by having the fortuity to be born in Langholm and live beneath the library. For MacDiarmid, its library did not serve as a refuge from what may be fancied to be the dull provinciality of Langholm; rather, the town and the knowledge that he gleaned in that library were his political basis and creative template for radical internationalism.[9]

'Ever since I was a boy I have been an incessant and omnivorous reader and lived in "a strong solution of books"', writes MacDiarmid in *Company* (11). He goes on to point out that such reading habits make it difficult to fully acknowledge all of his quotations for the book, their source presumably misplaced in memory and numerous haphazardly compiled old notebooks. This seemingly blasé attitude to the laws of copyright would be exposed most famously in the case of 'Perfect', a poem largely composed of words used in short story form by Glyn Jones but appearing under MacDiarmid's name in *The Islands of Scotland*. Having lost or deliberately laid aside his lyric talent with later prose-poems such as *In Memoriam James Joyce*, here he claims that he is striving 'to heal the breach / Between genius and scholarship, literature and learning' (*CP2*, 752). However, a writing technique that distils the essence of what he is reading at that period and then inventively infuses it into his own work actually forms the basis of much of his poetic oeuvre, from the early experiments in dictionary Scots lyrics to the lengthy 'prosetry' of knowledge. In a letter of 20 July 1970 to John C. Weston, Grieve agrees with the Professor of English that his '"scholarship" is spotty and promiscuous', while admitting to being 'a very industrious Autolycus' (*L*, 724). That MacDiarmid should confess his plagiarism to an academic through the use of a literary reference is cheekily apt. The pickpocketing pedlar of ballads in Shakespeare's *The Winter's Tale* took his name from the semi-divine grandfather of the famously cunning Odysseus, Autolycus, prince of thieves. Commenting on the nature of artist-as-thief, MacDiarmid's poetry, particularly his later work, is a concerted attempt to meld invention and quotation. His generalist reading stimulates a synthetic writing method that aspires to allusively express the inexpressibly elusive wisdom of the whole. This could be seen at once as a bid to outmanoeuvre the specialised, academic ferreting of sources, as well as being a harbinger of academia's own recycling of material in its capture and commodification of the rebellious creative spirit. As a poetic *modus operandi* it is surely conditioned by Grieve's autodidacticism, the roots of which can be traced to the Langholm Library.

MacDiarmid maintains in 'Growing Up in Langholm', 'I never made any conscious decision that I should be a writer. That was a foregone conclusion from my very early life' (*SP*, 269–70). He remembers Langholm Academy as being 'a great school' (*LP*, 228) where he was taught by the composer Francis George Scott (1880–1958), rated by MacDiarmid as 'among the strictly limited number of the best brains in Scotland to-day' (*LP*, 229). F. G. Scott worked at Langholm Academy from 1903 to 1912, but felt confined by the town and went to teach in Dunoon, becoming friends there with MacDiarmid's *bête noire*, the entertainer Sir Harry Lauder (1870–1950).[10] Despite his endorsement of school, it was actually in the Langholm Library that Grieve took responsibility for his own education as a nascent writer. MacDiarmid's autodidactic endeavours correspond to the traditional idea of the Scottish love of book learning. Writing for *Vox* on 30 November 1929 as 'A. K. L.', in 'Professor Trevelyan's National Lecture' he dismisses as merely 'a stale old platitude' the notion of 'the Scots being a race of scholars and metaphysicians' (*RT2*, 182). Here he is seeking to undermine stereotypes of the Scot perpetuated since the Union, but his personal example seems to confirm rather than disprove what he regards, at least for the purposes of this article, as a national myth. In his own case erudition originated and was fostered in a close-knit, local environment, a place with 'a strong local spirit' (*LP*, 16), which he projects as being a smaller version of Scotland as a whole.

Langholm is 'a microcosm of the entire Borderland' (*SP*, 269), but the town also 'presents all the manifold and multiform grandeur and delight of Scotland in miniature' (*LP*, 222). MacDiarmid points out in *Lucky Poet* that the Borders folk of his childhood didn't use English but spoke instead 'a racy Scots' (*LP*, 16), with local idiosyncrasies ensuring that even the neighbouring towns of Langholm, Canonbie and Hawick differed markedly in linguistic character. If his synthetic Scots is a modernist undertaking to culturally legitimise and connect such divergent, provocative vernacularism, then he understands his obsession with language itself to be 'distinctively Scottish (and so republican *au fond*)' (*LP*, 16). In 'Scots Unbound' MacDiarmid's vernacular illuminates how his poetry flows from the inspirational local source of Langholm, each individual poem converging in an overall creative design that he hopes will (re)form the nation:

> No' the Esk that rins like a ribbon there
> But gi'es and tak's wi' the cluds in the air
> And ootwith its stent boonds lies at the root   [*fixed*]
> O' the plants and trees for miles roondaboot,

And gethers its tributaries, yet pulse-beats back
Up through them and a' that mak's it helps mak'
Sae I wad that Scotland's shape 'ud appear
As clear through a' its sub-shapes here
As whiles through my separate works I see
    Their underlyin' unity

                                                (*CP1*, 343)

The active civic republicanism – Buchananite *vita activa* – of MacDiarmid in his local operations in Montrose, and on a national scale in Scotland, is impelled by his autodidactic engagement with the Langholm Library.[11] Allowing him a broader view of the world, one that grows from the local but refuses to renounce it, MacDiarmid's education was conducted by himself – not at a Scottish university with metropolitan values – through the civic virtue of a local library project. MacDiarmid's determination through his reading in the Langholm Library to make himself a poet-intellectual, combined with his inculcation of the pronouncedly independent community ethos of the town, provides the early local foundation of his lifelong aspiration to build Scottish self-determination.

'My first cause?': place/poetry/politics

'Out of the World and into Langholm', appearing in the *Voice of Scotland* of April 1946, a date that is important in situating the article's ideas, promotes the universal benefits of the provinces. 'The small town is a sort of protection against the disharmonies evolved around efforts for World peace and security', MacDiarmid begins by claiming, before making the case that the community ethos of a town that is compact enough for everyone to know each other is 'infinitely more preferable to the anonymity of the great cities' (*RT3*, 102). Written just after the end of the Second World War, MacDiarmid believes the merits of a place such as Langholm to be illustrative of 'how far we have gone astray in the modern world' (*RT3*, 102). He thinks that it is unhealthy for any large city, such as Glasgow, to predominate the national population, particularly in a small country such as Scotland. The resultant alienation and anomie of living in big cities both augurs and augments the destructive malaise of modernity, undermining not only the health of the individual psyche but also the nation's overall sense of itself. In a world recently numbed by the battle of the big battalions, MacDiarmid is equating the communitarian virtues of the small town with the possible international benefits accruing from the small nation. Arguing that a crucial 'basis of local life' lies in an awareness of 'local history', he believes the teaching of such history to be 'one of the best guarantees against the same destructive tendencies that are operating in our midst at the present time' (RT3, 103).

MacDiarmid's anti-metropolitanism is a nationalist response to the violent perils of imperialism. 'Out of the World and into Langholm' urges connection with the local environment as a preliminary step towards defusing the tensions of internationalism. But if it seems utterly improbable that millions will turn their backs on city living, MacDiarmid can also be questioned for what, implicitly at any rate, appears to be his unwillingness to allow for the more exciting and hopeful aspects of cosmopolitanism. Such reactionary traces are discerned by Christopher Hitchens in his critique of Philip Larkin's England, with its 'preference for the countryside over the town, an instinct for history and the nation, reservations about the "cosmopolitan", a dislike of the capital and the City, [and] a belief in the common sense of the folk'.[12] Clearly MacDiarmid is no little Englander, but his dislike of cities sees him stray occasionally into the braes of 'Scotshire' (SS, 200), that parochial place toured by Lewis Grassic Gibbon in 'Literary Lights' (1934). If Gibbon was keen not to belong to the Scottish Renaissance movement it was because he objected to what he perceived to be its bourgeois insularity. Despite describing himself as being 'some kind of Nationalist' in 'Glasgow', Gibbon decides that 'Scotland's salvation, the world's salvation lies in neither nationalism nor internationalism, those twin halves of an idiot whole. It lies in ultimate cosmopolitanism, the earth the City of God' (SS, 146). In subconscious self-hate at the particularity of his earthbound rootedness, Gibbon seeks the universal transcendence of nationality. MacDiarmid's politics, on the other hand, turn on the proposition that the local self and the small place are no encumbrance to universality, which is constituted after all by nothing more than an alliance of different localisms. Internationalism – indeed, Gibbon's mystical cosmopolitanism also – is impossible unless preceded in actuality by the imagined world community of nations. In 'Scottish Music', written for the Scottish Educational Journal and appearing on 10 October 1930 under the pseudonym 'A. L.', MacDiarmid succinctly states his case: 'True nationalism and true internationalism are complementary and indispensable to each other' (RT2, 243).

His birthplace in the Debatable Land of the Scottish Borders provided a dialectical source of inspiration throughout the poet's life. Langholm is a place he remembers in representation as being of Edenic childhood delight, but it is also somewhere Grieve had to leave to become MacDiarmid and imagine a Scottish Republic – this in spite (or because) of the fact that the roots of his politics stem from Langholm, his poetry possessed of an imagination that constantly returns home. 'All the chief elements of my life to-day, however developed and enriched by subsequent experience, were quick in me by at least my early teens,' writes a 48-year-old MacDiarmid, 'and I am now, despite my long absence from the scenes of my boyhood, more of a Langholmite than ever.' (*LP*, 39). This confession of the centrality of Langholm to the growth of the poet's personality was written in Whalsay. Previous to his time in Shetland, it was not until MacDiarmid actually left Scotland at the end of the 1920s that the significance of Langholm was revealed to him. Living in London and Liverpool between 1929 and 1931, it was the experience of separation from his first wife Peggy and their children that sent his imagination back to Langholm. Deprived of the poetically productive environment of Montrose, where his political activism had found a suitable local base, the chaotic narrative of *To Circumjack Cencrastus* (1930) bespeaks the disruptions in his personal life. A sense of geographic and emotional displacement prompted the need for his creative vision to refocus around memories of home.

In 'Kinsfolk' he admits that 'no' till lately ha'e the hame scenes played / A pairt in my creative thocht' (*CP2*, 1147). The poem begins by complimenting Langholm on its beauty, confirmed in 'Growing Up in Langholm' as 'the bonniest place I know' (*SP*, 268). Leaving Langholm because he was looking for more than mere 'scenic beauty' (*CP2*, 1147) the poet finds, however, that the pursuit of his vocation has left him doubly homeless, having lost both his childhood relations and his family by marriage. Uncompromising commitment to his craft has impaired his ability to sustain human commitments – a failing he defiantly renders as an artistic virtue. Rationalising, perhaps, in his lonely freedom, he claims that 'Maist bonds 'twixt man and man are weel ca'd bonds' (*CP2*, 1149). Whilst in Liverpool, where he briefly worked as Publicity Officer for a business federation called the Liverpool Organisation, MacDiarmid thinks not only of his wife and children in London, but also of his elderly mother and dead father. Deciding that his relationship with his parents was a 'maitter o' easy-ozie habit maistly, shy / O' fundamentals' (*CP2*, 1149), he ponders the contrasting conceptions of the family engendered by the working and leisure classes. 'Great hooses keep their centuried lines complete' (*CP2*, 1150), but there is no remembrance of things past for the poet, who is barely able to recall even his own father. Released from the necessity of work, the propertied succeed in perpetuating themselves in art – observe 'their forbears painted on their wa's' (*CP2*, 1150) – and through a family name distinguished almost purely by wealth. In contrast, the artist MacDiarmid, who has changed his name from the commonplace Grieve in order to be immortalised as a poet, 'canna signal to a single soul / In a' the centuries that led up to me' (*CP2*, 1150). In the last stanza, however, he finds his genealogical place at the forefront of a family tree deeply at odds with those traced by the upper orders:

> Reivers to weavers and to me. Weird way!
> Yet in the last analysis I've sprung
> Frae battles, mair than ballads, and it seems
> The thrawn auld water has at last upswung
> Through me, and's mountin' like the vera devil
>   To its richt level!

> (*CP2*, 1150)

Written in 1931, 'Kinsfolk' appeared as 'From Work in Progress' in that July's *Modern Scot*, but had to wait until 1970 and *Selected Poems* to find collected publication. As the first part of the projected *Clann Albann*, this Work in Progress was the unpublished *Muckle Toon*. 'Kinsfolk' is an important indicator of several key themes in the *Muckle Toon* explicable with reference to MacDiarmid's possible meanings when alluding to Peggy's departure having thrown him back on what he describes as 'my first cause?' (*CP2*, 1147). Defining cause as 'that which produces an effect',[13] MacDiarmid's first 'first cause' would of course be his parents. This first cause must be extended back into the familial past, however, as without the existence of his parents' parents – 'Graham, Murray, Carruthers, Frater' (*CP2*, 1149) – and so on, there would be no Grieve. Searching for notable ancestors in this line and failing to find any, the poet of 'Kinsfolk' is asking, who am I and where do I come from? Answered literally: Christopher Murray Grieve, born in Langholm, Scotland. But what of his art, that which constitutes his invented self, from where or what was it conceived? If his poetry is 'water flowin' frae an unkent source' (*CP2*, 1150) then this poet of Christian parents might be tapping a tributary of the divine creator; otherwise, in a modernist, secular universe, he is entirely self-generating, creating himself as he creates. The first cause (or cosmological) argument would have God as MacDiarmid's 'first cause' – if only the infinite regress of creators by which this theistic principle self-destructs hadn't licensed the atheist poet's self-creation as god-like modernist creator. It follows that, when defining cause as 'an ideal, principle, or belief',[14] Grieve's true 'first cause' is without doubt poetry: that which brought MacDiarmid into being. Yet poetry for MacDiarmid is continually, intimately, inextricably bound up with the political cause of radicalising Scotland, with his belief in an independent republic. Understanding the crucial early influence of Langholm on his work, Grieve identifies MacDiarmid as someone 'who found ready and waiting in himself by the time he came to write poetry a sound relationship between the political thinker in him and the artist' (*LP*, 231). MacDiarmid's 'first cause' – poetry and politics – originates in Grieve's 'first cause': the place he began.

Family, class and religion: the Calvinist roots of radical republicanism

Langholm is the 'secret reservoir' (*LP*, 20) that MacDiarmid draws upon when writing poetry, a place that is his 'touchstone in all creative matters' (*LP*, 3). His origins are clearly important to him: *Lucky Poet* opens with a brief look into the Grieve ancestry. W. N. Herbert discerns in the *Muckle Toon* a 'need for acknowledgement' and 'a plea to belong' in regard to MacDiarmid's psychological relationship to his working-class family and the wider Langholm community.[15] Whilst this is true, there is also a political challenge to certain community values, in particular those of religion, and the very notion of family per se. According to MacDiarmid, because his internationalist politics are native to Langholm and the Borders he was 'fed on out-and-out Radicalism and Republicanism when still a child' (*LP*, 231). This means that he uses the progressive political traditions of his birthplace (in this regard, as in others such as beauty, Langholm equals that which is best in Scotland) in order to attack the provincialised condition of Scotland.

MacDiarmid remembers having had 'an incredibly happy' (*LP*, 219) childhood in Langholm. But, despite parental love, he also writes of the 'incredible gulf' (*LP*, 224) between religious mother and blasphemous son. In *First Hymn to Lenin* (1931), MacDiarmid dons the guise of the fighting Borderer in order to question the religion of his childhood and the family life so important to the perpetuation of religion. This distancing from the bonds of family begins in 'At My Father's Grave', the poet declaring, 'I'm nae mair your son' (*CP1*, 299). It is not simply death that separates father and son, however, but the intellectual development of the poet and his adoption of a value system conflicting markedly with his father's religious convictions:

> It is my mind, nae son o' yours, that looks,
> And the great darkness o' your death comes up
> And equals it across the way.
> A livin' man upon a deid man thinks
> And ony sma'er thocht's impossible.

> (*CP1*, 299)

'First Hymn to Lenin' signifies where the poet's political ideas have taken him since leaving Langholm. The poem's internationalist advocacy

of violent revolution sits somewhat awkwardly with the rest of the collection, which proceeds into seemingly more placid local terrain, but he
is announcing with this opening salvo his intention of bringing the class
battle back home. By situating 'At My Father's Grave' directly after 'First
Hymn', MacDiarmid is proclaiming the death of his father's religion and
modestly reformist politics as inconsequentialities of the past, proposing
instead a modernist replacement in aggressive revolutionary action in the
name of the future. MacDiarmid not only goes further than his father in
political terms, advocating an extremist solution to capitalist iniquities;
he finds faith in a secular political philosophy that seeks to make sense
of – and then revenge – his father's death as the utter termination of an
incomplete life, a life that the poet will determinedly not repeat.

When recollecting the family's straitened circumstances in *Lucky Poet*,
MacDiarmid thought his father had earned – at best – thirty-seven
shillings a week. Perhaps this economic hardship is one reason that the
narrator of 'The Never-Yet-Explored' calls the start of the twentieth
century 'a terrible period' (*Annals*, 75). The death of Queen Victoria in
1901 inaugurated *la belle époque* and the lavish upper-class lifestyles of
Edwardianism, a social signifier of the yet further tightening of already
rigid class boundaries. Although 'At My Father's Grave' marks the intellectual difference between son and father as being as definitive as that
between life and death, in 'Fatherless in Boyhood' (1931; collected 1994)
MacDiarmid witnesses in his father's concerns 'the crude / Beginnin's o'
my ain deep interests' (*CP2*, 1250) in books, the political reformism of
the Trades Union and Co-operative movements, and religion. 'A laddie
when he dee'd' (*CP2*, 1148), says the poet of his father in 'Kinsfolk'.
'First Hymn' regards revolution as requiring (super)men such as Lenin,
grown beyond the childish opium of Christianity's stupefying ethic of
transcendence. The poet furnishes himself with a heroic father figure, the
revolutionary Russian Christ, to supersede his deceased working-class
father whose principles were hopelessly inadequate to the millenarian
task of modernity. MacDiarmid believed, however, that before he died in
1911, aged just forty-seven, the pious James Grieve 'was coming steadily
towards the Socialist position' (*LP*, 226). Alan Bold relates that,
unlike most other Langholmites, MacDiarmid's father held 'pro-Boer
sympathies' during the Second Boer War (1899–1902).[16] Concluding
'Fatherless in Boyhood', MacDiarmid almost reverts to the irreverent
attitude of 'At My Father's Grave', deciding that the real tragedy of his
father's death, or all his paltry remembrance of the event will allow, is
that it cannot be considered to fulfil the requisites of tragedy. In
Aristotelian terms, postman James Grieve's hard-working life lacked the
magnitude necessary for his death to constitute tragedy.

MacDiarmid brought his father's burgeoning radicalism and opposition to British imperialism to a high pitch. Son completed father in other ways contrary to, but inescapably influenced by, paternal inheritance: James wrote sermons, whereas MacDiarmid's often sermonic poetry is fired with the spirit of evolution, James proscribed Burns from the Grieve household while, denouncing his cult and influence, MacDiarmid would seek to replace Burns as Scotland's poet. Inspired by his father's civic example of extra-professional, active localism, MacDiarmid says in *Lucky Poet* that he was determined never to work for a wage but dedicate himself instead to a non-remunerative vocation; only 'public service', he emphasises, could be regarded as '*real* work' (*LP*, 226).

Such high-minded republican virtue was imparted to MacDiarmid by the self-conscious decency and uprightness of his Calvinist parents. Inculcated with a sense of being better than the other working-class children in Langholm, Christopher and his brother Andrew were taunted for the neatness of their appearance. Peter, the fictionalised quasi-Christopher of 'Murtholm Hill' (1927), revenges his exclusion from the boisterous community of boyhood by imagining that as an adult he will become 'a banker or a lawyer, or, at the vera least, a teacher' while the rougher children are condemned to 'be mill-haunds a' their days' (*Annals*, 145). Confirming his inner superiority, Peter finds ultimate redress in making friends with the minister, an indication that he is chosen. But it is more surely the minister's social standing – his niece, Barbara, dressed in fur and smelling of wholesome cleanliness – that excites Peter with a sense of his own worth; he is where he feels he belongs, with the gentry of the community.

MacDiarmid politically opposed the gentry and the class snobbery that found its local apex in the Church. He claims of his Langholm boyhood that it 'made me a man naturally fitted for Communism' (*LP*, 231), but the elect surety of specialness endowed by his respectable working-class, Calvinist upbringing remained. Feelings of being set apart from others were manifested in, and exacerbated by, his bookishness. So Peter of 'Murtholm Hill' sees himself as 'naethin' but a pair o' e'en and a brain lookin' on at life – but withoot ony share in't' (*Annals*, 149). In preference to playing with his brother, in 'Andy' (1927) Tammy tells of his enjoyment of reading and 'bein' alane – wi' his ain thochts' (*Annals*, 172). 'Old Miss Beattie' centres on a youngster whose intellectual precociousness and verbal dexterity is such that locals say of him 'the boy's lost his ain mooth and fund a minister's'; in turn he describes his parents as being 'different frae the feck o' folk – they were mair religious' (*Annals*, 137). Other short stories written in Scots and set in what appears to be a small town, such as 'A'body's Lassie', 'The Moon Through Glass' (both 1927) and 'The Stranger' (1934), deal with religion and the supernatural. The democratic assembly of Scots voices in 'The Purple Patch' (1924) gathered to discuss an inspirational sermon by the new Reverend of their church discover that his text, what they believe to be the true 'language o' God' (*Annals*, 134), has not only been plagiarised but used before by a previous minister.

The tone of these short stories is teasingly affectionate of what is perceived as being the couthie, kirk-induced limitedness of most Langholmites. In *First Hymn to Lenin*, however, MacDiarmid puts his sense of election, his book-learning and his knowledge of religion and local religiosity to more stirringly radical ends. 'Prayer for a Second Flood' craftily uses the religious imagery familiar to Langholmites in order to issue them a wake-up call to greater life:

> There'd ha'e to be nae warnin'. Times ha'e changed
> And Noahs are owre numerous nooadays,
> (And them the vera folk to benefit maist!)
> Knock the feet frae under them, O Lord, wha praise
> Your unsearchable ways sae muckle and yet hope
>   To keep within knowledgeable scope!

                                                        (*CP1*, 299)

Emphasising the spiritual parsimony of the Langholm congregation, the poet calls on God to cleanse this locality and so 'replenish the salt o' the earth / In the place o' their birth' (*CP1*, 300). While 'the salt of the earth' (Matthew 5: 13) originally referred to disciples of Christ, it has commonly come to mean the working class. MacDiarmid wants the people of Langholm to reactivate their 'tremendous proletarian virtue' – a quality he remembers as having 'saved' (*LP*, 232) him from the inhibiting theology of his parents – in order that the genesis of a revolutionary new world will be precipitated from a local setting. 'Some Day' (1923) is a short story imagining the possibility of 'RESURRECTION DAY at Sleepyhillock . . . a' the graves crackin' open an' the fowk loupin' oot' (*Annals*, 123), a scene revisualised two years later in 'Crowdieknowe' from *Sangschaw*. By 1933, with 'The Kernigal', MacDiarmid could only foresee 'this vain resurrection' of Langholmites, who 'seem to rise / Juist as they were, and sae belittle Daith' (*CP2*, 1275). Clearly he was more convinced of his powers of national revivification in the 1920s. The putative miracle worker of 'Some Day', trying to bring the local dead back to life (without the intermediating presence of a minister), is Hugh M'Taggert. Grieve in Montrose, attempting the renewal of Scotland, had become Hugh M'Diarmid only the year before. According to the reminiscences of Langholmite John Hyslop, published in 1912, 'instead of being in the main stream of life, as we thought,' Langholm and its folk 'were only as a pool the flood has left'.[17] MacDiarmid's radical localism, born in Langholm, aims to bring a political and ethical flood that will resituate the provinces in universal significance and so save the whole.

He continues the religious theme in 'Charisma and My Relatives', comparing himself to the Christ who transcends family relations. The poem is dedicated to the iron and coal merchant Peggy left MacDiarmid for: William McElroy. The poem's attack on Christianity and the family makes it a precursor of the radical spiritual individualism of 'Ode to All Rebels'. MacDiarmid claims that 'naewhere has the love-religion had / A harder struggle than in Scotland' (*CP1*, 301), an idea echoed in Grassic Gibbon's *A Scots Quair*.[18] Blinded to the 'epopteia' (*CP1*, 301) – the (Eleusinian) moment of spiritual illumination in which God is revealed to the initiate – by the mystifications of human entanglement, MacDiarmid calls upon his fighting Border spirit to free his fettered vision from the circumscriptive self:

Oorsels oor greatest foes. Yet, even yet,
I haud to 'I' and 'Scot' and 'Borderer'
And fence the wondrous fire that in me's lit
Wi' sicna barriers roond as hide frae'ts licht
    Near a'body's sicht.

                              (*CP1*, 302)

'Charisma' is MacDiarmid's bitter acknowledgement that his wife never really understood him: had she discerned the inimitable spirit burning within him, but imperfectly manifested in print, surely she wouldn't have left him for a man of McElroy's materialistic values? In sub-text, away from home and – very briefly – literally homeless in London, MacDiarmid is also angry at the neglect he has suffered in his quest to resuscitate Scottish identity.

MacDiarmid's grief over the loss of his wife and the children, a hurt that was to resound in his letters to Peggy throughout the 1930s, precipitated a crisis of identity that called him back imaginatively to his past in Langholm as he sought to find emotional resources with which to cope with the alienation of the present. 'Beyond Exile', a conventional poem written in Salonika in 1916, goes back to the war so that he can relive – in irony, sadness or last attempt at seduction? – the dream of seemingly more innocent times: returning home to Scotland and Peggy. Divorce from his family now forced him into an emotional and psychological debatable land, as well as bringing aspects of his Langholm childhood into questioning focus. Memories of the Muckle Toon are tinged with the adult acerbity of his personal life in 'The Liquid Light': 'The pairts o' Langholm the Esk reflects / Seem like maist women, better than they are' (*CP1*, 306). 'The Prostitute', whilst endorsing male sexual liberties as part of the ungainsayable totality of life, may also be a vengeful, sexually jealous dig at Peggy; a misogamist aiming to upset family convention grounded in religious dictate, MacDiarmid is playing (a somewhat louche) Christ accepting the sinning Magdalene. Resentful feelings about personal love are coincident with his desire to dispel religion's organised aura in 'Religion and Love', while 'The Church of My Fathers' impugns the neglect of the sacred sustained by Scottish Presbyterianism's traducing of the spirit.

As he embraced a spiritualised communism, *First Hymn to Lenin* represents the point at which MacDiarmid attempted to finally annul within himself the effects of childhood faith. Striving to escape the claustrophobia of familial conformity, in 'The Hole in the Wall' he asks for spiritual comrades:

You're a fechter tae? The best o' news.
The fecht sae faur frae owre
Has haurdly begun, and'll wax foraye
In proportion to oor power.

(*CP1*, 309)

As in 'Charisma', MacDiarmid sees himself as some sort of soldier of the spirit, a Christ-like genius attacking Christian conformism. This evolutionary zeal for the attainment of creative completion in every life, however ordinary, is proclaimed as in a newspaper advertisement in 'The Burning Passion': 'Wanted a technique for genius!' (*CP1*, 305). Lenin is again cited as humanity's pinnacle. Through communism History will begin anew in order that each individual human history need no longer start from scratch, but build on the best that has gone before by learning to truly learn from the past. Speaking to himself in 'Another Turn of the Screw' the poet's memory of his own past seems to be slipping, leaving him face-to-face with nothingness, but again he summons his Border identity to confront the abyss: 'Fear? What's fear to a Border man?' (*CP1*, 310).

For all his fighting talk, MacDiarmid was in bad shape at this point. His family's departure instigated a crisis that rendered nugatory the Christian ethos of his forebears even as their collective spiritual indomitableness still resided in the poet. Unable to will his personal life back into the shape he wants, MacDiarmid's faith comes to rest on the adamantine, impersonal will of communism, 'the flower and iron of the truth' ('First Hymn to Lenin', *CP1*, 298). Claiming that most Scots are completely unable 'to accept or conceive the artist's doom', MacDiarmid frankly characterises himself in *Lucky Poet* as 'an absolutist whose absolutes came to grief in his private life' (*LP*, 44). This suggests that the subjective unhappiness created by his domestic situation, experienced acutely during the dislocation of living in England, may have subliminally motivated his adoption of the replacement religion of communism.

'The Seamless Garment', a title alluding (John 19: 23) to Christ's tunic as symbolising the indivisible oneness of his ethic, aims to unify the ultimate poet (Rilke) with the consummate politician (Lenin) in a revolutionary rather than a Christian whole, 'a single reality – a' a'e 'oo" (*CP1*, 312). Addressing a family member as a political comrade (or vice versa), MacDiarmid admits that it is only recently that he has begun to think about the conditions of working-class work in Langholm. He asks the mill hands to find full expression as humans in the manner of his artistic and political exemplars:

> Lenin and Rilke baith gied still mair skill,
>   Coopers o' Stobo, to a greater concern
> Than you devote to claith in the mill.
>   Wad it be ill to learn
> To keep a bit eye on their looms as weel
> And no' be hailly ta'en up wi' your 'tweel'?
>
> (*CP1*, 312–13)

To keep pace with the technological advancement of the machinery they harness (and are harnessed by) MacDiarmid desires the cultural and political evolution of the worker. The assumption that this is possible whilst still being an operative seems dubious at best. A similar objection can be raised to the idea that the 'fricative work' (*CP1*, 314) of the unacknowledged and self-elected legislators parallels manual labour in authentic arduousness. This view is undermined somewhat in 'Second Hymn to Lenin' as MacDiarmid pessimistically concedes that culture has 'affected nocht but a fringe / O' mankind in ony way' and dismisses reputed geniuses as 'romantic rebels / Strikin' dilletante [*sic*] poses' (*CP1*, 324). Indeed, returning to Langholm as a point of radical reference, in 'The Oon Olympian', from *Scots Unbound*, he denounces Goethe's celebrated universalism as a bourgeois concern to maintain law and order – in and outside the cultural canon:

> Ridiculous optimist, maintain
> Your proofless unity o' the real.
> There's pluralisms abroad at last
> Ha'e a' sic follies in a creel.   [*state of confusion*]
>
> (*CP1*, 360)

'Depth and the Chthonian Image', also from *Scots Unbound*, ponders the significance of a dilapidated mill in relation to communist universalism and notions of transcendence, deploring 'Hoo few men ever live / And what wee local lives at best they ha'e' (*CP1*, 350). Harvey Oxenhorn's point that a failing of 'The Seamless Garment' lies in the provinciality of its setting implies that the working environment of those in small places like Langholm is less important than that of great centres of 'mass indus- trial and political conflict' such as 'Lenin's Petersburg, Rosa Luxembourg's Berlin – or the Glasgow of John MacLean'.[19] It is just such insular metro- politanism that MacDiarmid's Maclean-inspired Scottish Republicanism seeks to radically counter. From a local milieu, his internationalist politics supplant in faith the Christian vision.

First Hymn to Lenin ends with a poem dedicated to beginnings, Life itself and the poet's origins in Langholm. Returning to the Christian idea of the Flood, 'Water of Life' goes further back to 'that first flux in which a' life began', recovering an evolutionary memory 'o' the time / We ploutered in the slime' (*CP1*, 314). Accustomed to the 'perfect maze / O' waters' around Langholm that he swam in as a child, MacDiarmid claims to be 'amphibious still' (*CP1*, 314). This connects the poem to a 1927 prose piece 'The Waterside'. Here Langholm is constituted of different areas that determine the characteristics of their inhabitants, qualities that in turn symbolise a particular human epoch. Those living on the High Street of modernity are frantically full of the ignorant conceit of self, while the taciturn hillside dwellers, with a loftier view of their surroundings, seem more composed and religiously reflective. Neither bustlingly empty in the secular, contemporary sense nor stilled by the metaphysical con- templation of the age of belief, the people of the waterside exist by the instinct of primordiality: 'To dae onything ava they'd to use something faur quicker than thocht – something as auld as the water itsel'. And thocht's a dryland thing and a gey recent yin at that' (*Annals*, 156). In 'Water of Life' MacDiarmid rescues himself from drowning in the tumul- tuous sea of emotions he has been thrown into by the departure of his family through the adoption of the apparent senselessness of Langholm's waterside folk. This return to the water appears to advocate a retrogres- sive evolutionary step, but MacDiarmid's spiritual evolutionism runs counter to that capitalist code of competition the survival of the fittest. He is proposing we start over, as he must do in his personal life, in order to establish a revolutionary source of new standards:

> The promise that there'll be nae second Flood
> I tak' wi' a' the salt I've saved since then.
> Extinction? What's that but to return
> To juist anither Muckle Toon again?

     – A salutary process bringin' values oot
      Ocht less 'ud leave in doot.

(CP1, 317)

'Water of Life' is one of a number of water poems intended for the
Muckle Toon which were inspired by the River Esk and the Water of
Ewes and Wauchope, all in and around Langholm. 'Water Music' com-
petes in linguistic liveliness with the 'Anna Livia Plurabelle' section of
what became James Joyce's *Finnegans Wake* (1939), but 'Tarras', which
follows in *Scots Unbound*, comes closer to Joyce's evocation of Dublin's
Liffey as a mothering source of manifold renewal. MacDiarmid describes
'*This Bolshevik bog!*' (*CP1*, 337) by the River Tarras in Part One of the
poem, praising this fecund tract of earth as if it were a no-nonsense
woman; in the second section, 'Why I Became a Scots Nationalist',
Scotland is a frigid female who, initially against her own volition, grad-
ually succumbs to the poet's advances. MacDiarmid's communism
emerges naturally from his birthing ground, whereas Scotland is a more
difficult terrain for the nationalist to conquer. His politics cheek by jowl
in this two-piece poem, each Muse-like ideology exhibits a resolutely
masculine prerogative.

    'The Dog Pool', a hitherto uncollected poem from 1931, confirms this
by comparing the Esk with characteristics of two Scottish socialists, its
water being 'as black / As Maxton's hair and noisy as Kirkwood' (*CP2*,
1252). In 'The Point of Honour', from *Stony Limits* (1934; 1956), the
poet defines the '*onomatopoeic art*' (*CP1*, 388) that propelled 'Water
Music', seeking in the Esk's feminine spate the key to understanding his
art's mystery:

> *Nay, the last issue I have all but joined,*
> *But my muse still lacks – and so has missed all –*
> *The right temper, like yours, which goes to the point*
> *Of the terrible; the terrible crystal.*

(CP1, 390)

'The Point of Honour', like 'The Terrible Crystal', is in pursuit of
absolute clarity of poetic consciousness: 'Mid the elemental enemies –
cold, ravening brine – / The intellectual flame's survival I sing' (*CP1*,
389). Concerning Whitshiels, a wood close to Langholm, 'Whuchulls',
from *A Lap of Honour* (1967), acknowledges that the ostensibly undis-
cerning chaos of natural creation is 'where the Arts stert' (*CP2*, 1093).
In the same collection, 'By Wauchopeside' decides, however, that nature
and the memory of place, whilst important to MacDiarmid's art, are
inadequate to the evolutionary task of 'true poetry', which is concerned
with 'Revolutions in the dynasty o' live ideals' (*CP2*, 1084).

'The Scots Renaissance' (1933) locates the roots of the movement that MacDiarmid championed in Montrose in the 'wowf places' (*CP2*, 1274) of Langholm and the Borders. A Scots word meaning crazy or disordered in the mind, such wowf places are seen here as the provenance of an irrational energy and uncanny rebelliousness that revitalises by resisting the conformity of the current order. A short story published in 1927 when MacDiarmid was in Montrose, 'The Common Riding', begins with the reflection that ambition 'grows in the maist unlikely places' (*Annals*, 140). With the death of the usual carrier of the thistle in this Langholm festival, Yiddy Ballantyne offers to replace him. Obsessed with the Common Riding since he was a child, Yiddy is an 'eaten-an-spewed-lookin' cratur' (*Annals*, 140) – Elizabeth Grieve's description of a newborn Christopher, which MacDiarmid also includes in *A Drunk Man*.[20] Too slight to bear the weight of the thistle alone Yiddy none the less heroically brings it to Langholm's Market Place before expiring through the strain of a feat that he has lived only to accomplish. Including a description of the Common Riding, where 'The aucht-fit thistle wallops on hie' (*CP1*, 97), *A Drunk Man Looks at the Thistle*, from 1926, sees the poet sacrifice himself for the nation. Four years on *To Circumjack Cencrastus* still wonders, '*Sall Jewry breed a Christ / Gaeldom canna equal* [?]' (*CP1*, 245). Willingly crucified by the Thistle, Yiddy (Yid is Yiddish for Jew) represents MacDiarmid's desire to be the Celtic Christ. His visionary transfiguration of Scotland reached gestation in the provincial setting of Langholm.

The controversy over the site of Jake Harvey's Hugh MacDiarmid Memorial Sculpture was in a manner predicted by the author of 'The Monument'. The corten steel and bronze representation of an open book unveiled in 1985 near Whita Yett was originally proposed for the higher and more visibly exposed Whita Hill. From here, towering above the memorial to the radical poet, rises the column (1835) that commemorates the subject of 'The Monument', Sir John Malcolm, born in Langholm in 1769, a Knight of Eskdale and Governor General of Bombay. According to MacDiarmid in *Lucky Poet*, 'what I personally owed to the Langholm of that time was an out-and-out Radicalism and Republicanism' (*LP*, 225). His communism is the apotheosis of his spiritual and intellectual evolution, from the Calvinist autodidact in the Langholm Library to international modernist and Scottish saviour; emerging from his imaginative re-immersion in the Debatable Land of his Langholm childhood, it is his attempt to transcend churchy parochialism and so transform the values and politics of home. In 'The Borders', a late poem from 1967, MacDiarmid is sure that the cultural 'treasures' of humanity can still come 'frae the lanely places, / No' the croodit centres o' mankind yet' (*CP2*, 1424). From Langholm, his provincialist universalism was to be reborn in another 'wee Nazareth' (*CP2*, 1424) in Angus, north-east Scotland.

Notes

1. Robert Crawford, *Devolving English Literature* (Oxford: Clarendon Press, 1992), p. 247.
2. Walter Perrie, *Out of Conflict* (Dunfermline: Borderline, 1982), p. 16.
3. Ibid., p. 15.
4. George Ogilvie, *Broughton Magazine*, Christmas 1920, cited in Alan Bold, *MacDiarmid: Christopher Murray Grieve: A Critical Biography* (London: John Murray, 1988), p. 43.
5. Perrie, *Out of Conflict*, p. 15.
6. *The Langholm Library Heritage Project* (Glasgow: Glasgow Polytechnic in association with The Langholm Library Trust, 1992), p. 3; information on the Langholm Library is drawn from this anonymously authored booklet.
7. In conversation with the present author, the Langholm Library, 28 June 2005.
8. Andrew O'Hagan, 'Into the Ferment', in T. M. Devine (ed.), *Scotland's Shame? Bigotry and Sectarianism in Modern Scotland* (Edinburgh: Mainstream, 2000), p. 25.
9. Duncan Glen did well to reverse the local apophthegm 'Out of the World and into Langholm' when titling his book on the poet's birthplace *Hugh MacDiarmid; or, Out of Langholm and into the World* (Edinburgh: Akros, 1992).
10. See Maurice Lindsay, *Francis George Scott and the Scottish Renaissance* (Edinburgh: Paul Harris, 1980), p. 25.
11. See Roger A. Mason and Martin S. Smith, *A Dialogue on the Law of Kingship among the Scots: A Critical Edition and Translation of George Buchanan's De Iure Regni apud Scotos Dialogus* (Aldershot: Ashgate, 2004), p. l.
12. Christopher Hitchens, 'Something about the Poems', *Unacknowledged Legislation: Writers in the Public Sphere* (London & New York: Verso, 2001), p. 211.
13. Ian Brookes et al. (eds), *The Chambers Dictionary* (Edinburgh: Chambers, 2003), p. 240.
14. Ibid., p. 240
15. W. N. Herbert, *To Circumjack MacDiarmid: The Poetry and Prose of Hugh MacDiarmid* (Oxford: Clarendon Press, 1992), pp. 105, 107.
16. Bold, *MacDiarmid*, p. 24.
17. John Hyslop and Robert Hyslop, *Langholm As It Was: A History of Langholm and Eskdale from the Earliest Times* (Sunderland: Hills, 1912), p. 582.
18. For example, Chris says to her brother Will in *Sunset Song* (1932): '*I don't believe they were ever religious, the Scots folk, Will – not really religious like Irish or French or all the rest in the history books. They've never BELIEVED. It's just been a place to collect and argue, the kirk, and criticise God.*' Similarly, Robert Colquhoun, Chris's husband in *Cloud Howe* (1933), says:

'*Religion – A Scot know religion? Half of them think of God as a Scot with brosy morals and a penchant for Burns. And the other half are over damned mean to allow the Almighty even existence.*' Lewis Grassic Gibbon, *A Scots Quair* ([1946] Harmondsworth: Penguin, 1986), pp. 165, 295.

19. Harvey Oxenhorn, *Elemental Things: The Poetry of Hugh MacDiarmid* (Edinburgh: Edinburgh University Press, 1984), p. 136.

20. See Gordon Wright, *MacDiarmid: An Illustrated Biography* (Edinburgh: Gordon Wright, 1977), p. 21; and *CP1*, p. 104.

Chapter 3

'A Disgrace to the Community'

When Chris Grieve was born in Langholm at the end of the nineteenth century provincial Scotland was most famously associated in the national literary imagination with the couthie Thrums of J. M. Barrie (1860–1937), the author's fictionalised account of his Kirriemuir birthplace. Barrie established the Kailyard novel in *Auld Licht Idylls* (1888) and *A Window in Thrums* (1889). From a small Scottish town to triumph on the metropolitan stage, Barrie's career is archetypal of the lad o' pairts: up-and-out through talent and ambition, allied with a democratic Scottish education and Calvinist industriousness, to financial success in the city.[1] Aiming his modernist critical guns at a literary commercial giant, in the *Scottish Educational Journal* of 26 June 1925 Grieve writes that he believes, 'so far as Scottish literature is concerned, Barrie has long severed any effective connection he ever had with Scottish life or thought' ('Sir J. M. Barrie', *CSS*, 17).

Researching the roots and determining principles of those in positions of educational authority, Andrew McPherson concludes that, even as late as 1961, in Scotland 'the locus of social identity has indeed been that of the village or the small town and not that of the city'; this 'symbolic world bounded by Angus, standing for the East and North and with Kirriemuir at its heart', evinces 'a nation of small towns, and implicitly, therefore, a Protestant nation'.[2] MacDiarmid's politics of place oppose the parochial, sectarian values of what McPherson calls the 'Kirriemuir career'. Yet, in his life, Grieve clung to, creatively prospered in, and theoretically defended small-town Scotland. Championing the Scottish Renaissance movement, in the *Montrose Review* he describes 'Montrose as a Literary Centre' (*MR*, 23 September 1927, 5), and in 'Literary Angus and the Mearns' (1933), from the *Fife and Angus Annual*, he acknowledges 'the foremost place Angus holds in the new stirrings in Scottish letters' (*RT2*, 390). His decade in Montrose in the 1920s was pivotal in his efforts towards an internationalist

Scotland. MacDiarmid's modernist poetry in Scots and his espousal of a radical Scottish politics at a local and national level were crucially stimulated by his daily engagement with the Montrose community. Grieve manifested a civic republicanism in the town, most strongly through his work as a journalist with the *Montrose Review* and as an independent member of the town council. His professional working life in Montrose facilitated the finding of his poetic and political voice.

MacDiarmid had two spells in Montrose. He was demobilised from the British army as a non-combatant in the summer of 1919 and went to live with his first wife Margaret Skinner in St Andrews – a place both he and Edwin Muir found creatively unfavourable, but central in the 1930s to James Whyte's nationalist journal *The Modern Scot*. From the university town, MacDiarmid found employment as a reporter with the *Montrose Review*. He left his first stint in Montrose in October 1920 to work as a private tutor at Kildermorie Lodge in Ross and Cromarty. By November 1920 he had published a new group of Scottish poets in the first series of *Northern Numbers*. He also edited and wrote much of the *Scottish Chapbook* and began working on articles that would later be collected as *Contemporary Scottish Studies*, his modernist blast at Scotland's cultural Kailyard. Aged twenty-eight, he was tempted back to the *Review* in April 1921 by the promise of increased wages. Chris and Peggy moved into the first of three houses in Montrose at 19 Kincardine Street. By 8 September 1921 the couple had flitted to 12 White's Place. On 17 March 1922 they relocated to 16 Links Avenue, a council house that became the nerve-centre of the Scottish Renaissance movement.

MacDiarmid's modernist manifesto for Scottish cultural and political internationalisation, ambitiously implemented from Montrose, was mapped out during the First World War. Supposedly fighting for the rights of small nations, the British were also bloodily dealing with the Irish rebels of Easter 1916, such as the Edinburgh-born autodidact James Connolly (1868–1916). Writing 'Connolly, Bakunin, Mussolini, and Others' for the *Northern Review* of May 1924, Grieve recognises that Connolly's 'conjunction of revolutionary Socialism and rebel Nationalism' (*RT1*, 211) holds a significant message for those Scottish socialists still duped by the false internationalism of British Unionism. According to Grieve, Connolly 'divined that Socialism and Nationalism must come to terms – that the Marxian dispensation would not answer the needs of humanity' (*RT1*, 211). By 1927 Grieve was proposing a Scottish Home Rule motion to the local branch of the Independent Labour Party (ILP), arguing that, 'in view of the difference in political psychology and economic and social requirements between England and Scotland', self-government

> would be a short cut to Scottish Socialism, and would have important reper-
> cussions on Imperial and international affairs, or modify British, foreign, and
> imperial policy to a far greater extent than is presently possible by means of
> the Socialist opposition at Westminster. ('Montrose ILP and Scottish Home
> Rule', *MR*, 28 October 1927, 5)

MacDiarmid wants a nationalist movement enabling Scotland to find her true identity, not as a provincial handmaid to the colonialism administered in Ireland but as an independent nation resisting the capitalist metropolitanism governing imperialism. Integral to the formation of the National Party of Scotland (NPS) in 1928, MacDiarmid made an important visit to the Irish Free State in August of that year with the Hon. Ruaraidh Erskine of Marr (1869–1964) – a figure described by Grieve in the *Scottish Educational Journal* of 19 February 1926 as 'the very core and crux of the Gaeltacht' (*CSS*, 285). Meeting Éamon de Valera and W. B. Yeats in Dublin confirmed his wish for a Celtic confederacy against British imperialism, as did the 'eager interest in the new Nationalist developments in Scotland and in Wales' that he found amongst the Irish ('What Irishmen Think of Ireland: some prominent literary men' (1928), *RT2*, 194).

Inspired by Irish Republicanism to advance the Scottish nationalist cause, MacDiarmid was also politicised by Russia's 1917 Bolshevik Revolution. During his first period in Montrose in 1920 (the year in which the Communist Party of Great Britain was founded), C. M. Grieve gave a lecture to the Montrose ILP on 'Lenin – The Man and His Message and Methods' (*MR*, 13 February 1920, 5). This interest in Leninism precedes by more than a decade the writing of *First Hymn to Lenin* (1931), suggesting that W. N. Herbert is correct in his thesis 'that MacDiarmid's work displays at every stage of its complex progress a continuity of vision'.[3] Grieve joined the ILP in 1908 when he was unsuccessfully training to be a teacher in Edinburgh. By 1911 he was a junior reporter with the *Edinburgh Evening Dispatch*, but his radical journalism didn't find expression until later the same year with the *Monmouthshire Labour News* in South Wales. Before the Great War he worked briefly as a reporter in Clydebank and Renfrew (1912), Cupar (1912) and Forfar (1913) – 'on weekly local papers at that. I preferred these because in that way one is involved in every element of a community's life and gets to know practically everybody in the area in question' (*Company*, 24). MacDiarmid believed his radical republicanism derived from his upbringing in Langholm; it wasn't until he moved to Montrose in the 1920s, however, that such politics found a place to be practised.

'The man o' independent mind': Councillor Grieve of the *Review*

Effectively and ingeniously, MacDiarmid managed to interrelate his political and cultural activities in Montrose through his jobs as journalist and councillor. While not directly political in content, the Scots lyrics of *Sangschaw* and *Penny Wheep* and the metaphysical nationalism of *A Drunk Man Looks at the Thistle* are the poetic manifestation of the cultural and political ideas that MacDiarmid propagandised in various periodicals, such as the *Scottish Nation*, and through the pages of the *Montrose Review*.

Established on 11 January 1811 as the *Montrose, Arbroath and Brechin Review, and Forfar and Kincardine Shires Advertiser*, the *Review* is one of the oldest newspapers in Scotland. When MacDiarmid worked there this eight-page Liberal weekly would appear every Friday from its editorial and publishing offices in Montrose at 97 High Street. Like most provincial newspapers, it fused mainly local concerns with reports of the most significant national and international events. MacDiarmid also claimed to write for the *Montrose Standard* (1837–1964),[4] the ideological rival of the *Review*, but it is almost impossible to find traces of his pen in this Unionist, imperialist and Christian newspaper. His job with the *Review* was that of editor–reporter, which, according to Alan Bold, meant that he 'wrote most of the contents'.[5] Identifying his contribution to the paper is made problematical by the anonymity of the articles. The probability of a piece being by MacDiarmid centres on its radical political and cultural purposefulness, particularly in relation to Scotland. Glen Murray states that 'the principle of putting controversial and sometimes even quite arcane ideas before a wide audience in the columns of a newspaper was one he used repeatedly'.[6] In his utilisation of the *Montrose Review*, however, he primarily advanced issues of local and national democracy fundamental to the whole community.

MacDiarmid began working for Montrose Town Council on 13 March 1922 on a provisional basis, replacing Councillor James Davidson who had resigned.[7] In November of that year, C. M. Grieve sought the votes of the people of Montrose with this address in the *Review*:

Journalism rightly-conceived is a training in the understanding of public affairs and in the formulation and expression of opinion. Journalists have rendered public service to Montrose before. Having been requested to stand for the Town Council, it will be my earnest endeavour, if returned, to worthily follow these precedents. I am opposed to 'secret diplomacy' in public affairs. I believe that no work should be sent out of the town which can possibly be allocated locally, and that the Council should do all in its power to increase local prosperity and relieve unemployment. A negative policy of economy is not enough. A forward policy is needed, and, in the initiation and carrying-out of such, the services of a young man may be useful. Ability and public spirit are not the monopolies of the elderly. I do not believe that a caucus can fairly represent the electorate, and foresee danger to the public interest if this caucus secures a majority in the reduced Council. I respectfully solicit the suffrages of those who, aware of the grave issues confronting local authorities in these troublous times appreciate the need not only for men who are not afraid to speak their minds (except in Committee), but who actually have minds to speak. ('Montrose Municipal Election: to the Electors', *MR*, 3 November 1922, 4)

The budding young local politician shows an understanding of the importance of his journalistic work to a knowledge of and democratic commitment to community affairs. In a record poll he gained 1,279 votes.

MacDiarmid remembered himself as 'the only Socialist Town Councillor in Montrose' (*Company*, 158). According to Trevor Johns, however, MacDiarmid denied 'that he was standing as a Socialist. He admitted that he was a Socialist, but was not standing as an official Socialist candidate: he was an Independent.'[8] Exemplifying a Burnsian independence of mind in his work as a councillor, he was a successful local politician in Montrose in contrast to his attempts to shine on the national stage against such as Prime Minister Sir Alec Douglas-Home in 1964 and his repeated failure to win university rectorships. In the appointment of the office-bearers for Montrose Town Council Councillor Grieve was selected to work on several committees: the Water Committee, Dorward's House of Refuge Representatives, the Montrose School Management Committee (on which he was the lone council representative) and the Public Library Committee. He later became a Justice of the Peace in February 1926.

When he was standing for election to Montrose Town Council in November 1922 one of the main ideas that MacDiarmid proposed was that trade should stay local: 'I believe that no work should be sent out of town which can possibly be allocated locally' (*MR*, 3 November 1922, 4). On the same day that his election address appeared in the *Review*, a letter of his was printed in the correspondence column. 'Harbour Board Representation' concerns the building of new dock gates and the dredging of the harbour. Grieve's contention is that in commercial operations many local councillors are putting their concerns before that of the public and that as a result business in Montrose is suffering:

Montrose Harbour history is an amazing record of the 'rigging' of public affairs to suit private interests, and the desuetude of local trade is largely due to the selfish and short-sighted policy of men ostensibly representing the community but actually furthering their individual interests (and, on occasion, indulging their individual spleens) – regardless of the general consequences to the burgh, and employing when necessity arose the most unscrupulous means. (*MR*, 3 November 1922, 8)

That councillors pursued their own profit rather than that of the burgh was a claim MacDiarmid made again in 1975, referring in *Scottish Marxist* to the 'very great deal of graft going on' (*RT3*, 572) in Montrose Town Council. As an independent councillor in the 1920s, he proposed a socialist politics that believed in prioritising and transforming Montrose. His *Review* editorial of 25 January 1924 suggests a 'Montrose First' movement chiming with the election address pledge to keep trade local:

The essence of the contention advanced is that steps should be taken to ensure that no work that can be done locally should be sent out of town, and that all money earned locally should be spent locally – other things being equal. (*MR*, 4)

MacDiarmid's work as a councillor in Montrose gives the lie to his own (borrowed) statement that he is 'interested only in a very subordinate way in the politics of Socialism as a political theory; my real concern with Socialism is as an artist's organized approach to the interdependencies of life' (*LP*, 241).[9] From the *Review* throughout the 1920s we find MacDiarmid actively engaged in a local socialism, both in the council chamber and in public lectures and debates round the town. 'Proposed Wage Cuts', a letter he sent to the *Review* of 23 February 1923, rails against a 'reduction in the wages of officials and workmen' in Montrose:

The argument that such reductions in the remuneration of public employees are made in the interests of the ratepayers is entirely specious, and will not bear a moment's consideration. The present trade depression and widespread unemployment are mainly due to the reduction in the workers' purchasing power caused by wage-cuts. To the individual ratepayer the saving effected by the cuts now proposed will be negligible; but the cuts will not be negligible to those affected. A Town Council is not justified in a matter of this kind in falling in line with a tendency created by private employers; but should consider each case on its merits. So considered, with a full knowledge of present circumstances in Montrose, no one can contend that the town's officials and employees are overpaid to say the least of it.

Councillor Grieve goes on to state that the reduced wages' policy in a particular locality has universal implications:

No section of workers can have their wages reduced without endangering the standard of living of their fellows. Each wage-cut anywhere is triumphantly cited by employers and employing authorities elsewhere as a reason for further and further cuts, and so the vicious circle is kept going round. (*MR*, 4)

He again drew attention to the wages question at the monthly meeting of Montrose Town Council on Monday, 14 May 1923, protesting against the 'starvation wage' (*MR*, 18 May 1923, 6) of thirty-five shillings a week for full-time employees, and calling for it to be raised to at least £2. Believing such radicalism could find a more effective political home in a reconstructed national setting, at the same meeting Grieve proposed a motion that the Parish Council should be affiliated to the Scottish Home Rule Association (SHRA: established 1886). As a *Review* journalist he trumpets the councillor's case, arguing 'every bit as much as Ireland does Scotland need Home Rule' ('Round the Town', *MR*, 24 August 1923, 5).

From advocating increased wages in the council chamber, MacDiarmid moved to a more revolutionary stance in his public lectures. At an ILP meeting at the Co-operative Hall in Montrose on Sunday, 13 January 1924, Hospitalmaster Grieve gave a talk on 'The Dangers of Moderation':

> Mr Grieve said that they were diluting their principles and modifying their demands in a fashion that could have only one result – the stultification of their movement. They might gain social reforms very valuable in themselves, but that had nothing to do with their objective, which was the realisation of Socialism. If as a consequence of moderation, by means of better wages and conditions generally, they raised the working classes to conditions of comfort equal to those at present enjoyed by the middle classes, and so merely changed the proletariat into a bourgeoisie [*sic*] he would regard it as the greatest catastrophe in history. He regarded a Trade Unionist who voted Labour, but was not a Socialist, as a more dangerous enemy than the die-hard Tory. Mr Grieve concluded by reading some of the scathing social satires from Mr Osbert Sitwell's 'Out of the Flame' and poignant verses from Richard Dehmel, the German Socialist poet. (*MR*, 18 January 1924, 3)[10]

MacDiarmid combined his uncompromising socialist commitment to a particular locality with concern for the global through his participation in the Montrose branch of the League of Nations. As the organisation's Secretary, he attended an open-air 'No More War' demonstration at the Montrose Town House on Friday, 10 August 1923. The *Review* of 17 August reports that Councillor Grieve was appalled at the 'extraordinary lethargy' (*MR*, 7) shown in Montrose towards the internationalist and pacific aims of the League. Having been formed the previous winter the local branch still had only thirty members, whereas the less populous Ferryden had over sixty. MacDiarmid blames the ministers of Montrose for a lack of leadership:

> They had cut a sorry figure during the last War when they manifested themselves as mere 'blind leaders of the blind', impotent to give any message to the stricken peoples. If that was all that the Christian Churches could do after

2000 years of advocacy of Christianity, they might as well resign themselves to the continuance of war and the destruction of civilization and Christianity. The Churches were missing the greatest opportunity that had presented itself to them in the course of their history. He invited the local ministers to declare themselves on this urgent matter. (*MR*, 7)

When writing 'After Two Thousand Years', from *Second Hymn to Lenin* (1935), he must have remembered his political disillusionment with the kirks of Montrose:

> The Christians have had two thousand years
>   And what have they done? –
> Made the bloodiest and beastliest world ever seen
>   Under the sun.
>
> (*CP1*, 559)

It is apposite that MacDiarmid should have criticised religious involvement in the League of Nations Union so soon after he joined the organisation. Six months later, on Friday, 8 February 1924, MacDiarmid resigned from his offices as Secretary and Treasurer because he was no longer prepared to work with what he saw as the implacably conservative local churches. At this time, he was also beginning to write a lyrical Scots poetry that would challenge the Christian view of the universe.

Cosmological Modernism – *Sangschaw* and *Penny Wheep*

Advertised in the *Review*, a talk MacDiarmid gave on 17 February 1924 explored the potentially liberating cultural and political implications of exciting scientific breakthroughs:

> VISTAS OF SCIENCE – Hospitalmaster Grieve is to address Montrose Brotherhood in the YMCA Institute on Sunday afternoon, when he will deal with the great discoveries which have recently revolutionised scientific thought – relativity, the Bohr-Rutherford theory of atoms, etc. – and relate these to the individual outlook in general, and to religious belief in particular. (*MR*, 15 February 1924, 5)

The preoccupations of this lecture predate by some time the use of scientific vocabulary in MacDiarmid's poetry of fact, begun in Whalsay in the 1930s. However, it was made only a year or two before the modernist metaphysics of his first collections of poetry in Scots, *Sangschaw* (1925) and *Penny Wheep* (1926). As MacDiarmid illustrates in his talk, the electron nucleus model of the atom developed in 1913 by the Dane Niels Bohr and the son of a Scottish wheelwright, Ernest Rutherford (1871–1937), and the General Theory of Relativity that Albert Einstein proposed in 1915 and published the following year were not only of interest to scientists but paradigmatically shifted perspectives of subjectivity. According to Randall Stevenson, Einstein's new physics ensured that 'no law or observation can be universally reliable, but depends, among other factors, on the position of the individual observer'.[11]

Relativism was of interest to many modernists. In 1923 D. H. Lawrence writes in *Fantasia of the Unconscious* that 'Relativity means . . . there is no one single absolute central principle governing the world'; for Lawrence, 'There is only one clue to the universe. And that is the individual soul within the individual being. That outer universe of suns and moons and atoms is a secondary affair.'[12] Like other modernists, including Lawrence, MacDiarmid was influenced by the psychoanalytical work of Freud and Jung and their respective theories of the unconscious. But his Scots lyrics, whilst surveying the world from the new relativistic perspective, are not obsessed with the musty inner life of the world-weary modern. Suggesting that many modernists found Einsteinian relativism a threatening scientific development, Daniel Albright proposes that, none the less, 'the methods of physicists helped to inspire poets to search for the elementary particles of which poems were constructed', the result being what he experimentally terms 'poememes'.[13] Resisting modernist reactionism, MacDiarmid's Scots 'poememes' intimate the cultural and political opportunities of new beginnings. Sustaining a secular optimism, they wonder, with almost virgin senses, at grand natural phenomena such as rainbows, moonlight, mountains, sea and sky, as well as the more lowly beasts of 'Country Life'. 'The Bonnie Broukit Bairn' looks lovingly at the earth as a lonely child in a godless galaxy; 'Moonstruck' from 'Au Clair de la Lune' imagines the world as a child's spinning-top: 'When the warl's couped soon' as a peerie' (*CP1*, 24); and 'Somersault' from *Penny Wheep* wheels in energetic delight over a topsy-turvy modernist universe:

I lo'e the stishie
O' Earth in space
Breengin' by   [*rushing*]
At a haliket pace.   [*headlong*]
                               (*CP1*, 47)

The mental landscape here is certainly a relativistic one that questions Christianity, as 'the warld gaups at me like a saul frae its body, / Owre suddenly sundered!' ('Wheelrig', *CP1*, 30), but these poems largely sing a spiritual '*tune / Fu' o' elation*' and acceptance of the new materialist disorder ('Bombinations of a Chimaera', *CP1*, 64).

Adopting a cosmological viewpoint of the universe, the lyrics suggest a Creation from which God has mysteriously withdrawn leaving only small traces and clues to be discerned through the spiritually penetrating 'keethin' sicht' of the Scots words ('Au Clair de la Lune', *CP1*, 25):

> But mebbe yet the hert o' a man
> When it feels the twist in its quick
> O' the link that binds it to ilka life,
> A'e stab in the nerves o' the stars,
> 'll raise a cry that'll fetch God back
> To the hert o' His wark again?
> – Though Nature and Man ha'e cried in vain
> Rent in unendin' wars!
>
> ('Sea-Serpent', *CP1*, 50)

Chambers Dictionary defines the cosmological as 'according to the cosmology of general relativity, the principle that, at a given time, the universe would look the same to observers in other nebulae as it looks to us'.[14] Such a theory is at work in 'The Innumerable Christ':

> I' mony an unco warl' the nicht   [*unknown/ strange*]
> The lift gaes black as pitch at noon,
> An' sideways on their chests the heids
>   O' endless Christs roll doon.
>
> (*CP1*, 32)

'Ballad of the Five Senses' similarly decentres the Christian subject and opens up new ways of seeing. Perceiving 'wi' his senses five' the 'bonny warl' / That lies forenenst a' men' (*CP1*, 36) the balladeer understands that to see God he must move beyond mere sense perception:

> Oot o' the way, my senses five,
> I ken a' you can tell,
> Oot o' the way, my thochts, for noo'
> I maun face God mysel'.
>
> (*CP1*, 38)

The idea that the poet must encounter God alone, with no material intermediaries, is a reminder of MacDiarmid's ascetical Protestant lineage. This religious atheist moves beyond even that stark creed: 'I cam' unto a place where there / Seemed nocht but naethingness' (*CP1*, 38). The balladeer understands that such metaphysical emptiness has been filled by humanity in its own image; for the modernist creator, 'God Himsel'' is only 'A way o' lookin' at himsel'' (*CP1*, 40). If God is the reflection of humankind seen through the mirror of its own religious desires, then the exciting scientific discoveries occurring in MacDiarmid's lifetime, explored in his 1924 'Vistas of Science' lecture in Montrose, bring with them new modernistic approaches to subjectivity and reality. Such relativism allows the poet to speculate in cosmological fashion:

> And staun'in' as you're staun'in' noo,   [*standing*]
> And wi' things as they are
> Ye'd be as gin ye stude upon   [*if*]
> Anither kind o' star.
>
> (CP1, 39–40)

Just as Edwin Morgan's 'The First Men on Mercury' (from the 1973 collection *From Glasgow to Saturn*) craftily uses space travel to point to linguistic and concomitant forms of imperialism in this world, so MacDiarmid may have felt impelled to journey poetically to distant stars in order to imagine different political and cultural formations at home. Historically ingrained power systems of the United Kingdom connecting class, nation and language may seem more hopefully transient when seen under the aspect of eternity. Modernist relativity, opening up new ways of seeing, legitimising subjectivities other than the powerful, enables MacDiarmid's use of a local politics of language. His interest in science, which became more persistent as his Marxism hardened in the 1930s, is another means of loosening the grip of the prevailing cultural order. By going back to first principles, remapping the cultural geography with *Sangschaw* and *Penny Wheep*, what he seems intent on doing is undermining the Christian idea that God as eternal authority, representative of cultural and political orthodoxy, is central to the purpose of the universe, so clearing the way for the historical destiny of a metaphysical Scotland to be revealed by the poet-saviour of *A Drunk Man*.

In *A Drunk Man* Christ is central to the poet's concern that humans should strive to be more spiritually alive than the 'feck [*majority*] o' mankind' (*CP1*, 100), the poet-Christ becoming an unforgiving, Calvinistic *Übermensch*. The earlier lyrics identify the absence of God, but Christ is a dominant figure to whom an almost sad tenderness is displayed. 'O Jesu Parvule' shows the Christ child in his mother's arms – 'His mither sings to the bairnie Christ' – yet failing to find comfort, foreshadowing the sacrifice and pain he is to suffer in adulthood:

> 'Fa' owre, ma hinny, fa' owre, fa' owre,
> A' body's sleepin' binna oorsels.'   [*except*]
> She's drawn Him in tae the bool o' her breist
> But the byspale's nae thocht o' sleep i' the least.   [*precocious child*]
>   *Balloo, wee mannie, balloo, balloo.*
>
> (CP1, 31)

'I Heard Christ Sing' imagines the crucifixion and the song of the spirit that emanates from the lips of the physically broken Jesus, 'the bonniest sang that e'er / Was sung sin' Time began' (*CP1*, 19), while 'The Innumerable Christ' again links Christ's death-agony with the wail of sorrow he gives for humanity as a 'Babe' (*CP1*, 32). These poems suggest a clinging memory of, and affection for, the religion of MacDiarmid's childhood, but his political objection to the role of the local Montrose churches in the League of Nations in 1924 would have confirmed an atheist perspective also first identified in Langholm:

> My parents were very devout and as a boy, a small boy, I had to go to church several times every Sunday, and I had to go to Bible class and Sunday school and so on . . . And it wasn't until I was . . . about fifteen or sixteen, that I repudiated the lot. I didn't quarrel with my parents about it. There would be no point in that. But I just made it clear that I dissociated myself completely. I became a complete atheist, you see – and still am. But I'd had all this indoctrination that I'd been subjected to up till then and it's still part of my vocabulary. (Radio Telefis Eirann, 'The Arts: Hammer & Thistle', An Interview with Micheál O hUanacháin, 23 February 1978, *RT3*, 594–5)

The Scots lyrics are soaked in the 'vocabulary' of MacDiarmid's memory of Langholm. Unlike the evocative poems written about Langholm and Whalsay, the work produced in Montrose offers no obvious poetics of place. Indeed, the castigation of Montrosians in *A Drunk Man* from 1926 may have isolated him somewhat from those colleagues at the *Review* who were aware that Grieve had become MacDiarmid four years earlier:

> And in the toon that I belang tae
> – What tho'ts Montrose or Nazareth? –
> Helplessly the folk continue
> To lead their livin' death!   . . .
>
> > (*CP1*, 88)

The strain of his 'dooble life' (*CP1*, 236) as Scots poet-Christ – saviour of nation and language – and provincial journalist writing in English is evident in *To Circumjack Cencrastus*. Only with the retrospective 'Montrose' (1961) do we find poetic allusion to the town's positive influence on his work:

> 'Guid gear gangs in sma' book' and fegs!
> Man's story owes more to little towns than to great,
> And Montrose is typical of Scotland's small grey burghs
> Each with a character of its own time cannot abate.
>
> > (*CP2*, 1407)

MacDiarmid's time in Montrose was, in part, so productive because in a deep-rooted intellectual and emotional manner it reconnected him to the folk-memory of his earliest childhood in Langholm: the native Scots tongue, the religious imagery and the insistence on rural rather than urban settings. This last point is particularly pertinent when examining *Sangschaw* and *Penny Wheep*. In both collections only one poem, 'Glasgow' from *Sangschaw*, has an obviously city-based, industrial locale, and it is written in English. This intensely local colouring that flows through MacDiarmid's work flowered most abundantly in Montrose.

The lyrics in Scots anticipate – in less obviously intellectual but no less effective terms – the metaphysical concerns of *A Drunk Man*, but in a way that strongly connects them to the local community and the bonds of family in Langholm and Montrose that helped to nurture such work. Grieve told Norman MacCaig that Peggy 'made the poetry' (*NSL*, xiii) he wrote in Montrose, and 'The Bonnie Broukit Bairn' combines love for her as its dedicatee with concern for the Earth, while the paternal tenderness of 'From "Songs for Christine" ' is revealed '*In the licht o' the mune*' (*CP1*, 70). In a letter of 6 September 1926 to the sculptor and poet James Pittendrigh Macgillivray (1856–1938), Grieve confesses to being 'a perfectly hopeless fool in personal relationships' (*L*, 322). On leaving Montrose his personal world was to break apart with the split from Peggy and his children with her, Christine and Walter (born in 1924 and 1928 respectively), perhaps partly provoked by his excessive workload in the town. Marital breakdown would lead him to the starkly inspiring landscape of Shetland, writing along the way a Marxist poetry of a more alienated nature than the optimistic Montrose lyrics. 'The Watergaw', for instance, fuses the natural beauty of a rainbow, symbolising speculation as to a possible hereafter, with a poet thinking more sorrowfully and empathetically of his father's death than the later Leninist intellectual of 'At My Father's Grave'. Even the quirky publishing history of 'The Watergaw', first appearing in the *Dunfermline Press* in September 1922 as the work of Grieve's 'friend',[15] suggests something of the exuberant intimacy of MacDiarmid's creativity in Montrose. Many of the Scots lyrics also suggest loving relation with the countryside and farmland of rural Scotland, perhaps inspired by Langholm and the Scottish Borders, but surely marshalled into poetic life by the beauty of Angus.

> Wi' sae mony wild roses
> Dancin' and daffin',
> It looks as tho' a'
> The countryside's laffin'.

(*CP1*, 55)

As in 'Wild Roses', MacDiarmid's Scots lyrics can be reminiscent of Burns in their coupling of the natural radiance of the local rural scene with love for a girl among the rigs of barley.

These beautiful poems are written in a Scots not necessarily as artificial as the term 'synthetic' may imply. J. Derrick McClure argues that the 'MacDiarmidian Revolution' is actually following a Scottish poetic tradition: 'That MacDiarmid wrote in a wholly "synthetic language", or even one which is, as language, much more recondite than that of his immediate or his eighteenth-century predecessors, is simply untenable.'[16] The demotic nature of much Scottish literature indicates that many of the Scots words of *Sangschaw* and *Penny Wheep* would still have been used on the High Street and port of Montrose and the surrounding farmlands of Angus in the 1920s, just not in such stunning combination as appears in MacDiarmid's lyrics.

This point is borne out when examining the *Montrose Review*. As William Donaldson makes clear, the provincial press in Scotland was an assiduous carrier of poetry and fiction written in Scots, suggesting 'that use of the Scots language was much more extensive and important than might otherwise be concluded on the evidence of a book-culture produced for an all-UK literary market'.[17] In the *Review* of the 1920s the populist tradition of Scots writing uncovered by Donaldson from 1840 to 1900 is still active, if in diluted form. As a local journalist, MacDiarmid was soaked in this atmosphere of Scottish popular writing – a form his ultra-modernist tendencies would renounce but that, none the less, deeply informs his work in the 1920s. Declaring that 'the revival of Scots is only a half-way house' towards a modern return to Gaelic, in 'Towards a Scottish Renaissance: desirable lines of advance', MacDiarmid argues that, because 'popular journalism lives by pandering to the mob-mind', the cultural aims of the movement are hamstrung by the 'Londonisation' of the Scottish national press (*RT2*, 79). Working for the *Montrose Review* facilitated the adaptation of his synthetic Scots poetry, enabling him to draw from a populist localism inherent in the journalistic culture of provincial Scotland.

Writing in the *Nineteenth Century* in October 1929, just after he left Montrose, Grieve praises his own artistic endeavours in the town by claiming in 'Contemporary Scottish Poetry' that 'no language in which great literature had been produced had been so hopelessly degraded as Braid Scots before the synthetic method began to recondition it a few years ago' (*RT2*, 169). To 'recondition' implies no clean break with a populist past but an attempt to develop still workable linguistic material in the modernist culture of a new Scotland. Is the Scots language mere evolutionary 'Cast-offs' the poet of 'Gairmscoile' asks?

> But wha mak's life a means to ony end?
> This sterves and that stuff's fu', scraps this and succours that?
>
> (*CP1*, 73)

His politicised theory of evolution has no sympathy with the popular misconception of Darwinism: 'The best survive there's nane but fules contend' (*CP1*, 73). This local socialist councillor and nationalist poet-propagandist is opposed to such metropolitan universalism: 'We are told that Scots, and, even more, Gaelic, have had to give way owing to over-ruling economic tendencies – but had they? Are these tendencies good in themselves? Is mankind made for economics or economics by mankind?' ('Towards a Scottish Renaissance: desirable lines of advance', *RT2*, 78). He replies with the MacDiarmidian credo of the crucially symbiotic relationship between the particular and the universal, the core of his radical nationalism: 'The logical conclusion of the process our opponents defend is the negation of not only nationality, but of personality. In the last analysis this is a reductio ad absurdum of their case' (*RT2*, 78). For a poet identifying himself so closely with Scotland, the spirit of the nation, the Dedalusian conscience of the race, cannot be (re)created in a foreign tongue – 'Wull Gabriel in Esperanto cry / Or a' the warld's undeemis jargons try?' – but must come instead from the irrationally national '*herts o' men*' (*CP1*, 74). MacDiarmid wanted the Scottish Renaissance movement to 'profoundly alter the rhythm of Scottish life' ('Rhythm and Race (III), *CSS*, 401), and formed his Scots poetry to change the beat of what he hoped would become the native cadence. His switch from writing in post-Georgian English to lyrical Scots is galvanised by his immersion in the local concerns of the Montrose community. MacDiarmid's synthetic Scots is no reactionary, backward step, but a modernist stance that draws on the populist tradition of local Scottish poetry and fiction in order to radically refashion the cultural and political state of the nation.

> For we ha'e faith in Scotland's hidden poo'ers,
> The present's theirs, but a' the past and future's oors.
>
> ('Gairmscoile', *CP1*, 75)

Local News: Montrosian calls for a 'Scottish Renaissance'

Addressing Henrik Arnold Wergeland 'Gairmscoile' parallels the Norwegian *landsmål* he adapted in the early-nineteenth century with the synthetic method of the modernist Scots lyrics. Claiming in *Albyn: or Scotland and the Future* that Wergeland was 'conscious of the idiosyncratic power of the Scottish blood in his veins' (*A*, 8), MacDiarmid uses him accordingly, in poem and polemic, as an exemplar of what full cultural expression can achieve in giving voice to political aspirations. Wergeland's poetry was a symbol of Norway's striving for independence, finally gained in 1905. MacDiarmid could see firsthand in Ireland how promotion of the Irish language was significant in the development of the Free State in 1921–2. Douglas Hyde – who lectured in 1892 on 'The Necessity for De-Anglicising Ireland', and wrote the first modern play in Irish, *Casadh an tSugáin* (1901) – impressed with his *A Literary History of Ireland* (1899), and he drew contemporary sustenance from Daniel Corkery's *The Hidden Ireland* (1924), 'that wonderful study of the Munster poets' (*A*, 75). Imagining 'Scotland in 1980', in what proved to be the year after the failure of the 1979 Devolution Referendum, MacDiarmid's somewhat prophetic fear in 1929 is that the '*Hidden Scotland* remained hidden' (*A*, 75). Linguistic renewal could act as a catalyst for national revival. By using an intimately local language, the Scots poems written in Montrose work to uncover the seed of a tradition buried by cultural self-repression and a centralised, metropolitan polity.

In early 1922 a series of letters appeared in the *Montrose Review* on 'Home Rule for Scotland'. Writing to himself as editor, Grieve initiated this debate on 20 January by calling for backing in Montrose for the Scots National League (SNL, founded in 1919–20), the aim of which would be full self-government. He also drew comparisons with Ireland, where the Dáil had approved the Anglo-Irish Treaty on 7 January that would end imperial administration from Dublin Castle nine days later.[18] Underlining the demand for Scottish independence in 'Round the Town' on 27 January, he emphasises the necessity for local activism if national democracy is to be attained:

> It is to be hoped that the letter by Mr Grieve in the last issue of the 'Review' on the question of Home Rule for Scotland will arouse as much interest as will lead to Montrose doing its bit towards achieving the desired end. The issue is certainly of such pressing importance as to create a great national movement which will go irresistibly forward with growing power to its ultimate goal. And speedy success will rest upon participation in the demand by every city, town, and village in Scotland. (*MR*, 5)

Replying to Grieve's letter on 3 February, J. Spears Burt, the local secretary of the devolutionary SHRA, contends 'that the Scottish people have too much practical wisdom ever to follow the example of Sinn Fein Ireland in her demands for an independent republic' (*MR*, 4). In an important letter dated 3 February and appearing in the *Review* a week later, Grieve counters Burt's ca' canny position by backing the more militant SNL, arguing that 'even were Home Rule sufficient quite other tactics than those which have been pursued – or are likely to be pursued – by the Scottish Home Rule Association would be necessary to secure it' (*MR*, 10 February 1922, 4). Burt's claim that Scotland would be damagingly isolated if divorced from England and the Empire 'must appear singularly at variance with the tendency of the times' to those, such as Grieve, who far-sightedly discern the postcolonial significance of international postwar political movements:

> Moravia, Bohemia, and Hungary, tied, before the war, to the Imperialistic Austrian Empire took the first opportunity of freeing themselves from its toils. Bosnia, Croatia and Herzegovina likewise severed their connection with Austria, and joined, with their brother Slavs in Serbia, to form the Kingdom of Yugoslavia. Finland, Esthonia, Livonia, Lithuania, and Crimea, before the war, were part of the unwieldy Empire of the Czar; today, they are masters of their own destiny. Ireland, after a struggle lasting nearly 700 years, has once again taken her place among the free nations of the world. Poland is no longer divided in three. She too has regained her freedom. Malta has been granted a legislature of her own, and Egypt seems well on the way to the realisation of her national desires. Yet Scotland, the oldest country in Europe, remains a vassal State, governed from the capital of another country. (*MR*, 10 February 1922, 4)

Also cogently arguing for independence on economic and legal grounds, Grieve then briefly mentions 'the pre-requisites of a Scottish Literary Renaissance': 'the recovery of our ancient arts and crafts' and 'the preservation of Scottish national individuality' (*MR*, 10 February 1922, 4). This allusion to an incipient Scottish Renaissance precedes by six months its previously assumed first reference in the inaugural *Scottish Chapbook* of August 1922.[19] The poet's policy of an internationalist cultural movement with self-determining political designs is announced in the correspondence column of a local newspaper.

What is evident from the *Montrose Review* is that, on all fronts, MacDiarmid actively pursued the localism firing the use of Scots in his poetry. Indeed, being a provincial journalist substantially aided his industrious push for political and cultural change in Scotland. In *Albyn*, Grieve points out that 'all the daily, and practically all the weekly, papers are anti-Home Rule, just as they are all anti-Socialist'; in this environment of vested interests 'Scottish journalism is, therefore, almost wholly untrustworthy in relation to Scottish opinion' (*A*, 3). In the *Review*, and through the various periodicals he established, MacDiarmid sought to undermine such political bias.

Throughout 1923, when Grieve's first book, *Annals of the Five Senses*, was published, the *Review* carried syndicated articles from the *Scottish Nation*, established in that year from its editorial office at 16 Links Avenue and first advertised on 4 May:

> NEW ALL-SCOTTISH WEEKLY – Councillor C. M. Grieve, Montrose, is editing and publishing, and the Review Press are printing, a new weekly

entitled, 'The Scottish Nation', devoted to Scottish Nationalism, Progressive
Politics, and Scottish Arts and Letters. The first issue will be published on
Tuesday, 8th inst. The price is 3d, and the paper is available at all newsagents,
bookstalls, etc., throughout Scotland. (*MR*, 5)

Syndicated articles from many journals were sold to a number of different publications to be printed simultaneously. This allowed for a larger
and non-specialist readership to be reached, multiplying the potential
impact of one piece. In 1928 a polyphonic Grieve claimed that, through
'a special bureau formed for the purpose (in connection with the Scottish
Home Rule Movement)',[20] he was reaching up to forty local weekly
newspapers across Scotland by means of syndication.

Robert Crawford argues that 'there are strong formal connections
between the production methods underlying the text of the *Montrose
Review* and those underpinning the work of Hugh MacDiarmid'.[21]
Certainly, the editorial requirements of Grieve's job are reflected in a cut-
and-paste utilisation of recycled and plagiarised quotations in his prose
and poetry, particularly his longer English-language prose-poems. The
autobiographical narrator of 'A Limelight from a Solitary Wing' even
ascribes to himself a 'journalistic mind' (*Annals*, 88). But Grieve's editorial nous had potentially larger ramifications than the partial shaping of
MacDiarmid's creativity. He used the *Review*, and other local newspapers
through syndication, to assist in the dissemination of a propaganda programme for a Scottish Renaissance that couldn't possibly hope to win
wide support solely through short-lived, highbrow journals such as
the *Scottish Nation*, *Scottish Chapbook* and *Northern Review*.[22] In a
letter of 1 November 1923 to nationalist philanthropist R. E. Muirhead
(1868–1964), Grieve complains that the *Scottish Nation*, with an average
circulation since its inception six months previously of around 3,500
copies, is struggling financially because 'we antagonised advertisers at the
outset by our insistence on Scottish national politics and by labour sympathies' (*NSL*, 21). Advertising the *Scottish Nation* in 'Round the Town'
from 25 May 1923, the editor of the *Review* attempts to stimulate recep-
tion of Scottish nationalism by congratulating Grieve on his journal:

> It is inconceivable that Scotsmen and Scotswomen will not welcome their new
> weekly. By all the tokens, it is assured of such a vigorous measure of support
> as will give it a long and healthy life and so reward the public spirit and enter-
> prise of its promoters. No one who believes that mind is greater than matter
> can afford to miss a copy of 'The Scottish Nation' – if for nothing else than
> the fact of its promise of forcing the pace in the strife to compel an unrepre-
> sentative Parliament in which an alien, although neighbouring country is a
> 'Predominant' partner to hand over to Scotland her right to manage Scottish
> affairs in her distinctively Scottish manner. (*MR*, 5)

Such self-promotion must have been invaluable when launching the *Scottish Nation*. From a local setting, using a provincial press, MacDiarmid was aiming to become the voice of an internationalist Scotland.

Impatience with national powerlessness is betrayed by his assistance in the instigation of the Montrose Parliamentary Debating Society in 1923. A *Review* editorial recognises the Society as a local forum for serious political debate of national issues:

> Steps are now being taken to form a Montrose Parliamentary Debating Society as suggested by Mr W. D. M'Laren. The idea is less to encourage amateur oratory than earnest and effective thinking. To model such a Society at all closely on the 'Mother of Parliaments' would be to immerse its activities in a strangling mesh of procedure. Life is too short to fid-faddle in this fashion. A political debating Society concerning itself with the mass of minor issues would probably be short-lived in Montrose. (*MR*, 21 December 1923, 4)

Grieve sent a letter to the *Review* on 11 January 1924 repeating that the proposed Society would not mirror the London parliament as 'there will be no voting' and debates 'will be conducted by two sides equal in number, each side being given the same amount of time', but concludes 'Socialist policy either here or at Westminster can be positively espoused without fear' ('Montrose Parliamentary Society', *MR*, 4).

At the Society's first debate, on Monday, 28 January 1924 in Montrose Town Buildings, the unemployment issue was discussed. The socialists, headed by Grieve, proposed 'that unemployment is inherent in and indispensable to the capitalist state of society and is, in fact, a "vested interest" of it – and can only be abolished by the substitution of production for use for production for profit' ('Montrose Parliamentary Debating Society', *MR*, 25 January 1924, 5). Hospitalmaster Grieve advanced the Douglasite hypothesis that

> economically there was no unemployment problem. The masses of the people were short of money – but money, the want of which caused so much misery and distress, cost nothing to produce. The problem was to supply this costless product in a way which would maintain productivity while increasing the purchasing power of the people to an adequate extent. That could be done by destroying the present financial system and applying the social credit of this great nation to its proper purpose. (*MR*, 1 February 1924, 8)

Grieve is introducing locally ideas garnered from A. R. Orage's modernist *New Age*, something he was to repeat in a talk to the Montrose ILP on 'The Banking System with special reference to Major Douglas's New Economic Theorem and the Credit Reform Movement, and to the Gold Standard, the raising of the Bank rate, and international debts' (*MR*, 3 April 1925, 5), and again in 'Major Douglas and the New

Economics', a lecture to the Dundee Theosophical Society on 19 March 1928 (*MR*, 23 March 1928, 5). Founded in 1894 as a Liberal Party journal and becoming on Orage's acquisition with the help of Bernard Shaw in 1907 an avant-garde socialist weekly, by 1924 the *New Age* 'was a sectarian organ of Social Credit dedicated to the economic theories of Major C. H. Douglas (1879–1952)'.[23] The *Review* report of the 1924 unemployment discussion emphasises the spiritual basis of MacDiarmid's Douglasite economics:

> Hospital-Master Grieve led off for the Labour Party. Leaving it to his col-
> leagues to put forward immediate relief schemes, he dealt with their oppo-
> nents' schemes – more production, decreased wages, more thrift, etc. – and
> said that none of these would solve the problem. Socialism was the only cure –
> the substitution of a Christian commonwealth for a state of society founded
> on usury, by liberating human productivity from the stranglehold of the
> present financial system. They (the Socialists) intended by manipulating the
> social credit of this great country, not for private profit but to public advan-
> tage to create a state of society in which everything done would benefit every-
> body, and everything left undone would be a common loss, in which none
> would be permitted to have too much while others had too little, in which men
> would only be able to help themselves by helping their fellows, in which, in
> short, the glorious paradox of Christianity would be the principle of admin-
> istration. (*MR*, 1 February 1924, 4)

The 'principle of administration' of MacDiarmid's society would, in fact, be communistic. If this particular debate illustrates his desire for radical economic theories to find a local hearing, then the Montrose Parliamentary Society can be seen as a regional undertaking to fill a void in national democracy, demonstrating how MacDiarmid's active Montrose municipal-ism relates to his designs for a Scottish Republic. If true internationalism, rather than the imperialism of the metropolitan core, requires nationalism as its basis, then an independent nation needs a flourishing regional life.

On Tuesday, 1 April 1924, Grieve attended the Convention of the Royal Burghs of Scotland in Edinburgh City Chambers as Assessor for Montrose Council. In *Albyn* he describes the Convention as 'the oldest municipal institution in Europe' (*A*, 37). The Convention began in the 1550s and by 1973 had evolved into the Convention of Scottish Local Authorities (COSLA). According to Christopher Harvie the Convention was 'effec-tively a specialized Parliament',[24] in which role it petitioned against the loss of the Scottish Parliament in 1707. On the Scottish Home Rule debate, the *Review* of 4 April reports that

> Hospitalmaster C. M. Grieve, Montrose, moved an amendment that the
> Convention reaffirmed that there should be established a Scottish Legislature
> and Executive for the control of Scottish affairs, and that this resolution be

sent to the Prime Minister, the Secretary for Scotland, and each of the Scottish members of Parliament. He said he deprecated the introduction of party considerations into a matter of this kind. (*MR*, 6)

Despite the fact that he had condemned the SHRA only two years earlier as 'moribund', believing that 'no measure of devolution is worth a rap if it does not include the power of the purse' (*MR*, 10 February 1922, 4), the absence of a more radically coherent nationalist alignment in the early 1920s saw MacDiarmid continue to press for Home Rule as a necessary second best. At the 1924 Edinburgh Convention his frustration at the lack of a suitable vehicle for his nationalism is palpable: 'If there were a strong separatist movement he fancied the motion would have been framed otherwise' (*MR*, 4 April 1924, 6).

As an elected local representative with a socialist agenda he was still deeply immersed in community affairs. The *Review* of 4 April 1924, for instance, shows his involvement in a free breakfast scheme for selected pupils at Southesk School (*MR*, 6). However, being unable to find an organisation unifying aspirations for Scottish democracy must have raised doubts in MacDiarmid's mind as to the effectiveness not only of the current national political groupings but also of his own local council work. On 29 August 1924 it was announced that

Hospitalmaster C. M. Grieve has resigned from the various public bodies of which he is a member, intimating that he finds it necessary to do so for business reasons, although he does so with regret, as his heart has been in the work . . . He is the only Socialist member of the Council. ('Hospitalmaster Grieve Resigns', *MR*, 5)

In *Scottish Marxist*, MacDiarmid was to remember his experience as a councillor in Montrose rather differently some fifty years later from the formal tone of 'regret' of the *Review* notice:

I enjoyed the experience it gave me as a journalist, [as it] showed me aspects of local life and so on that I might not otherwise have had access to, but apart from that, from a purely political point of view, it was a very disillusioning experience. (*RT3*, 572–3)

Disenchantment may have seemed apparent to MacDiarmid in retrospect, but he clearly worked hard as a councillor and argued consistently from a socialist standpoint, opposing low wages, fee-paying schools and anti-trades-union legislation. He remained a member of the ILP and in Montrose on 12 October 1924 took part in a discussion on the 'Industrial Crisis' (*MR*, 17 October 1924, 5). The General Election of Wednesday, 29 October saw the fall of the first Labour Government as the minority administration of Ramsay MacDonald (1866–1937) was replaced by Baldwin's Unionists. With the Private Member's Bill for Scottish Home Rule proposed by Labour's George Buchanan also talked out of parliament that year, Grieve's decision to resign from Montrose Council had more to do with the development of his Scottish nationalism than with 'business interests'.

Significantly, only twelve days before the election, he was in the capital to deliver the inaugural lecture for the session to the University of Edinburgh Historical Association, 'History and Imagination, with Special Reference to Scottish Affairs'. Presided over by historian Sir Richard Lodge and Herbert Grierson (1866–1960), Regius Professor of Rhetoric and English Literature (1915–35), the lecture gave MacDiarmid an eminent institutional platform from which to expound his nationalist ideas. As an activist and autodidact, he used this opportunity to emphasise his scepticism as to the worth of the merely academic study of history:

> Mr Grieve contended that the true criterion of history was its power of making history and that Scottish history had hitherto lamentably failed to rise above a dead-level of mediocrity mainly because it lacked all sense of tendency, and art of significant alignment and anticipation. The essential instruments of history, redeemed by true purpose, then, were not so much laborious research as the creative spirit and imagination. The true test of history was its power of reinforcing and furthering the spirit that was the essence of its subject. Mr Grieve related his theme to the present tendencies towards a Scottish National Renaissance, and said that just as it was true that no Scottish imaginative artist had won to the second or even the third rank in English literature, writing in English, so for the same reason it might well be that the essence of Scottish History was inaccessible except to Braid Scots. ('Montrosian Lectures in Edinburgh University', *MR*, 24 October 1924, 5)

Quoting Benedetto Croce's dialectical dictum that 'the philosophy of History is the same as the history of Philosophy', MacDiarmid believes that Scotland as an historical entity, a nation with a living history, can only be exhumed in the creative consciousness of individuals of 'spiritual stature and imaginative insight' (*MR*, 24 October 1924, 5). Currently, the possibility of writing Scotland back into history is buried by the mere regurgitation of the defeats of Scottish history in English-language history books manifesting one of the very failures of that history: the loss of the Scots language. Scotland as an historical actuality remains dead on the page by the fact and manner of its academic telling. It is only the creative writer in Scots who can uncover the nation's 'essence', instituting the teleological drive towards regaining the full cultural, political and spiritual expression that was available before the Union. Regarding the writing of history as an aesthetic practice, MacDiarmid wants Scottish history to mirror his Scots lyrics by going back to find a native voice in which to express modernist methods of narrating the nation. Only by creatively re-imagining the national past will Scottish history get 'rid of that perpetual Provincialism which had hitherto condemned it to structural and spiritual obsolescence' (*MR*, 24 October 1924, 5).

The Scottish Christ – *A Drunk Man Looks at the Thistle*

Published on 22 November 1926, *A Drunk Man* is a denunciation of Scottish provincialism that grows out of the local environment in which it was born, placing that milieu within a universal metaphysic and aligning Scottish culture with international modernism. The poem displays a complicated relationship with Burns that can be understood as complementing MacDiarmid's argument for a dynamically contemporary and creative nationalist conception of Scottish history and culture.

Both Montrose newspapers carried articles every 25 January detailing the celebrations of local Burns clubs. As a member of the Montrose branch Grieve was often present, usually proposing a toast to 'the lasses o". His strictures against the Burns cult in *A Drunk Man* developed experientially out of how he believed Burns's immortal memory was exploited: the reports of Burns night in the *Montrose Standard* show that even the Imperial forces were toasted in his name.

The Drunk Man attacks the Burns cult for a philistine misappropriation of the past that frustrates current cultural developments:

No' wan in fifty kens a wurd Burns wrote
But misapplied is a'body's property,
And gin there was his like alive the day
They'd be the last a kennin' haund to gi'e

(*CP1*, 84)

Providing a Scottish counterpart to Wordsworth's wish that the spirit of Milton return to England in 'London, 1802', the Drunk Man exclaims, 'Rabbie, wads't thou wert here – the warld hath need, / And Scotland mair sae, o' the likes o' thee!' (*CP1*, 85). Burns's radical integrity is what all nations lack in the wasteland of 1920s modernity, particularly Scotland. The Drunk Man complains that 'Mair nonsense has been uttered in his name / Than in ony's barrin' liberty and Christ' (*CP1*, 84). Ostensibly equating Burns and Jesus, he is actually proposing that the more exacting political vision of his own modernist Christ–creator replace the Christian *demos* informing Burnsian socialism. If Burns is a potential spiritual saviour to Scotland then the Second Coming is MacDiarmid, asserting his almost typological belief that he is 'the likes

o' thee'. Believing 'critical revaluation of Burns is overdue' Grieve justi-
fies his selection in a brief introduction to his 1926 edition of Burns 'by
the fact that my ideas generally coincide with his, especially where these
are at odds with conventional opinion'.[25]

MacDiarmid certainly upset conventional Burnsians with his infamous
speech to the Glasgow branch of the Scottish National Movement on
21 January 1928. 'Burns from the Nationalist Standpoint' unfavourably
compares the effort to revive the use of Scots with a more successful language movement in Friesland. According to Grieve's *Review* report, this
is because

> grants such as were available in Friesland could not be given in Scotland owing
> to the fact that Scottish public monies were controlled by a predominately
> English legislature which, ever since the Union of Parliaments, had spent enor-
> mous sums annually on the teaching in Scotland of English language and lit-
> erature, but would not devote a penny piece to the teaching of Scots language
> and literature. Had a tithe of the money spent on the teaching of English in
> Scotland been spent on the teaching of Scots our national literary position
> would have been a very different one to-day. ('Montrose Speaker in Glasgow',
> *MR*, 27 January 1928, 7)

MacDiarmid's *coup de grâce* was that Burns should be forgotten for at
least twenty-five years, prompting Burnsians to assume that he was arro-
gantly launching a direct attack on the greatness of Scotland's national
poet.[26] His wish to see Burns assessed in light of international critical
standards rather than receive unquestioning adoration at home leads
MacDiarmid to want Scotland to temporarily forget the bard in order 'to
give it the chance of realising the aims for which Burns had wrought'
(*MR*, 27 January 1928, 7). If bourgeois British Scotland, epitomised by
the reactionary Burns Federation, uses a mythic Burns to bolster the
cultural–political status quo, then a nationalist revival must destabilise
his place in the canon so as to allow the real Burns and – crucially – the
next Burns to emerge in the Scottish Renaissance.

MacDiarmid believed he was the rightful inheritor of Burns's authentic
radical legacy. This is demonstrated in 'Ballad of the Crucified Rose' (lines
1119–1218 of *A Drunk Man*), which deals symbolically with the 1926
General Strike. Beginning at midnight on Monday, 3 May and lasting for
nine days of potentially revolutionary industrial disturbance, it centred on
miners' pay and conditions, but escalated to include most other national
industries and services. According to Harvie 'the strike cut at the roots of
revolutionary millenarianism; it also enhanced the notion of "British"
class politics, and so diminished the nationalist element in Scottish
Labour'.[27] Deeply affected by the strike's failure, and alienated by Labour
Unionism, MacDiarmid helped to found the NPS two years later.

The ballad uses Christian imagery and mythology to signify the betrayal of the strikers by members of the General Council of the Trades Union Congress, such as J. H. Thomas, Labour MP and Secretary of the National Union of Railwaymen. The red rose that emerges from 'a camsteerie [*ungovernable*] plant' is the organised spirit of labour that 'For centuries' has been buried in the seemingly unpropitious ground – 'yon puir stock' (*CP1*, 119) – of the politically disorganised working class. The plant craves a more beautiful form, masked until now in 'The thistle's ugsome guise':

> 'My nobler instincts sall nae mair
> This contrair shape be gi'en.
> I sall nae mair consent to live
> A life no' fit to be seen.'
>
> (*CP1*, 120)

All the ugly plant needs to become a red rose is 'needfu' discipline' (*CP1*, 120), something the workers achieve during the strike, so setting in revolutionary motion that which will enable them to live to their true spiritual potential. MacDiarmid plays with Burns's sentimental 'A Red, Red Rose', turning it into 'A reid reid rose' of radicalism transmuting 'The haill braid earth' (*CP1*, 120). Burns's 'Luve' is lyrically infinite, strong enough to last until the end of time: 'Till a' the seas gang dry, my Dear / And the rocks melt wi' the sun'.[28] MacDiarmid's radical ideal owes much to the spiritual evolutionism of his Calvinist background, and similarly seeks an aesthetic for the transcendence of materialist confines:

> The waefu' clay was fire aince mair,
> As Earth had been resumed
> Into God's mind, frae which sae lang
> To grugous state 'twas doomed.   [*ugly*]
>
> (*CP1*, 120)

The strike's failure is attributed to 'A coward strain in that lorn growth' (*CP1*, 121). The Drunk Man admits that the flaw that sees the strike founder is congenital to the plant:

> The vices that defeat the dream
> Are in the plant itsel',
> And till they're purged its virtues maun
> In pain and misery dwell.
>
> (*CP1*, 121)

That the plant needs purging can be interpreted in two seemingly divergent ways. Firstly, that the plant symbolises all humans, and the inherent flaw that prevents individuals and the societies they build from attaining perfectibility is the original sin of Christian myth. Or secondly, that it specifically signifies the working class, and the failure of revolution is due to a lack of unity and appropriate organisation within the Labour Movement, which leads to subsequent betrayal by union bosses. George Davie argues that this opposition between the anti-Pelagianism of Christianity and the Pelagian perfectibilism of the Enlightenment characterises MacDiarmid's oeuvre, with work before *To Circumjack Cencrastus* (1930) in the former camp and that poem as the *crise de foi* of an anti-Pelagian world-view.[29] However, the unifying principle behind MacDiarmid's politics of place seeks to heal the national schisms inherited from the Scottish Enlightenment with a metaphysical nationalism and breach the dialectical distortions of capitalism through a spiritual communism. This makes it impossible to split his work down the middle as Davie does between two ideologies that appear to be intractable. Kenneth Buthlay's statement that 'it is rash to give priority to MacD's politics' in 'Ballad of the Crucified Rose' due to its aesthetical and spiritual concerns is equally inappropriate.[30] MacDiarmid is unwilling to prioritise one of these contending positions over the other because he sees them as being dialectically linked, their synthesis of opposites finding expression in a radical Scottish Republicanism: 'I refuse to draw a distinction between the material and the spiritual. It requires much closer analysis and as soon as you begin to get at that kind of analysis then you're already in the realm of the political' ('The Arts: Hammer & Thistle', *RT3*, 590). He uses the symbol of the Cross to signify the spiritual martyrdom of a potentially revolutionary working class at its own hands – 'And still the idiot nails itsel' / To its ain crucifix' (*CP1*, 122) – while 'the Deils', sceptical reactionaries of human nature or Judas-like figures who have betrayed the Labour Movement, 'rejoice to see the waste' (*CP1*, 121). Twinning Christ and Burns in *A Drunk Man*, for MacDiarmid the spiritual and material, the political and poetic, are entirely synchronous.

The Drunk Man is a revolutionary Scottish Christ, crucified by the suffering of excessive self-consciousness and irrationalist intellection and hampered in his mission to save his people from themselves by 'the dour provincial thocht / That merks the Scottish breed' (*CP1*, 122). With all the Nietzschean scorn of an elect religious for his fellow earthbound nationals, the Drunk Man asks,

> Is Scotland big enough to be
> A symbol o' that force in me,
> In wha's divine inebriety
> A sicht abune contempt I'll see?

> > (*CP1*, 145)

Striving to 'mak' a unity' of 'My country's contrair qualities' (*CP1*, 145),
he turns for inspiration to Dostoevsky's Russia. C. M. Grieve JP pursued
this idea in a talk he gave to Montrose ILP on Sunday, 25 March 1927.
'Europe and Asia' argues 'that we must abandon the idea of maintaining
the predominancy of the white race. He regarded Soviet Russia as a
means of bridging the gulf between East and West' (*MR*, 1 April 1925, 5).
Seeking an East–West synthesis in a divided Scotland, the *Pictish Review*
of November 1927 sees Grieve use Dostoevsky's Russian Idea as a conceptual springboard to unify his own nation:

> In Scotland, as in every other country concerned with the maintenance and
> development or recovery of a national culture, it is becoming realised that sec-
> tionised interests are not only incapable of withstanding the great over-ruling
> tendency towards standardisation inherent in contemporary industrialism,
> dependent in the last analysis on cosmopolitan finance, but that that section-
> ising of interests is in itself merely an index of how far disintegration has
> already gone. Scottish interests have been deplorably 'atomised'. We have a
> whole series of isolated movements little related, and often antagonistic, to
> each other and making for nothing that is nationally synthetic. ('Towards a
> "Scottish Idea" ', *RT2*, 37)

As a visionary Dostoevskian idiot, the Drunk Man sees further than
the mass of his own people, rendered purblind by metropolitan capitalism's rationalised fracturing of the national *geist*. The spiritual sacrifice
of his art will expose the nation's provinciality:

> And never mair a Scot sall tryst,
> Abies on Calvary, wi' Christ,   [*except*]
> Unless, mebbe, a poem like this'll
> Exteriorise things in a thistle
>
> (*CP1*, 135)

The Drunk Man's soteriology aims to exteriorise the metaphysical mys-
teries of existence, uncovering Scotland's essence by refusing the interi-
orisation of linguistic and philosophical Scoticisms encouraged by the
Enlightenment. He asserts a fundamentally Scottish Republican cast of
mind and spirit that opposes the 'King and System' of England as something that 'Ootside me lies':

> For I stand still for forces which
> Were subjugated to mak' way
> For England's poo'er, and to enrich
> The kinds o' English, and o' Scots,
> The least congenial to my thoughts.
>
> (*CP1*, 157)

The strategic essentialism of MacDiarmid's nationalist theology enables resistance to cultural and political subjugation, but his nationalism

ultimately rests on an acceptance of the irrationality of nationality, an anti-essentialism aspiring to 'unite / Man and the Infinite!' (*CP1*, 98):

> He canna Scotland see wha yet
> Canna see the Infinite,
> And Scotland in true scale to it.
>
> (*CP1*, 162)

The poet-saviour of *A Drunk Man* must renounce Scotland's present incarnation – '*gin ye'd see / Anither category ye / Maun tine your nationality*' – if his '*sacrifice*' for the prospective nation is to be worthy of his infinite vision:

> *A Scottish poet maun assume*
> *The burden o' his people's doom,*
> *And dee to brak' their livin' tomb.*
>
> (*CP1*, 165)

The Langholm minister Thomas Scott Cairncross (1872–1961), a poet and novelist and a key figure for the young Christopher, introduced him to the poetry of Pádraic Pearse, executed leader of the 1916 Easter Rising who claimed '*Mise Éire*' – 'I am Ireland'.[31] According to Seán Farrell Moran, 'Pearse's notorious notion of the blood sacrifice on behalf of Ireland came from his merger of the myth of Cúchulainn's self-immolation and the Crucifixion of Jesus.'[32] MacDiarmid believed that Ireland could act as a nationalist exemplar for Scotland but was aware in 1927, writing in *Albyn*, that 'Scottish psychology differs from the Irish' (*A*, 38). Whereas Pearse led Ireland to sacrificial revolt through his mystical representation, MacDiarmid would be expelled from the NPS in 1933 for nationalist extremism and communism. Addressing 'The Difference' to Party Secretary John MacCormick (1904–61), he retaliates by echoing Pearse: 'I am Scotland itself to-day' (*CP2*, 1277). His work, particularly *A Drunk Man*, translates Irish Republican martyrology into a Calvinist variety of self-sacrifice, a lexical form of nationalist christophany in which the Scottish saviour appears through the word rather than in the image. The Drunk Man is a solitary anti-hero who could never have stormed the General Post Office in Dublin with the Irish revolutionaries – unlike (in combative mood) his creator, perhaps. Significantly, Grieve's poetic pseudonym was the gaelicised name adopted by another of the 1916 leaders executed by the British, Seán Mac Diarmada (originally John MacDermott), and MacDiarmid was born in 1922, the year twenty-six counties of Ireland gained national independence. Eschewing blood sacrifice, but giving his life for an art that will save the country's spirit, the Drunk Man transcends the one-dimensionality of a falsely materialist, earthbound nation in order to redeem his folk, freeing them to a true cosmological Scotland. Wishing to ensure Scotland's eternal future, he perceives that there can be no nation without the unending imagination of the community:

> I wad ha'e Scotland to my eye
> Until I saw a timeless flame
> Tak' Auchtermuchty for a name,
> And kent that Ecclefechan stood
> As pairt o' an eternal mood.

(CP1, 144)

It is telling that MacDiarmid, the modernist mystic, seeks to eternalise small-town Scotland in the form of Ecclefechan, birthplace of Victorian visionary Thomas Carlyle. *A Drunk Man* universalises Scotland from the provincial locality of Montrose.

Inconclusive Coda: the Kailyard's regress or towards a new Scotland?

The NPS, also called the Scottish National Party by MacDiarmid in the *Review*, was formally inaugurated at King's Park in Stirling on Saturday, 23 June 1928 – Bannockburn Day. Around two thousand 'delegates and adherents' were present to hear the 'principal speakers', names confirming the cultural origins of the nationalist movement: 'Mr R. B. Cunninghame-Graham JP, DL; Hon. R. Erskine of Marr, Mr C. M. Grieve JP, Montrose, and Mr Lewis Spence' ('Scottish National Party', *MR*, 29 June 1928, 5). Formed 'out of a widely expressed desire for a united front', the NPS was 'strictly non-sectarian' ('The National Party of Scotland', *MR*, 25 May 1928, 6). The NPS emerged from the Glasgow University Students' Nationalist Association, the SNL, Spence's Scottish National Movement (which had split from the SNL in 1926) and the SHRA.[33] Acknowledging the 'widespread apathy among the people in regard to the ideal of a self-governing Scotland', in 'Round the Town' of 1 June 1928 Grieve attributes this to 'the anti-Home Rule attitude of the daily press' (*MR*, 6), a bias of the Scottish national newspapers he tirelessly defied in the local *Montrose Review*.

However, after nine years of constant and interrelated activity on several different fronts, he left Montrose on 9 September 1929 in order to work for Compton Mackenzie's *Vox* in London. Grieve had been chafing against the confines of a provincial town for some time, complaining in letters to George Ogilvie that 'I can't get out of Montrose though, do what I will, but I loathe my work here' and, even more tellingly ([November 1925], *L*, 86),

> I am really feeling the need now, for divers reasons, of getting into a city and have during the past year tried to do so in all sorts of ways – but without success. I'm beginning to get desperate for I don't want to have to reconcile myself to Montrose – or the likes of Montrose – for good. (6 August 1926, *L*, 89–90)

Such frustration at the limits of small-town life is reflected in 'Frae Anither Window in Thrums' from *To Circumjack Cencrastus*. MacDiarmid vernacularises the painting 'From Another Window in Thrums', a modernist rendering by William McCance (1894–1970) of Barrie's *A Window in Thrums*. Barrie's novel exemplifies the characteristics of the Kailyard school that MacDiarmid and the Scottish Renaissance sought to usurp from its place of populist precedence, making it apposite that Tom Normand should link McCance's 1928 painting with the foundation of the NPS in the same year, believing 'From Another Window in Thrums' to be 'an inventive, subtle, ironic, and sceptical critique of the received vision of Scotland and Scottish culture'.[34]

Writing on 'William and Agnes M'Cance' for the *Scottish Educational Journal* of 20 November 1925, Grieve believes the work of husband and wife to be 'in accordance with a new or renewed realisation of fundamental elements of distinctively Scottish psychology', and approves of their 'ultra-modern tendencies manifesting themselves internationally' (*CSS*, 187). Seeking to supplant the Kailyard's retarding influence, the modernist Scottish Renaissance challenges the threat of the 'permanent provincialisation of our country' (*CSS*, 188). Walter Perrie sees MacDiarmid as an internationalist stifled by the Kailyard mores of Montrose:

> He hated Montrose and tried to find work in a more congenial, less provincial, environment but with little success. Montrose, a small town in Scotland still thirled, as Grieve saw it, to the cultural values of the Kailyard and suffering in its social and political life from the joint domination of the Kirk and English bourgeois hegemony, must have provided fertile soil for a good crop of discontent from someone whose ambitions lay in the direction of a highly intellectual poetry of European directions.[35]

'Frae Anither Window in Thrums' appears to confirm Perrie's view. Caught 'in the hauf licht' (*CP1*, 230) the elect poet damningly reiterates the lack of vision of this parochial environment fearing that 'The difference 'twixt the few and mony / In this puir licht seems sma' if ony' (*CP1*, 233). The Drunk Man's Christ-like sacrifice to save the nation's soul is vitiated by the poet of *Cencrastus*. Slumped in spiritual torpor, he calls to mind the self-crucifying nihilist Nikolai Stavrogin, Dostoevsky's ultimate nightmare in his anti-socialist *The Devils* (1871): 'Wan as Dostoevski / Glowered through a wudden dream to find / Stavrogin in the corners o' his mind' (*CP1*, 230). 'Stavrogin's Confession', unpublished till 1922, involves the rape of a young girl. Beyond a Christian ethic and unredeemable by love, he kills himself. Portending the revolutionary evils that will come to a Godless Russia, Stavrogin symbolises his nation's sick soul. Possessed of an existential boredom, the extremist Stavrogin suffers an acedia shared by the poet staring out of the office-window of the *Review* onto a Kailyard scene of unbearable inanity. With 'weans clamourin'' to be fed' (*CP1*, 237), the 'accursed drudgery' (237) of his job and the philistinism of his boss – 'Curse his new hoose, his business, his cigar' (235) – add to the poet's gloom, as he sits in darkness 'Huntin'' like Moses for the vital spark' (235) of creativity:

> Thrang o' ideas that like fairy gowd   [*full*]
> 'll leave me the 'Review' reporter still
> Waukenin' to my clung-kite faimly on a hill
> O' useless croftin' whaur naething's growed
> But Daith, sin Christ for an idea died
> On a gey similar but less heich hillside.
>
> (*CP1*, 237)

Such a negative summary of Montrose, coming at the end of his decade there, implies MacDiarmid's frustrated desire to transform the values of a place that nourished his own creative capacity and political imagination. MacDiarmid may have wanted his epitaph to be 'A disgrace to the community' (*LP*, 426), but his period in the town displays a dedicated striving to serve and radically transfigure Montrose and Scotland. In Montrose he found 'the true language o' my thochts' (*To Circumjack Cencrastus*, *CP1*, 239), producing the beautiful concision of the cosmological Scots lyrics and the lengthy metaphysical modernism of *A Drunk Man*. The level of energy involved in MacDiarmid's political work in Montrose is also inspiring, a civic commitment to local and national democracy illustrated by his industry as a socialist councillor and his part in establishing the NPS.

In 'The Angus Burghs', an article commissioned in 1953 by the *Montrose Standard* Press but never published, MacDiarmid recalls that in 1935, when he was in Whalsay, he opposed the implementation of the Local Government (Scotland) Act of 1929 – legislation that, by centralising power, stripped many local burghs of their ancient independence and characteristic singularity. His resistance to standardisation in politics – a battle he fought most avidly at local level – mirrors the poet's cultural aims for Scottish modernism. MacDiarmid believed that 'in the 'Twenties Angus (and particularly Montrose) was the cultural centre of Scotland'.[36] Montrose was, indeed, a place where an exceptional group of writers and artists converged. Many were Montrosians, such as William Lamb (1893–1951), who sculpted Grieve in 1927, and the painter Edward Baird (1904–49), who shared MacDiarmid's desire for a Scottish Republic and whose shifting portrayals of Montrose – brought to their highest pitch with *Unidentified Aircraft over Montrose* (1942) – depict the centrality of his local environment to the development of his art; Baird would paint Fionn Mac Colla in 1932 as the Montrose-born novelist finished *The Albannach*.[37] Violet Jacob, writing from the House of Dun near Montrose, shows a concern to represent the whole community, imagining the lives of ordinary Montrosians in collections of poetry such as *Songs of Angus* (1915) that merge the vernacular with modern folk song, as well as in novels and short stories. Willa Muir would return to the town with husband Edwin for summer breaks, and Grieve would meet the Muirs, as well as F. G. Scott, Compton Mackenzie, Pittendrigh Macgillivray and Neil Gunn. MacDiarmid thought Montrose 'very conducive to creative work',[38] and a place that helped to cultivate the politically and culturally progressive Scottish Renaissance; however, it was his vital presence there that brought such diverse talents into focus as a movement.

Considering the scale of his operations in Montrose, Grieve must be slightly disingenuous when writing to Macgillivray on 10 February 1925, 'I even sacrificed my own career – staying so long down here on a little local paper, simply because it gave me more leisure for my efforts on behalf of Scottish nationalism and letters' (*L*, 313). He understood, in a letter from Shetland in 1936 to his second wife, Valda, that 'my journalistic instinct *is* part of my life and has been a very important and indeed deter-minant part of it' (*NSL*, 123). His work for the *Montrose Review* demon-strates the extent to which MacDiarmid engaged with the community in which he lived, continually attempting to bring radical concerns to bear within the local milieu through his journalism and using this to attempt internationalist reconstruction of the national stage. MacDiarmid's job with the *Review* placed him at the hub of the town's affairs. Such intimate connection with the community fired his best poetry in Scots. It also encouraged the development of a Scottish Republican politics that would be fully realised in Shetland, yet enabled his propaganda efforts for a Scottish Renaissance to find greater scope than would have been possi-ble in the isolation of Whalsay or in a larger, less easy to dominate urban environment. This is one reason MacDiarmid never prospered in cities, and why his activities in Montrose in the 1920s decreased substantially in Shetland. 'Montrose' confirms this, MacDiarmid writing that the town 'has the right size too – not a huge / Sprawling mass', so 'it is possible to know / Everyone in it' (*CP2*, 1407). Without a university education he may have struggled to find work on a national newspaper, whereas a provincial press is keener to find journalists it can mould to its local requirements. MacDiarmid reversed these terms, availing himself of the local *Montrose Review* to further his internationalist aims for the national movement.

It would be impossible to wholly fathom the influences that brought about the great explosion of energy that characterises MacDiarmid's time in Montrose, but his direct involvement in the community through his work as a journalist and councillor was a pivotal influence on the evolution of his poetry and politics.

Notes

1. For the career trajectory of the lad o' pairts, and the myth (or otherwise) of the democratic intellect see David McCrone, *Understanding Scotland: The Sociology of a Stateless Nation* (London & New York: Routledge, 1998), pp. 95–120; and, R. D. Anderson, *Scottish Education since the Reformation* ([Stirling]: Economic and Social History Society of Scotland, 1997).
2. Andrew McPherson, 'An Angle on the Geist: Persistence and Change in the Scottish Educational Tradition', in Walter M. Humes and Hamish M. Paterson (eds), *Scottish Culture and Education 1800–1980* (Edinburgh: John Donald, 1983), pp. 218, 228, 233.
3. W. N. Herbert, *To Circumjack MacDiarmid: The Poetry and Prose of Hugh MacDiarmid* (Oxford: Clarendon Press, 1992), p. xi.
4. See Alan Bold, *MacDiarmid: Christopher Murray Grieve: A Critical Biography* (London: John Murray, 1988), p. 120.
5. Ibid., p. 120.
6. Glen Murray, 'MacDiarmid's Media 1911–1936', in *RT1*, p. xiii.
7. See Montrose Town Council minutes, in Angus Archives, M/1/1/31, 1921–2, p. 129.
8. Trevor W. Johns, 'MacDiarmid the Montrosian', *Montrose Review*, 17 April 1986, p. 14.
9. This footnote from *Lucky Poet* 'is an unacknowledged quotation from Lincoln Kirstein, writing about Gaudier-Brzeska', Kenneth Buthlay (ed.), *A Drunk Man Looks at the Thistle* (Edinburgh: Scottish Academic Press, 1987), p. 91.
10. MacDiarmid became Hospitalmaster on 9 November 1923, a job entailing the distribution of funds to charitable causes. I am grateful to Fiona Scharlau of Angus Archives for her explanation of the role of Hospitalmaster.
11. Randal Stevenson, *Modernist Fiction: An Introduction* (Hemel Hempstead: Harvester Wheatsheaf, 1992), p. 70.
12. D. H. Lawrence, cited in Stevenson, *Modernist Fiction*, p. 71.
13. Daniel Albright, *Quantum Poetics: Yeats, Pound, Eliot, and the Science of Modernism* (Cambridge: Cambridge University Press, 1997), p. 1.
14. Ian Brookes et al. (eds), *The Chambers Dictionary* (Edinburgh: Chambers, 2003), p. 341.

15. Cited in Bold, *MacDiarmid*, p. 137.
16. J. Derrick McClure, *Language, Poetry and Nationhood: Scots as a Poetic Language from 1878 to the Present* (East Linton: Tuckwell, 2000), p. 100.
17. William Donaldson, *Popular Literature in Victorian Scotland: Language, Fiction and the Press* (Aberdeen: Aberdeen University Press, 1986), p. xii.
18. See R. F. Foster, *Modern Ireland 1600–1972* (London: Penguin, 1989), Ch. 20: 'The Takeover'.
19. C. M. Grieve, 'Book Reviews', *Scottish Chapbook* I:I, August 1922, p. 28, cited in Margery Palmer McCulloch (ed.), *Modernism and Nationalism: Literature and Society in Scotland 1918–1939, Source Documents for the Scottish Renaissance* (Glasgow: ASLS, 2004), p. 53.
20. C. M. Grieve, letter to George Ogilvie, 20 January 1928, cited in Murray, *RT1*, p. xvi.
21. Robert Crawford, 'MacDiarmid in Montrose', in Alex Davis and Lee M. Jenkins (eds), *Locations of Literary Modernism: Region and Nation in British and American Modernist Poetry* (Cambridge: Cambridge University Press, 2002), p. 53.
22. 'MacDiarmid edited the [*Scottish*] *Chapbook* (14 issues, monthly, August 1922–November/December 1923), *The Scottish Nation* (34 issues, weekly, 8 May–25 December 1923) and *The Northern Review* (4 issues, monthly, May–September 1924)', Alan Riach, 'Editor's Commentary', *A*, p. 360.
23. Bold, *MacDiarmid*, p. 154; see, also, pp. 47–8.
24. Christopher Harvie, *Scotland: A Short History* (Oxford: Oxford University Press, 2002), p. 68.
25. C. M. Grieve (ed.), *Robert Burns 1759–1796* (London: Benn, 1926), p. iii.
26. See Bold, *MacDiarmid*, pp. 229–30.
27. Christopher Harvie, *No Gods and Precious Few Heroes: Twentieth-Century Scotland* (Edinburgh: Edinburgh University Press, 2000), p. 94.
28. Robert Burns, 'A Red, Red Rose', in Andrew Noble and Patrick Hogg Scott (eds), *The Canongate Burns: The Complete Poems and Songs of Robert Burns* (Edinburgh: Canongate, 2001), p. 412.
29. See George Davie, *The Crisis of the Democratic Intellect: The Problem of Generalism and Specialisation in Twentieth-Century Scotland* (Edinburgh: Polygon, 1986), Ch. 7: 'John Anderson and C. M. Grieve' and Ch. 8: 'Drunk Man or Lucky Poet?'.
30. Buthlay (ed.), *A Drunk Man Looks at the Thistle*, p. 91.
31. Pádraic Pearse, *Selected Poems / Rogha Dánta*, intro. Eugene McCabe and Michael Davitt (Dublin: New Island, 2001), pp. 46–7; see *LP*, p. 222, and Bold, MacDiarmid, pp. 30–3 for MacDiarmid and Pearse.
32. Seán Farrell Moran, *Patrick Pearse and the Politics of Redemption: The Mind of the Easter Rising, 1916* (Washington, DC: The Catholic University of America Press, 1997), p. 194; Moran sees Easter 1916 as a mythic revolt against the modern positivism of imperial Britain.
33. See Murray G. H. Pittock, *A New History of Scotland* (Stroud: Sutton, 2003), pp. 269–70.
34. Tom Normand, *The Modern Scot: Modernism and Nationalism in Scottish Art 1928–1955* (Aldershot: Ashgate, 2000), p. 7.
35. Walter Perrie, *Out of Conflict* (Dunfermline: Borderline, 1982), p. 16.
36. Hugh MacDiarmid, 'The Angus Burghs', in Alan Bold (ed.), *The Thistles*

Rises: An Anthology of Poetry and Prose by Hugh MacDiarmid (London: Hamish Hamilton, 1984), p. 220.

37. According to Jonathan Blackwood's Portrait of a Young Scotsman: A Life of Edward Baird 1904–1949 (London: The Fleming-Wyfold Art Foundation, 2004), the three heads of Unidentified Aircraft appearing beneath Montrose actually belong to one local man, Baird's friend Peter Machir, here representing all Montrosians; NPS meetings were said to be held at Machir's home in the town's Wharf Street.

38. The Thistle Rises, p. 220.

Chapter 4

At the Edge of the World

Leaving Leith on Tuesday, 2 May 1933 on the *St Magnus* bound for Shetland, MacDiarmid was sailing against the tide of urbanised modernity.[1] Only three years previously, on 29 August 1930, the *HMS Harebell* carried the last people from Hirta, the main island of St Kilda, most westerly of the Hebrides. Refused permission to film on St Kilda by owner Lord Dumfries, director Michael Powell headed for Foula off the west coast of mainland Shetland. After a seven-year ordeal of frustrated planning and four gruelling months of filming, *The Edge of the World*, Powell's dramatisation of the evacuation of St Kilda, was finally released in 1937.[2] Blending an almost mystical romanticism with a realist's grasp of the importance of location, Powell's experimental film movingly marks the tragedies of depopulation in all of Scotland's island groups.

Calling the St Kildan evacuation 'a very curious matter', MacDiarmid's 'The Modern Scene' (1934) pushes beyond Powell's film to question the political purpose of peripheral clearances:

> St Kilda, as Professor Mathieson has shown, is perhaps the most fertile island in the whole of Europe and, given proper methods, could feed all Glasgow, while it could also have been the centre of a prosperous fine wool industry. It is not impossible that its otherwise incomprehensible, and totally unnecessary and unjustifiable evacuation, is accounted for by reasons of 'higher policy' of which the public knows nothing and even the Press only enough to take the hint and say nothing. (*SS*, 40)

MacDiarmid thought that 'British civilization does not know what to do with the lonely places' (*LP*, 215), but the strategic placing of military bases, far from densely populated centres of importance such as London, is one possibility eluded to in 'The Modern Scene'.

From Welwyn Garden City and Whalsay, Lewis Grassic Gibbon and MacDiarmid believed that their respective 'distance from the Scottish Scene would lend them some clarity in viewing it' (*SS*, 11). Having fled south from his native Mearns, the diffusionist Gibbon continued to resist a nationalist solution to Scottish problems. MacDiarmid left mainland Britain to live in a place often cartographically boxed up and shipped south rather than finding accurate representation in its unaccommodating position on the map (on a line of latitude level with the southernmost point of Greenland, and six hundred miles north of London).[3] But it was while in Shetland that he located a Scottish Republican tradition opposing centralisation, a politics of place that also posited a controversial and radically internationalist remedy to the crisis of civilisation of the 1930s.

'I was aince a Scot': journeys to the edge

Worried about his excessive drinking in Edinburgh after his split with Peggy, the poet Helen Cruickshank (1886–1975) initiated MacDiarmid's move to the dry island of Whalsay. Comprising around 950 people in 1933, many of whom made their living from fishing, Whalsay is roughly five miles long and two wide. The Grieves stayed initially with the Scottish Republican Dr David Orr at Anchor Cottage then moved to a four-roomed cottage at Sodom ('southerly homestead') near Symbister, vacant through the death of a tubercular child.[4] Using tea and orange boxes that Valda covered with bits of old cloth to fashion furniture and a bed, Sodom looked 'out over a tangled pattern of complicated tideways, *voes*, and islands with snaggled coasts to the North Shetland mainland and the Atlantic' (*LP*, 45). The beauty of Whalsay was in stark relief to their new home, which was 'a humble dwelling' and 'a drab looking place' according to islanders, even after everything had been painted in black and red.[5] MacDiarmid contrasts the ascetical conditions of 'my shabby / Little cottage here on the bare hillside' with 'the blizzard that encompasses all life today' in 'the Money Age' ('A Shetland Cottage', *Revolutionary*, 34). According to Bold, 'Politically, MacDiarmid saw Whalsay as a microcosm of an unjust society.'[6]

Despite joining the Communist Party of Great Britain (CPGB) in 1934, when MacDiarmid socialised he did so with what was known in Whalsay as 'da gentry',[7] a group including the laird William A. Bruce and his wife Elizabeth (sister of Herbert Grierson), Dr Orr, the minister, teachers, shopkeepers and clerks of the local council. The ancestors of the Bruce family at Symbister House 'gained possession of Whalsay from its crofter-owners and brought in a period of harsh rule. In the 19th century the punishment for any small misdemeanour was exile from the island.'[8] Although by the 1930s such severe class power was no longer exercised some of the older residents would still bow when they met the gentry. It was 1946 before there was no separate table for the Whalsay elite at the celebration of a local wedding.[9] This mixing with the middle and upper orders prompts Brian Smith's belief that 'MacDiarmid's communism was a pose' that the islanders were able to see through: 'The people of Whalsay were never under any illusions about MacDiarmid's political or social affiliations. They regarded him as a member of what they called "da Gentry circle".'[10] For his part, MacDiarmid believed that land-lordism had imparted Shetlanders with a 'duality' manifesting itself in a 'secret radicalism and an external sycophancy' (*Islands*, 61). Decidedly open about his own radical republicanism, he was notorious for a fla-grant anti-monarchism, one Whalsay resident remembering 'Auld Grieves' (as the islanders knew him) wanting to see the whole Royal family pitched into a red-hot boiler, another that he said Queen Victoria had been 'just a cow'.[11]

Such iconoclasm was combined with genuine concern for the eco-nomic difficulties Shetland faced. 'Life in the Shetland Islands' (1934) fears that Shetlanders are 'fighting . . . a losing battle' to retain tradi-tional living and work practices: 'The fishing, upon which they princi-pally depend, is in a bad way; the population is rapidly declining; crofts are falling into desuetude and the ground is being increasingly acquired by big sheep-farmers' (*SP*, 88). Despite Shetland's geographical isolation, the propensity of international capitalism to dissolve local differences cannot be held at bay; MacDiarmid is optimistic, however, that Shetland can recover somewhat through the development of its untapped eco-nomic and cultural potential. Perhaps surprisingly, he recommends the stimulation of tourism – that postmodern simulacrum of the history of place – as a means of revival.[12] As a travelling correspondent for the *Scots Observer* at the Faroese National Festival of St Olaf in the summer of 1933, MacDiarmid had been impressed with what he believed to be a national resurgence. By following the Faroese example Shetland can also re-establish its own identity:

> The Faroes did this by breaking off alien ties opposed to their true national development; and by putting their activities once more upon their natural basis and developing them in accordance with the dictates of a true local economy, they have risen to their present healthy and happy condition. (*SP*, 97)

The phrase 'breaking off alien ties opposed to their true national development' is a succinct summation of MacDiarmid's essentialist Scottish nationalist credo. In this sense, Shetland was something of a test case for MacDiarmid's Douglasite economic plan for a separatist Scotland: 'Given the measure of independence they have, the island economy is in curiously surreptitious enjoyment of a measure of Douglasism – of economic nationalism within the present framework of international interdependence and high finance.' (*SP*, 90).

For MacDiarmid, Douglas was a builder of theories 'which could only have been discovered by a Scotsman, related as they are to essential factors alike in the old Gaelic commonwealth and its subsequent pre-Union Scottish policy and financial practice' ('Major C. H. Douglas', *SS*, 157). Writing as James Maclaren for the *Scottish Educational Journal* of 30 March 1934, he claims in 'Scotland and Europe' that Douglas's 'ideas have called into being strong movements in most of the civilised countries of the world' (*RT2*, 369). In 'The Future' (1934), MacDiarmid regards Douglasism as being 'the alternative to Fascism and the complement and corrective of Communism' (*SS*, 340). Douglas's Social Credit proposals interested many modernists, such as Ezra Pound and the young Edwin Muir. MacDiarmid saw Social Credit as a means to break the anti-evolutionary power of 'a banking system that from its lying books / Refuses to lift its eyes' ('Genethliacon for the New World Order', *CP1*, 404). In 'Song of the New Economics', 'anti-Douglasite arguments' are compared to 'the Simian speeches / Against the human developments' that 'orthodox economists are using' (*CP1*, 397). Despite his approval of Douglas, MacDiarmid didn't contribute to a debate on Social Credit that ran throughout 1934 in the correspondence column of the *Shetland Times*. However, combining what he regards as the internationalist economics of Douglas with an avid regionalism, in 'Life in the Shetland Islands' he hopes that Shetland will 'become the theatre of an exceedingly interesting politico-economic-cultural movement' (*SP*, 98).

He may still have been preaching the importance of the peripheries, but the active localism of MacDiarmid in Montrose is much less evident in Whalsay. This is partly due to the personal crisis he suffered in the 1930s. MacDiarmid could write humorously to Frank O'Connor on 21 June 1939 that 'I am pent up here on the edge of the Arctic Circle and cannot get away' (*NSL*, 163), but the sometimes frustrated sense of living at the geographical margins – *in* Scotland but not *of* it – combined dangerously with being mentally, physically and emotionally at the edge. The Grieves had little money as the poet had no regular income. Given their poverty, MacDiarmid's deliberate unemployment was a source of bewilderment to some islanders: 'He wis a very clever man – but he did nae right work un dey wir just fantin.'[13] That they were 'fantin', or starving, and had no earnings meant existing on handouts from the islanders: 'Dey wid nivver have survived without da kindness a folk. Dey owed money ta some aa shops.'[14] MacDiarmid recognised halfway through his time in Whalsay that 'I could not have lived anywhere else that is known to me these last four years without recourse to the poorhouse' (*LP*, 45). They were also permanently behind in the payment of rent to the laird. With an apologetic letter of 2 August 1940 to Bruce, Grieve encloses a Peter Cheyney detective novel to be returned to Mistress Bruce and £2 12s: 'I am sorry that owing to the effect of war-time conditions on my work this payment is so long overdue.'[15] As living at Sodom cost 27s a year, this represents two years rent and means he was almost a year overdue: Bruce had not been paid since 1938.

Work was difficult given his precarious health. Islanders said that on his arrival in Whalsay MacDiarmid looked thin and unwell.[16] In 1935 a complete breakdown led him to Gilgal psychiatric hospital in Perthshire, a fitting place for the author of *Stony Limits* to reach his spiritual nadir – Gilgal is Hebrew for 'circle of sacred stones'. The cause of MacDiarmid's illness has been difficult to define, but his letter of 20 September 1935 to Valda from Gilgal suggests that he was syphilitic:

> With regard to Peggy and you suspecting my trouble, you could not possibly – for I had no suspicion of it myself, never a single moment's, and no reason to have any. I knew that in 1915 I'd a slight dose of Gon. [gonorrhoea] I'd driven underground with violent boozing and that I'd no notion where it had gone – but there is no proven case of suppressed Gon. turning into Syph. [syphilis] and of Syph. I never had the slightest sign – chancre, rash, etc., all of which are invariably present. So how on earth could I suspect? (*NSL*, 100)

Marrying Valda on 12 September 1934 didn't immediately lessen his hurt at rejection by Peggy. He accuses his first wife of having 'completely disoriented my work' (21 October 1939, *NSL*, 170), partly due to her failure to return his books – 'the changed nature of my poetry was intimately connected with my loss of them' (1 June 1936, *NSL*, 118). In a long letter of 26 March 1937, while grateful 'for all the help you gave me at Montrose', he claims: 'Our rupture has not only cost me dear – but Scotland dear, for it destroyed the pith of my poetry and the very core and kernel of all my work' (*NSL*, 136). 'Ode to All Rebels' remembers the '*bonny sangs*' (*CP1*, 494) written in Montrose, whilst bitterly attempting to exorcise the memory of Peggy:

> *Scotland, when it is given to me*
> > *As it will be*
> *To sing the immortal song*
> *The crown of all my long*
> > *Travail with thee*
> *I know in that high hour*
> *I'll have, and use, the power*
> *Sublime contempt to blend*
> *With its ecstatic end,*

As who, in love's embrace,
Forgetfully may frame
Above the poor slut's face
Another woman's name.

(CP1, 489)

A poem of 1937 tells of the opening of 'That awful abyss' when thinking of his first wife and children, and a consequent unwillingness to 'set
out / Once more on difficult paths of thought' (*Revolutionary*, 32) for
fear of falling again into the same void. When writing to Peggy from
Whalsay an unbalanced MacDiarmid is also writing to justify himself,
attempting to reason his way through emotional trauma and fathom the
roots of his creativity. Unable to attend his mother Elizabeth's funeral in
April 1934 while he was in Cornwall with Valda, alienated from his
brother Andrew, MacDiarmid must have felt the loosening of his personal ties to Scotland; being spurned by Peggy, his Scots Muse, was the
greatest blow. No longer in productive touch with a community in such
a way as he was in Montrose, the rebel spins off the edge of the world:

Victim o' nae dialectic system, o' nae
Intricate web o' human beliefs to gainsay
Ocht that but for it I'd naturally think, feel, or dae,
Lookin' back on a' that – a' that ither men
Are and dae and think – I feel just as when
A clean man amang ither men first comes to ken
    Some o' them ha'e venereal disease,
Vague, terrible phenomenon o' a warld no' his ain;
    And the diseased men's callousness sees . . .

('Ode to All Rebels', *CP1*, 504)

'On a Raised Beach' offers an antidote of acceptance for the very
despair that prompts spiritual crisis. What in a letter to Valda he calls the
'curiously beautiful' ([8 May 1933], *NSL*, 53) barren landscape of
Whalsay is synthesised with the asceticism of a metaphysical hyper-
reality that refuses to be undermined by life's superfluities. As alleged
inspiration for the poem MacDiarmid concocted a three-day stay alone
on the uninhabited West Linga, with its raised beach at Croo Wick, an
island west of Whalsay that could be seen from his cottage. The poem
drew genuine sustenance from the 1933 geological survey of Shetland
conducted by G. V. Wilson, whose five-strong team included Thomas
Robertson, with whom MacDiarmid became friends. Composed mainly
of gneiss and schist with some intrusions of granite, Whalsay and West
Linga are over 420 million years old,[17] scientific findings appealing to
MacDiarmid's materialist theory of the earth, his desire in 'On a Raised
Beach' to 'get into this stone world now' (*CP1*, 426).

Newly arrived in 1933 and writing on the 18 October for *New Britain*, in 'The Shetland Islands' MacDiarmid describes a place where 'scores of crofts are falling into desuetude; the fishing has dwindled to vanishing point – soon there will be nothing but the bare stones left' – a depopulated scene that he appears to relish:

> Frequently a Shetland vista gives one the illusion of not being on part of the habitable earth, but of some burnt-out star. The end of the world; well, it will come to that some time, won't it? As well, perhaps, to reckon with a foretaste of it now. Why wait in parts where infinitely more irrelevances have still to be shorn away before the true goal of all this complicated terrestrial process manifests itself? (*RT2*, 510)

As here, 'On a Raised Beach' projects an emotional landscape onto Shetland. An 'Austerely intoxicating' place of the mind where 'a man must shed the encumbrances that muffle / Contact with elemental things', in Shetland MacDiarmid returns to first principles in every sense:

> Death is a physical horror to me no more.
> I am prepared with everything else to share
> Sunshine and darkness and wind and rain
> And life and death bare as these rocks though it be
> In whatever order nature may decree,
> But, not indifferent to the struggle yet
> Nor to the ataraxia I might get   [*tranquillity*]
> By fatalism, a deeper issue see
> Than these, or suicide, here confronting me.
> It is reality that is at stake.
>
>   (*CP1*, 428)

Addressing readers in quasi Biblical terms such as 'O we of little faith' (*CP1*, 430), 'We must be humble' (425), 'We have not built on rock' (431), the poem's questioning of contemporary civilisation's foundations bears comparison with choruses from T. S. Eliot's pageant play *The Rock* (1934). In *The New English Weekly* of 18 October 1934, however, MacDiarmid accuses Eliot of being 'a very meticulous priest of the devilry which arises as the class struggle develops' ('Denis Saurat: supernatural rationalist', *RT2*, 507). Eliot's Christianity may obviate societal divisions but MacDiarmid's eco-Marxism acknowledges that the reality of the stones, the very basis of life, cannot be grasped without engaging with the masses: 'Intelligentsia, our impossible and imperative job!' (*CP1*, 432). In 'The Shetland Islands' he describes his current home as a place that constitutes 'the end of the old world; and the beginning of the new!' (*RT2*, 512). This proved to be true on an emotional as well as an ideological level. By travelling north to Shetland, MacDiarmid, as poetic shaman, journeyed deeper into an interior reality.[18] From personal crisis came an ascesis, a self-discipline and self-knowledge from which emerged a belief in a politics to revolutionise reality during the crisis of civilisation of the 1930s. Like Ewan in *Grey Granite* (1934), a novel Gibbon dedicated to MacDiarmid, 'On a Raised Beach' moves from geological prehistory to establish the meaning of History in the political philosophy of communism.[19]

John Maclean and *Red Scotland*

MacDiarmid's communism hardened in the 1930s in opposition to the rise of European fascism. The Spanish Civil War (1936–9), according to Frederick R. Benson, 'represented the intellectual as well as the emotional climax of the turbulent 1930s' and was important to the intelligentsia because it 'provided the first violent test, at least for most European and American radicals, of the usefulness of Marxism as a means of ordering experience'.[20] MacDiarmid's Spanish poem, *The Battle Continues*, written mainly in Whalsay but not published until 1957, is a sustained attack on Roy Campbell, a South African poet of Scottish descent. A convert to Catholicism who failed his entrance examinations for Oxford, Campbell wrote eleven poems on the war in Spain, including *Flowering Rifle* (1939), and falsely claimed to have fought for Franco.[21] That the anti-Republican Campbell is of Scottish blood particularly raised MacDiarmid's ire, as if a right-wing Scot constitutes a false ideological calculation:

> Scotland, thank God, gave scores of her sons
> To the Republican cause in Spain,
> Sent out her doctors and nurses,
> Ambulances and foodships.
> Ninety per cent of the Scottish people
> Were whole-heartedly for the Republican cause,
> – Hating like Hell all you have fought for and praised.
> Are all these people wrong, Campbell,
> And only you right?
> You were always a braggart, Campbell,
> But in the eyes of Scotland you rank
> With Judas and Sir John Menteith
> And the executioners of William Wallace
> And the Judge who sentenced John Maclean.
>
> (*CP2*, 943)

Arguing that 'no creative artist has ever belonged / Or ever can belong to the Right' (*CP2*, 921) MacDiarmid sees Campbell as a false Scot, a betrayer of the true Scottish political tradition of radical republicanism. If 'Poetry is a progressive art' (921) then the fascist Campbell has 'done literature dirt' and 'swindled the Muse' (920). As such, MacDiarmid groups his work with 'Auden, Spender, Allott, Grigson, / The Woolfs, the *New Statesman* clique' – for him 'All Left Fascists, so very pointedly unrevolutionary' (*CP2*, 979).

The beginning of the Spanish conflict in 1936 was also the year Routledge turned down *Red Scotland*, originally called *What Lenin Has Meant to Scotland*. Discerning the fascist threat nearer to home, in a 1936 letter to the *Daily Record* MacDiarmid accuses Edwin Muir of 'intervening with the prospective publishers and inducing them not to publish my book' (*NSL*, 127) because of its criticism of him. MacDiarmid was to return Muir's alleged affront many times over in contempt for *Scott and Scotland*, dismissing it as 'a restatement of the literary case of Scottish Unionism – that hireling caste employed by English Imperialism to perpetuate the provincial status of Scotland' (*LP*, 199). He ridicules Edwin as a 'nyauf' in 'On an Opponent of Scots Literature' and finds it suspicious that the renaissance of a Scottish literary tradition is condemned by Muir as deeply reactionary: 'Strange that anti-Fascism should here alone be at one / With the English Ascendancy policy!' (*Revolutionary*, 13, 14). *Red Scotland* was due to appear in the same 'Voice of Scotland' series as *Scott and Scotland*, but Routledge refused it because they deemed it to be overloaded with quotations, uncommercial and libellously anti-royal.[22] In a letter to Routledge's Frederick Warburg on 17 June 1935 Grieve writes of his belief that his book would be 'likely to create a sensation in Scotland' (*L*, 541). While critics still debate the implications of Muir's disavowal of a distinctly Scottish tradition it is ironic, given its aim of resuscitating the censored and languishing tradition of radical Scottish Republicanism, that MacDiarmid's potentially powerful book was itself suppressed.

In *Red Scotland* MacDiarmid has 'cut himself off almost entirely from personal contact with the self-styled intelligentsia' of the nation, living instead ' "off the dole" among the crofters and fishermen' of Whalsay (*RS*, 49). Claiming that 'there is nothing more lawless than the law', MacDiarmid denounces 'the private ownership of land' as representing 'the perpetual civil war in our midst' (*RS*, 41). Alluding to the prospect of war with England and subsequent 'civil war in Scotland', he warns that 'militant methods would be necessary' (*RS*, 23) to defeat reactionary forces. Sectarianism is a politically retarded measure of a divided nation and 'the powers that be are secretly fomenting the potential civil war between the Catholic and Protestant factions in Scotland' (*RS*, 26). 'What England did in Ireland will be child's play to what it will do in

Scotland' (*RS*, 26) if Scots unify to break the Union. A paranoid MacDiarmid seems to be on high alert for open conflict, with Spain a live issue and his memory of the recent Anglo-Irish War (1919–21). In Scotland, however, perhaps the most menacing political development of 1936 was the opening of St Andrew's House in Edinburgh.[23]

Heavily influenced by John Maclean, whose biography MacDiarmid began but never completed, the political philosophy of *Red Scotland* derives from Maclean's August 1920 declaration for a Scottish Workers' Republic, in which the 'communism of the clans must be re-established on a modern basis'.[24] Born in Pollokshaws of parents who had been cleared from the Highlands as children, MacDiarmid wrote of Maclean, 'The unification of Scotland – Highland and Lowland, rural and urban – was complete in himself.' (*Company*, 147). Transferred from his first teaching post for refusing to teach Christian doctrines, Maclean was sacked in 1915 for advocating pacifism during the war. With the success of his classes on Economics and Industrial History in Glasgow from 1906 to the Rent Strike of 1915 to encourage him, Maclean founded the Scottish Labour College in 1916. Arrested just prior to the organising conference, Maclean was convinced, according to his daughter Nan Milton, that 'he had been singled out for special punishment by the government, that the greatest "crime" that he had committed in their eyes was the teaching of Marxian economics to the Scottish workers'.[25] MacDiarmid found in Maclean the most notable modern representative of a Scottish Republican tradition fusing nationalism and socialism. Influenced by James Connolly, who founded the Irish Socialist Republican Party in 1896 and printed the 1916 Proclamation of the Irish Republic on the presses of his radical journal the *Workers' Republic*,[26] both Maclean and MacDiarmid believed national self-determination and international socialism to be inseparable imperatives of revolutionary progress. Reinforcing Maclean's anti-imperialism, MacDiarmid argues that 'the secession of Scotland will be one of the deadliest blows that can be struck at English Imperialism – a blow at the very heart of Empire' (*RS*, 239). He confirms that 'the only Scottish publicists of my time for whom I have any respect' are Maclean, Connolly, and Keir Hardie (1856–1915), founder of the Scottish Labour Party (1888) and the ILP (1893) (*RS*, 66).

Red Scotland repudiates the Scottish National Party while still finding a nationalist place for radical internationalist politics, arguing that 'Scottish Nationalists are increasingly recognising that Scottish Nationalism and Socialism must go together' (*RS*, 257). MacDiarmid believes that 'the Communist Party is right in regarding the official National Party of Scotland as a Fascist organisation' (*RS*, 31). The 'bourgeois propaganda' of 'romantic Nationalism', with its 'Heather and

Tartan sentimentality', is political 'trickery by which the workers are rendered well-nigh incapable of seeing their real interests' (*RS*, 259). Scotland should be independent not only through its historical national status but due also to its contemporary industrial importance, there being 'no question of the proletarian significance of Glasgow' (*RS*, 240). An independent Scotland would not become a small reactionary state, a bulwark of capitalism and bourgeois culture, but a bastion of socialism and scientific progress. Utilising Patrick Geddes's terms, he believes that presently 'Scotland is still stuck in the grimy and forbidding ruts of the paleotechnic age'; however, 'The neotechnic age is now dawning. Its basis is the long distance transmission of electric power' (*RS*, 84–5). The radical nationalism of a Scottish Republic would be progressive and internationalist in orientation, not aristocratic like Polish nationalism or imbued with the philistinism of the SNP:

> Communism means death to the national cultures in so far as those elements in existing national cultures are concerned which 'embrace all classes', are rooted in the past, or founded on alleged transcendental values. It will be found that the Scottish Nationalist elements I represent are not alien to Communism to the slightest degree in any of these respects. (*RS*, 247)

MacDiarmid does not endorse the Scottish nationalists because they are bourgeois and reactionary, but the radical republicans that he supports must ensure that they are free of 'this collective hypnosis of the Scottish people' (*RS*, 221): adherence to imperialist English nationalism disguised as British internationalism. The powerful spell of this ideology, fostered through an anglicised Scottish educational system, has 'advantages to our Capitalist society' (*RS*, 221) in obscuring the distinct economic, political and cultural concerns of Scotland.

Frustrated by the metropolitan centralism of the CPGB and the 'corruption of the London communists', in 1920 Maclean attempted to establish a Scottish Communist Party 'as a prelude to a Scottish Communist Republic'.[27] His failure to construct a radical party within a distinctly Scottish context was hindered when his mental health was brought into question by Scottish communists in the CPGB. MacDiarmid claims such tactics are 'no new expedient in politics', particularly in relation to Scottish Republicanism:

> Thomas Muir and Fletcher of Saltoun have similarly had doubts cast on their mental soundness, and one of the intentions in resorting to this infamous expedient in respect of Maclean was, undoubtedly, an anxiety to represent his advocacy of Workers' Republicanism as a new and unheralded departure and hide the fact that, on the contrary, Maclean came at the end of a long sequence of Scottish Radical and Republican thinkers. (*Company*, 139)

Writing 'John Maclean, Scotland, and the Communist Party' for the *Scots Socialist* in 1941, MacDiarmid alleges that denials by Willie Gallacher (1881–1965) – a founding member of the CPGB in 1920 – that H. M. prison authorities mistreated Maclean arise from the fact that 'Scottish public life under English ascendancy is full of sinister little Tory–Socialist alliances' (*RT3*, 43). Although never imprisoned, MacDiarmid believed that he was similarly persecuted, explaining his Shetland exile in *Lucky Poet* as an inability to gain employment in Scotland due to his revolutionary politics. MacDiarmid's comparison in 'John Maclean (1879–1923)' of Maclean with Christ and his criticism of the CPGB's treatment of him led to his own expulsion from the Party in November 1936. That MacDiarmid's politics have also suffered accusations of cranky contradictoriness makes it apt that during his own breakdown he found sustenance in Maclean. What is eccentrically impressive about MacDiarmid's lionising of Maclean is that concern with the potential international ramifications of his Scottish Republicanism comes from a poet situated so far from the incendiary radicalism of industrial Glasgow during the Depression.

In Shetland MacDiarmid continues the ideological reconstruction of Scotland begun in Montrose by renouncing the 'so-called Scottish Renaissance Movement' (*RT3*, 10). Appearing in the inaugural edition of the *Voice of Scotland* for June/August 1938, 'The Red Scotland Thesis: Forward to the John Maclean Line' condemns Muir and former ally James Whyte's *Modern Scot* as belonging to the 'St Andrews school of polite literature' (*RT3*, 10). Writing to Sorley MacLean (1911–96) on 28 March 1938, Grieve explains that he is looking for material for 'a new quarterly devoted to Scottish Literature and Politics (i.e. Scottish Republicanism à la John Maclean)' (*NSL*, 152), provisionally titled in his next letter to 'Sam' of the 9 May the '*Scottish Republic*' (*NSL*, 153). As the unsigned editorial of the first *Voice of Scotland*, 'The Red Scotland Thesis' heralds 'THE END OF SCOTTISH NATIONALISM AND THE BEGINNING OF THE SOCIAL REVOLUTION IN SCOTLAND' (*RT3*, 9). Social change can only occur, however, if 'we unhesitatingly affirm that Scotland is a nation'; this requires opposition to 'the entire *ethos* in the United Kingdom which has far too long resisted effective penetration by Socialist analysis' (*RT3*, 13). Acclaiming the 'splendid "documentary film" work' of John Grierson (1898–1972), MacDiarmid's new '*line represents a complete break with recent Scottish cultural developments, and the realisation that further such developments must of necessity be revolutionary*' (*RT3*, 11). Directing *Drifters* (1929),[28] filmed partly in Shetland, Grierson's modernist realism illustrates the conflicting needs of the local fishing industry and its international markets. As he seeks to engage with the actualities of the 1930s, MacDiarmid argues from the marginality of Whalsay that poetry should be 'equipped to join issue at every point with modern intellection' (*RS*, 297). In Maclean and Grierson he identifies radical new Scottish weapons with which to challenge capitalist globalisation.

Hitler and the 'Defence of the West' (with a view from Military Intelligence)

In a letter of 12 October 1938 to the *Criterion*, MacDiarmid contends that a malign embodiment of modern capitalism is 'the urbanisation of the mind', its cure being 'that the greater part of the population, of all classes (so long as we have classes), should be settled in the country and dependent upon it' (*NSL*, 155). Citing psychologist Raymond B. Cattell's *The Fight for our National Intelligence*, which he asked Bill Aitken to bring with him to Whalsay upon its publication in 1937,[29] MacDiarmid notes that in the remotest areas intelligence is highest; Scots are cleverer than the English, but Edinburgh and Glasgow lower the national average. Despite claiming in *Scottish Scene* that 'if one is to live in Scotland it is necessary to live in Edinburgh' ('Edinburgh', *SS*, 94), 'Edinburgh' damns a capital 'too stupid yet / To learn how not to stand in her own light' (*CP1*, 646). Another poem originally from *Lucky Poet* accuses Glaswegian 'hoodlums' of having a 'terror of ideas' and a 'hatred of intellectual distinction' ('Glasgow', *CP1*, 647, 648). 'Dìreadh II', published in 1974 but also written during his time in Shetland, yearns for the 'real Scotland' of 'the leaping salmon' and 'soaring eagle', not the Scotland of Glasgow and Edinburgh with 'the loathsome beasties climbing the wall/And the rats hunting in the corners' (*CP2*, 1175). For MacDiarmid the paralysis of internal colonisation and the detritus of industrialism defile Edinburgh and Glasgow. Scotland can only be seen whole from its edges.

MacDiarmid may not have been aware that Cattell, innovator of IQ and personality tests, was a member of the English Eugenics Society in 1937,[30] but if he read Cattell's book fully he would have known that *The Fight for our National Intelligence* supports German sterilisation policy and racial engineering. Writing to Valda in 1936, he is anxious to discuss the 'vital matters' ([20 June], *NSL*, 125) raised in geneticist Hermann J. Muller's recently published *Out of the Night: A Biologist's View of the Future*. Quoting from Muller, MacDiarmid explains in *Lucky Poet* that a social revolution combined with the application of the American scientist's theories could end the waste of human potential under capitalism:

I believe with Professor H. J. Muller that scientific development and a better social order can tap genius in every human being and create a society in which men like the greatest philosophers, poets, and scientists in human history will no longer be, as they have always been hitherto, very rare exceptions, but the rule – most men will be of a stature like that of Plato or Homer or Shakespeare. And I believe that is coming, as the result of scientific discoveries, very speedily – the time when the earth will be occupied by 'a race of people all of whom come up to the level of what we now call "genius" '. (*LP*, 237)

Given MacDiarmid's dream of a communist utopia peopled by creative geniuses, it is ironic that Muller, who was a member of the Communist Party until Stalin and Trofim D. Lysenko proscribed eugenic research, eluded the Soviet purges to work at the University of Edinburgh's Institute of Animal Genetics from 1937 to 1940.[31] However unrealistic his ambitions for the cultural evolution of humanity, MacDiarmid employs science as an authoritative means of undermining the reactionary notion that identity is fixed and unchangeable. In 'To the Younger Scottish Writers', he claims to have found 'nothing whatever in contemporary biology / Either the science of heredity or of genetics' to undermine the idea that human nature is capable of 'the revolutionists' / Advocacy of profoundly-altered social systems' (*CP1*, 637).

An interest in contemporary scientific developments in the field of eugenics was shared by reactionary and progressive intellectuals of a period in which it would prove to be a hideously significant factor in European politics. As Donald J. Childs comments, some modernists were attracted to eugenics as a means 'to assume responsibility for a creation recently orphaned by the death of God'.[32] In the introduction to *The Golden Treasury of Scottish Poetry* MacDiarmid refers to the Spanish essayist and novelist Angel Ganivet, who 'diagnosed the disease from which his country was suffering as ἀβουλία, or lack of will-power, and preached the need of a spiritual renaissance'; he believes 'that Scotland is deep in the grip of the same disease and in like need of a national awakening' (*GT*, xv). Evoking Nietzsche's will-to-power, MacDiarmid relates Scotland's condition to the interwar crisis of European liberalism.

In *The Islands of Scotland*, dedicated to the nationalist Orr, he conceptualises his view of European political developments:

I had always been interested in the great question of North versus South, though the breaking of the old European balance and the titanic emergence of Russia – the East – seemed (and still seems) to me to call for an attempt on the part of the Gaelic elements of the West – Ireland, Scotland, Wales, Cornwall, Brittany – to put forward the Gaelic idea as a complement and corrective to the Russian, making an effective quadrilateral of forces; and in the establishment of Saorstat Eireann and other happenings I hailed what appeared (and appears) to me to be the true 'Defence of the West', essential to the conservation of European culture. (*Islands*, 48–9)

Published in June 1939, just before the outbreak of World War Two, that *The Islands of Scotland* heralds the continuance of European civilisation in the emergence of Saorstát Eireann, the Irish Free State, may seem ironic given Irish neutrality during 'the Emergency'.[33] However, Éamon de Valera's policy finds some theoretical similitude in MacDiarmid's Defence of the West.

'The Caledonian Antisyzygy and the Gaelic Idea', first published in the *Modern Scot* (1931–2) the year before he went to Shetland, illustrates the extremes that MacDiarmid will go to in order to find a place for his self-confessedly playful vision of the Scottish genius as a balancing mechanism in world affairs during the thirties. Included by Duncan Glen in his 1969 *Selected Essays of Hugh MacDiarmid* it has yet to be collected in the Carcanet edition of MacDiarmid's complete works. Beginning by citing G. Gregory Smith's idea of the contradictory nature of Scottish literature, MacDiarmid, somewhat uncharacteristically, emphasises the absence 'of a truly *British* tradition' due to 'English ascendancy', before asserting a proto-postcolonial vision heralded by the Irish:

> Ireland's breakaway – its power to sunder itself in the teeth of the entrenched English power – is one of the happy signs that all may not yet be lost. I welcome like tendencies in India, Egypt, South Africa and elsewhere, and think it is high time Scotland in particular was realizing what it is all about in terms not only of the crucial and immediate problems of our own country but in terms of world politics.[34]

Corresponding to the Defence of the West, the Gaelic Idea champions the national difference of smaller nations threatened by imperialism, something MacDiarmid was keen to take literally in his own cultural praxis. When asking Sorley MacLean's help with translations for his *Golden Treasury*, for instance, he is 'particularly anxious that the Gaelic side should be thoroughly well represented' (9 August 1934, *NSL*, 79). The inclusion of Gaelic (and Latin) poetry in this anthology undermines the notion that Scottish culture began with its anglicisation, just as the many poems attributed anonymously emphasise the oral origins of the Ballad and the impersonality of the ancient Celtic bardic system, each traditions of Scottish cultural commonality. In *Islands* he admits, 'Whatever the general considerations might be, however, my personal concern was not with Gaelic but with Scots and against southern English.' (49). Even minding that concern, and his desire for Scottish unity and freedom to be resurrected upon a creative Scottish myth, 'The

Caledonian Antisyzygy and the Gaelic Idea' finds the hymnist of Lenin on indefensible fascist terrain:

> Scottish nationalists – especially in view of the ascendancy in Anglo-Scottish politics of a Labour-cum-socialist electoral majority in Scotland, or, at all events in the more densely populated and commercially and industrially important centres, and the particular hatred which Scottish nationalism inspires in Labour-cum-socialist circles – ought to consider carefully the principle which Hitler and his National Socialists in Germany oppose to Marxism. Hitler's 'Nazis' wear their socialism with precisely the difference which post-socialist Scottish nationalists must adopt. Class-consciousness is anathema to them, and in contradistinction to it they set up the principle of race-consciousness.[35]

The historical reality of the East–West synthesis of MacDiarmid's Gaelic Idea was the German–Soviet pact made by Hitler and Stalin on 23 August 1939. Writing to fellow communist Sorley MacLean on 5 June 1940, he insists that

> although the Germans are appalling enough and in a short-time view more murderously destructive, they cannot win – but the French and British bourgeoisie can, and is a far greater enemy. If the Germans win they could not hold their gain long – but if the French and British bourgeoisie win it will be infinitely more difficult to get rid of them later. (*L*, 611)

MacDiarmid's amanuensis in Whalsay, Henry Grant Taylor, who as a conscientious objector was imprisoned for ten days in 1941 for failing to turn up to a National Service medical, recalled that 'when the blitzkrieg started' the poet was 'rather delighted': 'I don't know if he knew a very great deal about National Socialism or what it implied but he thought somehow that the old order was being smashed up.'[36] In a letter to Bill Aitken of 13 September 1939, however, his fear that the war 'can only make for a bestial submergence and perhaps final dissolution of all decent values' (*NSL*, 167) suggests he was only too aware of the threat to civilisation. Aitken remembers Michael Grieve being given paternal encouragement to proclaim 'Buy the *Daily Worker*, Join the United Front Against Fascism and War!'[37]

Expelled from the CPGB for nationalist deviation on 23 February 1939,[38] MacDiarmid's response to World War Two bears ostensible similarity to those Party members who, as Jonathan Glover relates, thought 'democracy and fascism were not importantly different' and that 'the British Empire was as bad as Nazi Germany'.[39] 'On the Imminent Destruction of London, June 1940' sees the capital of the Empire as 'the centre of all reaction' (*Revolutionary*, 42), the City having 'flourished like a foul disease / In the wasting body of the British Isles' (43). Alleging

that Scotland was unprotected from German attack, MacDiarmid writes
in another poem that

> The leprous swine in London town
> And their Anglo-Scots accomplices
> Are, as they have always been,
> Scotland's only enemies.
>
> (*Revolutionary*, 45)

Due to such controversial views the Secret Intelligence Service investigated MacDiarmid as a potential threat to the state, sending two soldiers
to Whalsay in May 1940. Stuart Bruce, brother of Whalsay's laird, had
written to the Home Office alerting them that MacDiarmid, along with
Grant Taylor and Dr Orr, had convened a meeting in Orr's house of all
those islanders who had been called up; Bruce presumed the intention to
have been that of dissuading them from going to war.[40] Rumours spread
throughout the island that the poet was to be arrested and Grieve wrote
a letter of complaint on 29 May to the Senior Military Officer in Lerwick
threatening to take legal action and have questions asked in the House
of Commons.[41]

MacDiarmid's politics were clearly taken seriously by Westminster. A
secret government file, now held in the National Archives, had, in fact,
been opened on Grieve as far back as 1931 when he was in London.
Special Branch were concerned that he would use the Unicorn Press, a
small publishing firm in High Holborn, of which he was then director, to
disseminate communist propaganda as they knew him to be consorting
with the so-called Fleet Street Communists, but they also investigated him
at this time when he delivered a lecture at Eustace Miles Restaurant on
'The Essentials of Scottish Nationalism' to the London Branch of the
National Party of Scotland.[42] From this point onwards, until 1943, after
MacDiarmid had left Whalsay to undertake war work in Glasgow, some
of his letters, particularly to and from the Communist Party, were intercepted and copied and a trace was kept on his activities and those of his
correspondents, including both of his wives. Peggy was still being watched
in 1940, eight years after divorcing Grieve.

Reports occasionally have the air of an Ealing Comedy, unwittingly
exposing the old-school-tie network of British Intelligence and the superficial, caricatured responses of its operatives to those outside the Establishment. Employing identikit categorisations, one file has a Special
Branch officer informing MI5 that the poet, with his slim build, long hair,
black suit and trilby, has 'the appearance of an artist';[43] in another a
Secret Service operative stationed at Scottish Command in Edinburgh
and writing to the War Office in London with regard to Grieve's activities

in Shetland closes a letter by asking his correspondent if they had attended Rugby, the prestigious English Public school, together.[44] But the intimate trawling through MacDiarmid's personal affairs, such as his divorce from his first wife, even his final rupture with his brother Andrew, demonstrates that his politics were not taken lightly by the state. When it became clear to him, whilst on Whalsay, that he was being watched, as would be a criminal, he faced the authorities with his usual vigorous directness. Military Intelligence (namely MI5 and German specialists MI12) may have been spying on MacDiarmid, but in his characteristically forthright, if wayward, manner, he explicitly refuted any implication that he was a German or Russian spy. In the mistaken belief that a Captain Hay of Lerwick was responsible for sending the investigating party to Whalsay, Grieve writes to him on 5 June 1940,

> Not only am I quite entitled to hold Communist meetings if I want to, but the present War is being fought on behalf of Civilisation, Freedom and Democracy – of which not even the Germans but skunks like you are the deadliest enemies.[45]

Such rhetoric almost landed MacDiarmid on the Invasion List, which contained the names of those who would be interned if the Germans were to land. Only the isolation of Whalsay kept him from inclusion as a suspect – as he was in a place impossible to leave in a hurry and among a population conspicuously loyal to the Crown, it was deemed that MacDiarmid's location sufficiently contained any security risk the expression of his politics may have held for the Censorship. When he moved to Glasgow, where he continued to warn of the perils of what he regarded as English fascism's grip on Scotland, his case was reassessed.[46] Whilst it was concluded that he was 'genuinely anti-Nazi', in relation to the war his Scottish nationalism was regarded as a greater risk to British state security than his communism.[47]

Writing to their Glasgow and West of Scotland Branch on 28 April 1941, Grieve sought to join the National Council of Civil Liberties.[48] This was primarily to seek their support in protesting against conscription of Scottish nationals as contravening the Act of Union, but perhaps also because he was conscious that his individual rights might soon need the armoury of legal protection. In police raids on Scottish Republicans in 1941 MacDiarmid's typescript 'A Brief Survey of Modern Scottish Politics in the Light of Dialectical Materialism' was seized from the Glasgow home of the editor of the *Scots Socialist*. Writing on 25 May to Tom Johnston (1882–1965), historian, cofounder in 1906 of the ILP paper *Forward* and then Secretary of State for Scotland (1941–5), Grieve vehemently denies any political link to Nazism:

The whole thing is a base English Imperialist manoeuvre to throttle and libel the now rapidly growing Scottish Socialist Republican Movement – and to divert public attention from the pro-Nazi Fifth Column traitors who are not to be found in our ranks but in the ranks of our aristocracy, plutocracy, and the Government itself, where there are plenty who will sell us out to Hitler if they get a chance (*NSL*, 192).[49]

In the paranoid political atmosphere of the period, a cartoon in the Glasgow *Evening Times* (established 1876) could caricature the Scottish Renaissance as a Nazi movement; under the leadership of Hamish McHitler, the Scottish National Original Socialist Conservatives, or 'Snoskies', sweep to victory in the General Election of 1940.[50] In reality MacDiarmid was seeking political and cultural rapprochement with anti-imperial nationalists closer to home, particularly in Wales.[51]

MacDiarmid's Defence of the West is his ideational cognisance that national particularity is universally threatened in the 1930s by *all* imperial 'isms'. So, in an unpublished book from 1936 on Scottish literature and the Renaissance movement, he sketches a chapter 'In which, to learn of Scotland, it is necessary to go to the Russians, the Chinese, and the Red Indians'; in this newly ordered landscape, 'the Hebrides – Orkneys – Shetlands – Faroes are found to be in the centre of Europe'.[52] But with war threatening just before the publication of *Islands*, such decentring of the political map of Europe may be less appropriate. He performs a perilous balancing act by playing off Russian communism against gaelicism in an attempt to offset the supremacy of anglophone, capitalist imperialism – regarded by MacDiarmid as simply a domestic brand of fascism. MacDiarmid would skit the crushing stupidity of Nazism in 'While Goering Slept' *(Revolutionary*, 41), but even in his ultimate opposition to German fascism his Defence of the West renders him unable to contain his hostility towards the main power fighting the Nazis. 'The man is a menace', is the view from the files of British Military Intelligence.[53]

As W. H. Auden's 'low dishonest decade' rumbled toward its ominous apotheosis on 'September 1, 1939',[54] European civilisation's symposium of democratic nationality was in dire need of defence. Auden began the decade imagining 'New styles of architecture, a change of heart', but in 1939 resignedly admitted that 'poetry makes nothing happen'.[55] After Yeats, Ireland may have 'her madness and her weather still',[56] but the Republic also has political independence and cultural confidence, both partly shaped by his poetic project of national reinvention. Affirming 'I Am with the New Writers', MacDiarmid in Whalsay recognises that

This renewed impetus
Towards the local and the vernacular

Implies a changing conception of culture,
No longer a hothouse growth but rooted.
If all the world went native
There would be a confusion of tongues,
A multiplication of regionalisms.

(CP1, 653)

With the Gaelic Idea MacDiarmid puts Scotland strategically first, fearful that the nation disappear from its place on the international map of cultural and political distinctiveness. The geopolitical edges of Britain, from Shetland in the northeast to Cornwall in the southwest, supply him with ammunition against British centralisation.

On the island archipelago of Shetland, 'Scotland's greatest exclave' (*Islands*, 69), MacDiarmid discovers the essentially fragmented nature of all national cultures, isolated in the sea of their own historical identity yet linked to other cultures by the very fluidity of that sea. He understands the connections Shetland has to mainland Scotland through language, religion, education, media and markets, while believing that its distinctive Scandinavian heritage 'ought to be encouraged by all possible means, and especially by a recovery of the old Norn tongue' (*Islands*, 59). His experience of the islands allows a clearer view of Scotland. On seeing Scotland whole, MacDiarmid discovers that there are many Scotlands, each different and difficult of combination:

> Scotland in its history and literature resembles very much a many-roomed house, in the different apartments of which, at one and the same time, entirely different activities are going forward, while the people in any one of these rooms have little or nothing in common with those in the other rooms, so that a time at which, on a given summons, all of them would assemble together is unthinkable. Such a general assembly has never, in fact, taken place in the history of Scotland to date, nor does it ever seem likely to do so . . . Scotland is broken up into islands other than, and to a far greater extent than merely, geographically; and it is perhaps not unreasonable to wish that the process had been physically complete as well, or, at least, to speculate upon the very different course not only Scottish, and English, but world history would have taken if the whole of the mainland of Scotland had been severed from England and broken up into the component islands of a numerous archipelago (*Islands*, 7–8).

Like its islands, Scotland may be perceived to be peripheral to metropolitan concerns. However, the Gaelic Idea rescues the geopolitical extremities from political and cultural desuetude by positing their potential to spiritually regenerate the materialist insularity of the centres of civilisation. A Scottish place unlike mainland Scotland, Shetland is conceptually moulded by MacDiarmid to politically challenge a metropolitanism that subsumes difference and patronises or ignores what it terms the provinces. Theoretically, this may be one reason why he chose to live in small places, in order to make a virtue out of the marginal and show that art, like life, happens everywhere: 'I am no further from the "centre of things" / In the Shetlands here than in London, New York, or Tokio' ('In the Shetland Islands', *CP1*, 574).

The Islands of Scotland can be seen as a nationalist response to *A Journey to the Western Islands of Scotland* (1775), topographically extending yet ideologically troubling the assured Enlightenment metropolitanism of Johnson and Boswell's tour of lonely places incompatible with British civilisation. Concurring with the Estonian theosophist Count Hermann Keyserling that 'one of the least intelligent prejudices of the Darwinian age was that life progresses by means of progressive adaptations' (*Islands* 22–3), when really 'non-adaptation is the nerve of all progress' (23), MacDiarmid believes that the truly evolutionary perpetuation of political and cultural particularity – the Defence of the West – can only come through the 'non-adaptation' to the metropolitan norm of that which is different.

Shetland's black sheep

MacDiarmid's idea that restoring the Norse roots of Shetland will facilitate its regeneration demonstrates his nationalist belief in the international value of difference. A more specific aim of his desire to recreate an autochthonous culture is regional resistance to the centralisation of the British state. It was Ordnance Survey cartographers' anglicisation of the Norse place names of Shetland that rendered MacDiarmid's Sudheim home as Sodom.[57]

The Islands of Scotland was reviewed in the local press, with the focus on MacDiarmid's nationalism in its application to Shetland. While noting his 'perfervid nationalism' in 'Whither Shetland: Hugh MacDiarmid on the Present and Future', 'R. W.' in the *Shetland Times* of 1 July 1939 maintains that reversing the 1468–9 mortgaging of Shetland from Scandinavia to the Scottish Crown would have no effect on present 'economic prosperity', which 'will have to be deferred indefinitely if it is to depend on a revival of the ancient Norse language' (8). In the *Shetland News* of 13 July 1939, 'The Plight of Scotland: Its Islands, Agriculture and Fisheries' displays equal scepticism that the cultural retrieval of a Norse Shetland would benefit the economy and agrees with 'R. W.' that the example of Faroe is misguided. However, the review gives MacDiarmid credit for a political theory 'that has nothing exclusive or arrogant about it, like so much nationalism on the Continent to-day, but is at bottom an appreciation of individuality and variety in the scheme of things' (6).

The *Shetland Times* (1872) and *Shetland News* (1885) were established during the late nineteenth-century burgeoning of interest in the Norse past of Shetland, a period in which cultures across Europe sought their roots in a classicism that may have owed more to an invention of tradition than any genuine rediscovery of the past.[58] The formal organisation of Up Helly Aa, a pagan festival held in January celebrating the Norse origin of Shetland, also began at this time. Perhaps reminded of Langholm's Common Riding, in the *Shetland News* of 8 February 1934 MacDiarmid declared Up Helly Aa to be 'a really marvellous spectacle' that 'links past and present and reveals the distinctive and timeless background against which the generations come and go' ('Mr C. M. Grieve on Up-Helly-Aa', 4). The economic distress of the 1930s saw Lerwegian socialists question what they saw as the false consciousness of working-class participants in Up Helly Aa, a festival they believed masked class differences behind the myth of a unified racial origin.[59] Similarly, neither Shetland newspaper could be entirely comfortable with the MacDiarmidian diagnosis of Shetland's economic ills as being attributable to a refusal to embrace a Norse past when both owed their existence to a period in which such a cultural resurgence had done nothing to stave off the present economic gloom.

A considered response was lacking in MacDiarmid's reaction to the pragmatic reviews of *The Islands of Scotland* in the Shetland press. His letter of 30 June 1939 to the *Shetland Times* scorns the scepticism of 'R. W.' over the likelihood of a 'renaissance along Norn-autonomous lines':

> I quite agree that ninety-nine people out of a hundred would share this 'common-sense view'; but in precisely the same way the vast majority of Russians in 1916 would have regarded the overthrow of the Czarist regime and the establishment of the USSR as a dream outside the bounds of all probability, while the hundreds of thousands of German Socialists a few years ago would have found the possibility of Hitler's Nazi's coming to power as just as fantastically incredible. ('The Islands of Scotland', 8 July 1939, 8)

Barely berthed in Shetland when he wrote 'The Future of Scottish Poetry' for the *Scots Observer* on 24 June 1933, he adjures young Scottish poets to acquaint themselves with Rilke, Valéry, Blok, and Rimbaud:

> Without a knowledge of these, anyone professing a serious concern with modern poetry is in a position similar to that of a would-be scientist who has not grasped the work of Planck, Bohr, and Einstein, or a political aspirant who has no effective knowledge of Lenin, Mussolini or Hitler. (*RT2*, 210)

In each case, MacDiarmid's extremist sense of contemporary political developments is akin to Rimbaud's revolutionary injunction from hell that 'one must be absolutely modern'.[60] MacDiarmid's Defence of the West may seek to guard marginal cultures from the engulfing power of imperialism, but could his own marginality have rendered him oblivious, particularly as late as July 1939, to Hitlerite anti-Semitism, a Nazi policy that would seek to eradicate that which is different? He was criticised by the visiting communist Bob Cooney and Peter Jamieson of the Lerwick Unemployed Workers' Movement for what they perceived to be the reactionary, racial basis of *The Islands of Scotland*.[61] Calling Cooney's analysis 'cheap claptrap' in a letter of 31 July 1939 to the *Shetland News*, Grieve castigates 'the customary anti-intellectualism of his type, and that deplorable theoretic inadequacy which is the curse of the British Communist movement' – a dialectical fallacy he purports to correct in his own politics: 'as a Scottish Nationalist I am on thoroughly good ground as a Communist and have no use whatever for bourgeois Nationalism' ('C. M. Grieve Replies to a Critic', 3 August 1939, 5).

MacDiarmid continued to rile Shetlanders through his criticism of their literature. In a letter of 7 July 1939 to the *Shetland News*, he claims,

> The question of Shetland literature is not a matter of taste at all, but of simple fact. I feel sure I have read everything that falls into this category, but in case I have overlooked anything of the very slightest value, I challenge your reviewer to mention any Shetland literary work that is not beneath contempt. I insist not only that there is none, but that there is not a single county in Scotland which has not produced a body of writing in prose and verse immensely superior to anything and everything that has ever been produced in the Shetlands, and, even so, of no more than local value and hardly removed from doggerel. ('Mr C. M. Grieve and "Shetland News" Reviewer', 20 July 1939, 7)

He responded to correspondence from the likes of Shetland poet John Nicolson (1876–1951) with threats of litigation, claiming that the 'entirely impersonal' nature of his 'wholly disinterested' literary criticism exempted him from personal abuse; 'I have no grudge against the Shetlands at all' he maintained, persisting in his incorrect use of the definite article, 'otherwise I would not choose to live here' (*Shetland News*, 3 August 1939, 5).

He ran into similar conflict during the Shetland dialect debate of 1941. In a letter of 1 August to the *Shetland News*, Grieve said that while not a member of Walter Robertson's Shetland Poetry Circle, which encouraged the use of Shetland dialect in literature and the teaching of Shetland culture and history in schools, he was 'entirely sympathetic to the dialect movement, and to the promotion of the Poetry Circle'. Answering allegations

of interference, he claims to have no 'intention of intruding on their particular little cabbage-patch – though the provincialism they show in regard
to such intrusion by non-Shetlanders is a poor augury for the success of
the movement'. Flustered by accusations of egotistical self-promotion he
again countered by deriding the quality of Shetland literature, retorting
that his writing on Shetland was 'not likely to be in periodicals which have
any circulation in Shetland, nor to be of a nature Shetlanders will appreciate' ('Hugh MacDiarmid and Mr John Stewart', 7 August 1941, 2). His
one positive contribution to the debate encouraged the retrieval of local
vernacular culture: a letter of 27 August to the *Shetland News* urging
further research to 'uncover additional remains of that lost balladry' of
Shetland, such as 'King Orfeo' and 'The Great Silkie of Sule Skerry',
'undoubtedly the high water marks of Shetland popular literature'
('Shetland Balladry', 4 September 1941, 3). Other than brusquely defending his creative reputation he took almost no part in the Shetland dialect
debate, which repeated many of the same issues he had been through in
Montrose and again in 1936 when confronting Muir.

The egoistical MacDiarmid may have felt less threatened on the
margins. By situating himself in a place where he could believe that his
is the most authoritative voice, his desire to construct a template for difference failed to encounter the stubborn opposition of the diverse accents
of city life. On his arrival in Whalsay it was remembered that 'Grieves'
was 'of a "townie" appearance'.[62] In Shetland, and particularly Whalsay,
it was MacDiarmid who unwittingly represented the metropolitan, his
individualism at odds with a community proud of its traditions, possessed of what Christopher Harvie describes as a 'toughly independent
localism'.[63] Spending several days aboard *The Valkyrie* in June 1936,
MacDiarmid considered the herring catch 'ane o' the bonniest sichts in
the warld' ('With the Herring Fishers', *CP1*, 437), yet his 'Shetland
Lyrics' find merely solitary revelation in the North Sea from which
Shetlanders earn a living. Claiming to 'like these Shetland fisherman – at
least when they are on the job' (*LP*, 52), the alienated poet of 'Deep-Sea
Fishing' confirms his creative vocation in distinction to their 'coarser
lives':

> Aye, and I kent their animal forms
> And primitive minds, like fish frae the sea,
> Cam' faur mair naturally oot o' the bland
> Omnipotence o' God than a fribble like me.

> (*CP1*, 438)

MacDiarmid lived in a community whose acts of practical kindness
probably kept his family alive but which was small enough to be acutely

aware of their eccentricities, both good and bad: the excitingly emanci-
pated dress and behaviour of Valda, and the rumour that the Grieves
kept their son Michael (born in 1932) tied in his crib when they went
out.[64]

According to the anthropologist Anthony Cohen 'identity in Whalsay
is produced by a process of social construction in which the person identified takes a somewhat passive role'.[65] Cohen explains that in Whalsay

> individuality (in the sense of idiosyncrasy) is recognised and legitimised within
> strict limits, but is again generally explained by the person's structural con-
> nections to the community. Thus the colourfulness of local personalities is cel-
> ebrated, but the colours fall within a finite spectrum of recognisability and
> permissibility. Beyond this range a person would be dismissed as peculiar,
> incomprehensible – 'He's always been a bit funny, like.'[66]

This traditional egalitarianism of Whalsay may help explain why, in a
letter of 17 September 1941 to the *Shetland News*, MacDiarmid felt the
need to insist that he was 'not a trouble-maker', having remained 'almost
entirely aloof from the life of the island, frequently going for months at
a time without exchanging so much as a single word with anyone outside
my own household' ('Mr C. M. Grieve and his Critics', 25 September
1941, 4). In 'Bedrock', this detachment from the people of Whalsay
enables a solitary alliance with the Shetland landscape and its elements:

> I've as little need here
> For a' ither folk
> As the sea and the wind and the light
> And the skerries o' naked rock.
>
> (*Revolutionary*, 28)

MacDiarmid helped to organise a cottar's resistance to increased rents in
1939,[67] but his general isolationism may not have been seen as a virtue
in Whalsay and contrasts sharply with his active communitarianism in
Montrose.

Writing to Neil Gunn in 1935, he admits to thinking 'often of the
Montrose days when I was so active and constantly in touch with you
and others'; in Whalsay 'even letters are few and far between while I go
months at a time without seeing a newspaper' (*L*, 256). Financially dis-
tressed during the war, he asks poet and playwright Albert Mackie
(1904–85) to look out for journalistic posts in Scotland, emphasising,
'What I'd like best would be a reportership on a local weekly paper'
(8 March 1941, *NLS*, 188). MacDiarmid knew the value to his poetry of
engagement with a community, and the perils of too great an isolation in
Whalsay:

I do my best work when I have most irons in the fire, and the fact that here I had all my time to myself and had 'nothing to do but write' for a long time made it almost impossible for me to do anything at all (*LP*, 45).

In *The Islands of Scotland*, he claims to live in Shetland because he is 'intent upon the connection between solitude and universality' (6). However, according to Bill Aitken, who provided MacDiarmid with new books such as Wyndham Lewis's *Men Without Art* (1934), *Letters from Iceland* (1937) by Auden and MacNeice, Cecil Day Lewis's edition *The Mind in Chains: Socialism and the Cultural Revolution* (1937) and David Jones's *In Parenthesis* (1937), 'he was very conscious of the fact that Shetland was remote' and so 'relished the contact with someone from the outside world'.[68] Perceived to be different by the islanders, with 'In the Shetland Islands' he retorts, 'To be exclusively concerned with the highest forms of life / Is not to be less alive than "normal" people' (*CP1*, 575). Writing to Aitken on 28 January 1938, he is 'anxious to get' (*NSL*, 151) a copy of Christopher Caudwell's *Illusion and Reality*, published posthumously in the year of his death fighting Franco in 1937. Caudwell argues that 'in a revolutionary period culture expresses the aspirations of the revolution or the doubts of the dispossessed'.[69] From his exilic home in Whalsay, MacDiarmid's poetry exhibits both revolutionary ardour and the loneliness of loss.

> I was better with the sounds of the sea
>   Than with the voices of men
> And in desolate and desert places
>   I found myself again.
> For the whole of the world came from these
> And he who returns to the source
> May gauge the worth of the outcome
> And approve and perhaps reinforce
> Or disapprove and perhaps change its course.
>   ('From "The War with England' ", *CP1*, 454)

Internal Exile

Purportedly writing from the 'uninhabited isle' of Bruse Holm ('Letter to R. M. B.', *CP2*, 1272), MacDiarmid contends that 'Nae man, nae spiritual force, can live / In Scotland lang', adjuring Robin McKelvie Black, editor of the nationalist-Douglasite *Free Man*, to 'leave it tae' and 'Mak' a warld o' your ain like me' (1273). Insisting that it has no literary culture and should return to its Norse roots, MacDiarmid evacuates Shetland of contemporary substance in order to find a transcendent solitude through which to mourn the spiritual emptiness of Scotland: 'There is nae ither country 'neath the sun / That's betrayed the human spirit as Scotland's done' (1273). Contrasting Shetland and Scotland with Faroe, he argues in 'The Future' that 'the relative happiness and prosperity of the Faroes is due to the fact that the material and the spiritual have gone hand in hand' (*SS*, 339). For MacDiarmid, Scotland's betrayal of the local and the universal proceeds from the logic of the Reformation, a religious movement initiating the spirit of capitalism that will extinguish the cultural difference of place. Economic progress and political independence can only come when the nation is reconnected to its organic cultural life.

From a Shetland that he believes should re-find its Norse origins MacDiarmid rediscovers a Gaelic Scotland. 'In Memoriam: Liam Mac'Ille Iosa' conjures the 'Lost world of Gaeldom' (*CP1*, 415) from a Scottish past where 'Shibboleths of infinity' (414) were expressed on the tongue of cultural distinctness.[70] Espousing a mystical Celtic communism that opposes the anglicised materialism of contemporary Scotland, MacDiarmid seeks freedom in the individual liberation of the creative spirit:

> O come, come, come, let us turn to God
> And get rid of this degrading and damnable load,
> So set we can give our spirits free play
> And rise to the height of our form. There is no going astray,
> More than there is for the rose shining full-blown,
> Full to perfection with itself alone.
> Come, let us obey the creative word.
>
> (*CP1*, 415)

Face set against history in 'Lament for the Great Music' he stands still in artistic isolation comparing his loneliness to the neglect for the music of the pibrochs. Exiled in a land disconnected from its cultural past, aware that the severance of culture and nationality cuts destructively at the roots of the individual self, he protests,

> These denationalised Scots have killed the soul
> Which is universally human; they are men without souls;
> All the more heavily the judgement falls upon them
> Since it is a universal law of life they have sinned against.
>
> (*CP1*, 472)

Made solitary through being unable to find a place for his art in an environment that has forsaken its traditions, the poet withdraws from his own culturally impoverished local community, believing, none the less, that he serves the universal community by continuing to narrate the particularity of national difference in his poetry. For Andrew Gurr, 'Exile as the essential characteristic of the modern writer anticipates the loss by the community as a whole of identity, a sense of history, a sense of home.'[71] Unlike the modernist exile Joyce, MacDiarmid challenged his country's creative stasis by staying at home; for the poet in Whalsay, it is Scotland that is deracinated:

> My native land should be to me
> As a root to a tree. If a man's labour fills no want there
> His deeds are doomed and his music mute.
> This Scotland is not Scotland.
>
> (*CP1*, 472)

In 'Charles Doughty and the Need for Heroic Poetry', first published in *The Modern Scot* in 1936, MacDiarmid alludes to the '*timeless* music' of the pibrochs (*SP*, 126). His italics are designed to highlight, firstly in literal terms, the un-symphonic, a-rhythmical inner structure of the great music, its architectonic formlessness. On a symbolical level, however, a concern with how pibroch music actually works as a sound has enduring significance in what such a sound says of the culture from which it emerges. For MacDiarmid, the epical nature of pibroch music represents a rebellious acoustic proclaiming the classlessness of an independent Celtic society. (Although not directly mentioned in the 1747 Act of Proscription, it is not for nothing that after Culloden the bagpipe has acted as a mythic signifier for the free expression of a suppressed Scottish tradition and identity.) In 'Lament for the Great Music' Time is suspended in a mystic synchrony; the poet synthesises the lost cultural traditions of the past with his political aims for the future in a postcolonial dialectic opposing the Enlightenment idea of progress as a straight line whereupon History could not have been otherwise. History is, rather, 'the struggle of a nation into consciousness of being' (*CP1*, 476). When writing on 'Ossian' Macpherson, MacDiarmid argues in *Scottish Eccentrics* that 'English literature is not open to fundamental revaluations of its bases' (*SE*, 244). By bringing the Gaelic past into the Scottish present he seeks to redeem the Scottish future, positing a radical reorientation of Scottish to English culture.

Celtic Communism, or the trouble with Auden

MacDiarmid's spiritual Celtic communism breaks the borders of the theoretical communism adopted by metropolitan intellectuals in the 1930s. He was sceptical of middle-class, public-school-educated writers, particularly the Auden group, who professed what he thought only a shallow, fleeting radicalism. He has read 'Auden, MacNeice, Day Lewis', but is disappointed not to hear 'the authentic call' of communism, explaining, 'You cannot light a match on a crumbling wall' ('British Leftish Poetry, 1930–40', *CP2*, 1060). In *Red Scotland* MacDiarmid argues of the Auden set that 'what their work really marks is a stage in the break-up of British Imperialism and a return to English Nationalism' (*RS*, 97). Writing from Whalsay on 6 June 1938 to John Lehmann, editor of *New Writing*, Grieve believes that, unlike the bourgeois Marxists of the South, 'the advantage of belonging to the working class' (*L*, 595) lends his poetry and politics an authenticity absent from their work:

> I view with deep suspicion the whole nature and tendency of the left wing literary movement in England – knowing that you have only to scratch it to find English Chauvinism and a 'superior' inability to believe that any good can come out of anywhere but Oxford and Cambridge. (*L*, 594)

Auden went to Christ Church, Oxford, 'the domain of aristocrats and Etonians'.[72] His mordantly flippant 'Song for the New Year' (1937) says 'farewell to the drawing-room's civilised cry' and illustrates to what his social milieu is forced to bid good-bye 'Now matters are settled with gas and with bomb'.[73] Arguing in *Lucky Poet* that Auden, Spender and Day Lewis are promoted on the basis of an English ascendancy policy at the expense of superior Celtic talents such as Dylan Thomas and himself, MacDiarmid points out that the teaching of English literature in Scottish schools is not mirrored by the teaching of any Scottish literature, even Burns, in England. The fostering of a supposedly socialist poetry by imperial England he describes as 'an impudent bluff', particularly as 'the silent sabotage of its own nationalities' problems continues not only unchecked but relentlessly intensified' (*LP*, 169).

According to Martin Green, 'Auden never opened a newspaper before 1930'.[74] Green's sardonic observation exposes a real tension in much of the radical poetry of the 1930s between the public sphere of politics and Press and the private life of the individual, most famously expounded in the epigrammatic epigraph to Auden's *The Orators* (1932):

> *Private faces in public places*
> *Are wiser and nicer*
> *Than public faces in private places.*[75]

In 'The Prolific and the Devourer' (1939), whilst admitting to his own 'political ambition', Auden gives an 'anti-political' cry for freedom from the glasshouse-like ubiquity of totalitarianism, recognising that 'the Enemy was and still is the politician, i.e., the person who wants to organise the lives of others and make them toe the line'.[76] Seeing himself as a double man, in 'The Conflict' (1933) Cecil Day Lewis uses images of war to evoke the unrest of being torn between individual and communal realms:

Yet living here,
As one between two massing powers I live
Whom neutrality cannot save
Nor occupation cheer.[77]

Caught in 'no man's land' between the outer of political ideology and the inner of creative truth, the poet realises that 'only ghosts can live / Between two fires'.[78] Christopher Caudwell argues that 'the bourgeois poet sees himself as an individualist striving to realise what is most *essentially* himself by an expansive outward movement of the energy of his heart, by a release of internal forces which outward forms are crippling'.[79] For Caudwell, the clash between the illusion of radical commitment and the social reality of middle-class individualism illustrates the false consciousness of those poets who briefly used their work to propagandise for a class to which they did not belong and whose advancement would threaten their own class power. A reversion to spiritual concerns, seemingly expressive of the artistic integrity of bourgeois poets (and therefore of Poetry per se), actually indicates a return to genuine class-consciousness.

Writing of British intellectuals' thorny relationship with the creed, Neal Wood claims that 'communism is an experience of an extremely intense personal nature'.[80] Applying a transcendental mysticism to the material circumstances of urban poverty, 'In the Slums of Glasgow' illustrates the spirituality of MacDiarmid's communism:

I am filled forever with a glorious awareness
Of the inner radiance, the mystery of the hidden light in these dens,
I see it glimmering like a great white-sailed ship
Bearing into Scotland from Eternity's immense,
Or like a wild swan resting a moment in mid-flood.
It has the air of a winged victory, in suspense
By its own volition in its imperious way.
As if the heavens opened I gather its stupendous sense.

(*CP1*, 564)

'Ode to All Rebels' exclaims, 'The revolutionary spirit's ane wi' spirit itsel'!' (*CP1*, 502). However the *abhyasa*, or Yogic practice of oneness and spiritual equality of 'In the Glasgow Slums' sits uneasily with the revolutionary violence of the Cheka excused in 'First Hymn to Lenin'. Indeed, the dedicatee of 'First Hymn', D. S. Mirsky, arrested in 1937, died in a Stalinist Gulag two years later.[81] In another poem relating to Lenin's Secret Police, MacDiarmid claims that since the leaders of all political systems 'are murderers and thieves' he should be allowed his 'own special variety of Hell' (*Revolutionary*, 26).

Interviewed by Walter Perrie on 29 September 1974, Grieve dismissed Auden as 'a complete wash-out' for his renunciation of communism ('Metaphysics and Poetry', *SP*, 281). MacDiarmid retained his belief in communism long past its fashionable period and, in Montrose, had a serious interest in Leninism predating by a decade that of most of the English literary intelligentsia. Calling Stalinism 'a mere bagatelle' in comparison to the depredations of capitalist imperialism, he rejoined the CPGB in 1957 after many Western intellectuals had left in disgust at the Soviet invasion of Hungary.[82] History, indeed its touted postmodern end in the victory of global capitalism, has not proved kind to MacDiarmid's belief that communism offered the only universal hope for the future. But as an adversary of the metropolitan intellectuals of the 1930s he so distrusted, MacDiarmid remained in stubborn adherence to his communist ideal – even through the very real horrors of Lenin's Cheka and Stalin's Great Purge – by rooting its internationalist opposition to capitalist atomisation in the politics of a specific place:

> I am the heir of the great Scottish Republican and Radical traditions and have never been affected by the social stratification, the public-school system, and the other peculiar traditions of England which Auden and his friends manifest so markedly. (*LP*, 170)

The spirituality of MacDiarmid's communism counters the metropolitan manufacturing of class culture, whether that be represented in the boosting of the Auden set in the interests of bourgeois consumption, or in the production of trash culture designed for the masses. Faithful to a political doctrine utterly anathema to the monarchical British state, communism represents for him a credo akin to the austere egalitarianism of Calvinism, a spiritual 'conversion', or 'a revolution indeed', allegedly made in a Glasgow slum, but written in the winds of Whalsay (*CP1*, 563).[83]

Notes

1. See Brian Smith, 'Stony Limits: The Grieves in Whalsay, 1933–1942', in Laurence Graham and Brian Smith (eds), *MacDiarmid in Shetland* (Lerwick: Shetland Library, 1992), p. 43.
2. *The Edge of the World* (1937), film, directed by Michael Powell. UK: British Film Institute, 2003. See also Michael Powell, *Edge of the World: The*

Making of a Film (London: Faber & Faber, 1990) first published by Faber in 1938 as *200,000 Feet on Foula*.

3. James R. Nicolson, *Shetland* (Newton Abbot: David & Charles, 1972), p. 11.
4. Jakob Jakobsen, *The Place-Names of Shetland* ([1936] Orkney: The Orcadian Ltd, 1993), p. 53.
5. Information gathered from interviews of Whalsay residents in 1991 by Loretta Hutchison and Jacqueline Irvine of Whalsay History Group, Whalsay, Shetland (courtesy of Jacqueline Irvine).
6. Alan Bold, *MacDiarmid: Christopher Murray Grieve: A Critical Biography* (London: John Murray, 1988), p. 285.
7. Whalsay History Group.
8. Hamish Haswell-Smith, *The Scottish Islands: A Comprehensive Guide to Every Scottish Island* (Edinburgh: Canongate, 1996), p. 373.
9. Whalsay History Group; see Smith, in *MacDiarmid in Shetland*, p. 68.
10. Brian Smith, 'Writing about MacDiarmid in Shetland', in *The New Shetlander*, 212, (2000), Lerwick, Shetland Council of Social Services, p. 11.
11. Whalsay History Group.
12. For an examination of heritage tourism in Scotland, see McCrone, Morris and Kiely, *Scotland – the Brand: The Making of Scottish Heritage* (Edinburgh: Polygon, 1999).
13. Whalsay History Group.
14. Ibid.
15. GD.144/179/8, Shetland Archives, Lerwick.
16. Whalsay History Group.
17. See Nicolson, *Shetland*, p. 19.
18. See Peter Davidson, *The Idea of North* (London: Reaktion Books, 2005) for the journey north as one of personal revelation, 'a journey into austerity and truth, a journey that leaves illusions behind', p. 240.
19. For a brief discussion of 'On a Raised Beach' as an atheist poem see D. M. MacKinnon, *The Problem of Metaphysics* (London: Cambridge University Press, 1974), pp. 164–70.
20. Frederick R. Benson, *Writers in Arms: The Literary Impact of the Spanish Civil War* (London: University of London Press, 1968), pp. 3, 19.
21. See Hugh D. Ford, *A Poet's War: British Poets and the Spanish Civil War* (Oxford: Oxford University Press, 1965), p. 180.
22. See Bold, *MacDiarmid*, p. 339.
23. See Murray G. H. Pittock, *A New History of Scotland* (Stroud: Sutton, 2003), p. 273.
24. John Maclean, 'All Hail, the Scottish Workers' Republic!', *In the Rapids of Revolution: Essays, Articles and Letters 1902–23*, ed. Nan Milton (London: Allison & Busby, 1978), p. 218; see RS, p. 255.
25. Nan Milton, *John Maclean* (Bristol: Pluto Press, 1973) p. 118.
26. See Donal Nevin, *James Connolly: 'A Full Life'* (Dublin: Gill and Macmillan, 2005); also, James Connolly, *Labour in Irish History* (Dublin: Maunsel, 1910), and Desmond Ryan (ed.), *Socialism and Nationalism: A Selection from the Writings of James Connolly* (Dublin: At the Sign of the Three Candles, 1948).

27. Maclean, 'The Irish Tragedy: Up Scottish Revolutionists!', *The Vanguard*, November 1920, reprinted in *In the Rapids of Revolution*, p. 220.
28. *Drifters* (1929), film, directed by John Grierson. Scotland: Panamint Cinema, 2003.
29. W. R. Aitken, interviewed by Brian Smith, Dunblane, 11 August 1991, Shetland Archives, Lerwick, SA3/1/331/1&2, 2, p. 6.
30. See Eugenics Society Members List <http://www.eugenics-watch.com/briteugen/eug_cacl.html> [accessed 29 March 2005].
31. See Nobelprize.org <http://nobelprize.org/medicine/laureates/1946/muller-bio.html> [accessed 29 March 2005].
32. Donald J. Childs, *Modernism and Eugenics: Woolf, Eliot, Yeats, and the Culture of Degeneration* (Cambridge: Cambridge University Press, 2001), p. 4.
33. See Terence Brown, *Ireland: A Social and Cultural History 1922–2002* (London: Harper Perennial, 2004), Ch. 6: ' "The Emergency": A Watershed'.
34. Duncan Glen (ed.), *Selected Essays of Hugh MacDiarmid* (London: Jonathan Cape, 1969), p. 62.
35. Ibid., p. 70.
36. Henry Grant Taylor, interviewed by Brian Smith, Galashiels, 16 August 1991, Shetland Archives, Lerwick, SA3/1/332/1&2, 1, p. 16.
37. W. R. Aitken, interviewed by Brian Smith, SA3/1/331/1&2, 1, p. 19.
38. See John Manson, 'The Poet and the Party', *Cencrastus*, 68, pp. 35–8.
39. Jonathan Glover, *Humanity: A Moral History of the Twentieth Century* (London: Pimlico, 2001), p. 270.
40. See letter from R. Stuart Bruce to H. M. Home Office, 27 April 1940, in The National Archives (NA), KV2/ 2010 2S1020.
41. See NA, KV2/ 2010 2S1020.
42. Special Branch report, 16 February 1931, NA, KV2/ 2010 2S1020.
43. Special Branch report to MI5, 19 September 1934, NA, KV2/ 2010 2S1020.
44. Letter, 14 June 1940, NA, KV2/ 2010 2S1020.
45. Letter, 5 June 1940, NA, KV2/ 2010 2S1020.
46. Letter from Scottish Regional Security Officer, Major P. Perfect to Miss R. Retallack, Oxford, 15 February 1942, NA, KV2/ 2010 2S1020. Grieve lectured to the Scottish Secretariat Study Group on 'Postwar Scotland – The Struggle to Live', concentrating on 'The Position of Scottish Culture', on 22 March 1942 (Glasgow Police report, 12 March 1942), and to the same group, in commemoration of the Declaration of Arbroath, on 5 April 1942 (Special Branch report, 10 April 1942), NA, KV2/ 2010 2S1020.
47. Letter from Major P. Perfect to Miss R. Retallack, 24 February 1942, NA, KV2/ 2010 2S1020.
48. Letter from C. M. Grieve to James R. B. Christie, Secretary of the National Council for Civil Liberties, 28 April 1941, NA, KV2/ 2010 2S1020.
49. For proof of the truth of MacDiarmid's contention that some among the British aristocracy were indeed supporters of Nazism see Laura Thompson, *Life in a Cold Climate: Nancy Mitford: A Portrait of a Contradictory Woman* (London: Review, 2003).
50. See Richard J. Finlay, *Modern Scotland 1914–2000* (London: Profile, 2004), plate 8.

51. See *NSL*, letter 89, p. 143.
52. NLS MS27065/ 36.62.
53. Letter from Major P. Perfect to R. Brooman-White, 6 June 1941, NA, KV2/ 2010 2S1020.
54. W. H. Auden, 'September 1, 1939', *Selected Poems*, ed. Edward Mendelson (London: Faber & Faber, 1979), p. 86.
55. Auden, 'Sir, no man's enemy, forgiving all/But will his negative inversion, be prodigal . . . Harrow the house of the dead; look shining at/New styles of architecture, a change of heart.' ('Petition'); 'In Memory of W. B. Yeats', *The English Auden: Poems, Essays and Dramatic Writings 1927–1939*, ed. Edward Mendelson (London: Faber & Faber, 1986), pp. 36; 242.
56. Auden, 'In Memory of W. B. Yeats', *The English Auden*, p. 242.
57. See Liv Kjørsvik Schei and Gunnie Moberg, *The Shetland Story* (London: Batsford, 1988), p. 104.
58. See John R. Baldwin (ed.), *Scandinavian Shetland: An Ongoing Tradition?* (Edinburgh: Scottish Society for Northern Studies, 1978), p. 30.
59. See Callum G. Brown, *Up-helly aa: Custom, Culture and Community in Shetland* (Manchester: Mandolin, 1998), p. 162.
60. Arthur Rimbaud, *Collected Poems*, trans. Oliver Bernard (Harmondsworth: Penguin, 1986), p. 346.
61. See Smith, in *MacDiarmid in Shetland*, p. 60.
62. Whalsay History Group.
63. Christopher Harvie, *Fool's Gold: The Story of North Sea Oil* (London: Hamish Hamilton, 1994), p. 172.
64. Whalsay History Group.
65. Anthony P. Cohen, 'A Sense of Time, A Sense of Place: The Meaning of Close Social Association in Whalsay, Shetland', in Anthony P. Cohen (ed.), *Belonging: Identity and Social Organisation in British Rural Culture* (Manchester: Manchester University Press, 1982), p. 38.
66. Ibid., p. 24; see, also, Anthony P. Cohen, *Whalsay: Symbol, Segment and Boundary in a Shetland Island Community* (Manchester: Manchester University Press, 1987).
67. See Smith, in *MacDiarmid in Shetland*, pp. 60–1; also, *NSL*, letter 114, pp. 165–6.
68. W. R. Aitken, interviewed by Brian Smith, Dunblane, SA3/1/331/1&2, 1, pp. 4, 15.
69. Christopher Caudwell, *Illusion and Reality: A Study of the Sources of Poetry* (London: Lawrence and Wishart, 1973), p. 57.
70. Pseudonym of William Gillies (1865–1932), Liam Mac'Ille Iosa was born in Galloway, but brought up in London where his father was a merchant banker. Co-leader of the Scots National League with Erskine of Marr, he was involved in Fianna na h-Alba, a group that planned military action for the political liberation of Scotland.
71. Andrew Gurr, *Writers in Exile: The Identity of Home in Modern Literature* (Sussex: Harvester, 1981), p. 14.
72. Richard Davenport-Hines, *Auden* (London: Heinemann, 1995), p. 52.
73. Auden, 'Song for the New Year', in Robin Skelton (ed.), *Poetry of the Thirties* (Harmondsworth: Penguin, 2000), p. 47.

74. Martin Green, *Children of the Sun: A Narrative of 'Decadence' in England after 1918* (London: Constable, 1977), p. 332.
75. Auden, *The Orators, The English Auden*, p. 59.
76. Auden, 'The Prolific and the Devourer', *The English Auden*, p. 399.
77. C. Day Lewis, 'The Conflict', in *Poetry of the Thirties*, p. 200.
78. Ibid., p. 200.
79. Caudwell, *Illusion and Reality*, p. 70.
80. Neal Wood, *Communism and British Intellectuals* (London: Victor Gollancz, 1959), p. 217.
81. See G. S. Smith, *D. S. Mirsky: A Russian–English Life, 1890–1939* (Oxford: Oxford University Press, 2000).
82. 'Why I Rejoined', *Daily Worker*, 28 March 1957, p. 2; cited in Bold, *MacDiarmid*, p. 411.
83. For an analysis of the similarities between these beliefs see Edwin Muir, 'Bolshevism and Calvinism' (1934), in Andrew Noble (ed.), *Edwin Muir: Uncollected Scottish Criticism* (London & Totowa, NJ: Vision and Barnes & Noble, 1982), pp. 123–30.

Chapter 5

'Ootward Boond Frae Scotland': MacDiarmid, Modernism and the Masses

High modernism was cosmopolitan and elitist. Many of its canonical literary artists left their country of birth, seeking in foreign metropolises for new experimental perspectives that they believed could not be envisioned in the philistine provinces of home. In *A Portrait of the Artist as a Young Man* (1916), James Joyce sends Stephen Dedalus into Continental exile 'to forge in the smithy of my soul the uncreated conscience of my race'.[1] Intended to 'Hellenize Ireland',[2] the linguistically intimidating modernism of Joyce's *Ulysses* (1922) was a pan-European creation, written in Trieste, Zurich and Paris between 1914 and 1921. Born in St Louis in 1888, T. S. Eliot travelled to England looking for knowledge and experience, searching also for the traditional culture he thought lacking in the United States. Ironically, European civilisation was in the process of being fragmented not only by the Great War but also by the American populism from which the Harvard- and Oxford-educated poet wished to flee. Eliot's idea that the centres of Western culture cannot hold – the 'Falling towers' of 'Jerusalem Athens Alexandria / Vienna London' are 'Unreal' – is of regret to a modernist concerned with upholding conservative values.[3] Ezra Pound was born in Idaho in 1885 but moved to London in 1909 in a cultural bid to 'MAKE IT NEW'.[4] He established Imagism in 1912 with H. D. and Richard Aldington, and coedited the influential Vorticist review *BLAST* with fellow radical reactionary Wyndham Lewis before being attracted to Italy by Mussolini's Fascism.

Christopher Schedler confirms that 'modernism is a metropolitan art, a product of the same forces that produced the modern metropolis',[5] those shaping forces being chiefly industrialisation, global capitalism, technological progress and imperialism. Schedler contends that, alienated by the conflicting and competing identities of the hostile urban world of the metropolis, an exiled modernist such as the early Eliot reaffirms his self through the development of a depersonalised art that refuses recognition of the Other. To radicalise Schedler's argument, Eliot was reacting against the metropolitan masses created by capitalist industrialisation. If the universalised Self is equated with the metropolis of the imperial core and the Other is the colony, then the capitalist power that captures the periphery also universally colonises the masses.

Living for most of the 1920s and '30s in the marginal locations of Montrose and Whalsay, MacDiarmid decentres the geography of exilic metropolitan modernism by creating work of continuing international importance whilst remaining resolutely national, declaring in *Scottish Scene*: 'I have no faith in these young men who flee to London or Paris. If anything of consequence to Scottish literature is to be done it will be done by young writers living in Scotland' ('Edinburgh', *SS*, 93–4). Calculatedly rooted, it is this geopolitical marginality that enables MacDiarmid's critique of the metropolitan fabrication of capitalist mass culture.

Whilst ostensibly sharing many of the elitist modes of metropolitan modernism, the internationally radical alignment of MacDiarmid's Scottish Republicanism locates his relation to the masses in a different ideological home. MacDiarmid was a self-declared cultural elitist, yet also a lifelong socialist. He believed that high art could be produced only by the few, while desiring that such art should be presented directly to the many. MacDiarmid the modernist mandarin of the working class and socialist elitist may sound like a contradictory position; indeed, the inconsistencies apparent in such a stance are usually assumed to be the ideological transgressions of a poet of Whitmanesque propensities. But, in actuality, the dialectical distortions, the apparent contradictions of MacDiarmid's political position *vis-à-vis* modernist elitism inhere in the fluctuating nature of market capitalism and its mass culture and are not the essence of the poet's politics and personality. Writing high art from the peripheries, MacDiarmid's poetic journey from the elect irrationalism of *A Drunk Man Looks at the Thistle* through the mystical communism of the 'Hymns to Lenin' to the hieratic materialism of *In Memoriam James Joyce* shows the poet's evolving awareness of the ideological shortcomings of elitist metropolitan modernism and his attempt to understand and combat the economic and political forces underpinning such alienated reaction.

Born in 1892, MacDiarmid entered the world and grew to maturity during a time of rapid societal change, particularly in education. According to John Carey 'the difference between the nineteenth-century mob and the twentieth-century mass is literacy'.[6] Carey cites Bernard Shaw's complaint that the 1871 Education Act (1872 in Scotland) created new readers seemingly uninterested in the cultural products of the intelligentsia. Instead, they would turn to mass circulation newspapers such as the *Daily Mail* (established by Lord Northcliffe in 1896) for informative entertainment. Considering his rural, working-class background, MacDiarmid would have been an obvious beneficiary of the drive to increase literacy and extend educational opportunities. Like many other modernists, however, the autodidact poet was uneasy about the cultural consequences of a compulsory education.

Carey argues that 'the principle around which modernist literature and culture fashioned themselves was the exclusion of the masses, the defeat of their power, the removal of their literacy, the denial of their humanity'.[7] The intellectual and artist, confronted with the loss of their authority under a system of universal education, regain cultural pre-eminence by separating themselves from the masses; the modernist now possesses individuality of a special, qualitative kind, while the mass, sheer quantity by definition, lacking determination and form except that given it by the intellectual, is Other. This has clear anti-democratic political implications. If the majority does not consist of individuals, but is only an amorphous creation of the intellectual minority, then the majority can very easily be ignored or moulded to suit the political dictates of an elite.

The intellectual invention of *hoi polloi* is as old as Western culture itself. Elitism is eminent in the rule of the philosopher-king in Plato's *Republic*, for instance. Under capitalism the exclusion of the vulgar masses has remained synonymous with high cultural praxis. Coleridge's clerisy functioned as an elite to defend the timeless value of the spirit against the unpredictability of massive material change. Carlyle saw the 'Sign of the Times' in 1829 as being the incompatibility of culture with the ordinary lives of most of the population. Matthew Arnold's *Culture and Anarchy* was published in 1869 at the height of industrialisation and only two years after the Second Reform Act in England (Scotland's came in 1868). Converting social divisions into cultural distinctions, Arnold 'seeks to do away with classes; to make the best that has been thought and known in the world current everywhere' through the 'inward spiritual activity' of art.[8] Written as a polemical attempt to unify Britain at a time of class discord Arnold's work posits culture as a means to an understanding of 'our best self' that in turn 'suggests the idea of *the State*'.[9]

T. S. Eliot is the modernist inheritor of this anti-industrial conservative tradition.[10] With the decline in importance of Christianity under contemporary capitalism, Eliot's cultural wasteland has become a definitive modernist trope. Culture for Eliot is 'that which makes life worth living'.[11] Through the degeneration of religion, however, culture is failing to develop. Consequently, the cultured, those who in Eliot's elitist society naturally become members of 'the dominant class', will experience a waning of their power.[12] In compensatory response for this loss of authority, and in a bid to regain it, the cultural elite depicts those who do not share their traditional values, and who neither understand nor care that Western civilisation is in decline, as being spiritually and intellectually dead:

Under the brown fog of a winter dawn,
A crowd flowed over London Bridge, so many,
I had not thought death had undone so many.[13]

Michael Tratner's claim that 'modernism was an effort to escape the limitations of nineteenth-century individualist conventions and write about distinctively "collectivist" phenomena' fails to address the almost pathologically negative attitude of modernists such as Eliot to the masses.[14] Eliot wrote *The Waste Land* after a nervous collapse that necessitated psychotherapy.[15] Given the poem's centrality to modernism, questions arise as to the nature of the highly individualised artistic personality and the modernist imagination. Carey pinpoints the importance of Nietzsche's thought to many modernists, yet the German was a lonely, almost pathetic, figure plagued by bad health who eventually succumbed to insanity. Does 'illness act as a short cut to reality',[16] creating a seer cut off from ordinary humanity? Or, as Cyril Connolly asks of Pascal and Leopardi, 'did their deformities encourage the herd to treat them thoughtlessly, and so create in them a pejorative impression of human nature?'[17] The very terms of Connolly's question suggest that the philosopher and poet stand above 'the herd', in spite of their 'deformities'. In attempting to define how an artist or 'highbrow' is created, W. H. Auden suggests, 'we only think when we are prevented from feeling or acting as we should like',[18] thus echoing the Freudian view of the creator as neurotic. He proceeds with the acidic comment that 'most people, however, fit into society too neatly for the stimulus to arise except in a crisis such as falling in love or losing their money'.[19] For Auden, ordinary people never think except when their own interests are at stake; disinterested thought can only come from the real intelligentsia. But if the artist and thinker are a 'self-elected elect' cut off from society,[20] made different by their powers of perception, what exactly is their value for those who 'fit into society too neatly'? Does the intelligentsia merely speak to itself?

The Self-Elected Elect

For the intellectual of the self-elected elect culture has a quasi-religious mission, one aphorised by MacDiarmid in 'Art and the Unknown': 'The function of art is the extension of human consciousness' (*SP*, 39). For this spiritual evolutionist 'art is therefore the most important of human activities; all others are dependent upon it'. (*SP*, 39). First appearing in the *New Age* in 1926, the essay strikes a characteristically modernist note: 'Comprehensibility is error: Art is beyond understanding.' (*SP*, 39). Or at least, it is beyond understanding for the masses: 'If great art is compatible with big popular appeal, it can only be in so far as it contains elements unthinkable to the public' (*SP*, 41). For MacDiarmid, ' "Popular art" is a contradiction in terms' (*SP*, 42).

'Art and the Unknown' could stand as a prose manifesto for *A Drunk Man* published in the same year, a modernist poem constituted by many similar ideas as to the almost religious importance of art and its impenetrability to the masses. *A Drunk Man* maps the modernist dislocation of a post-imperial Scotland, examining the nation's sick soul through the disordered senses of its artist-saviour. It is the overly sensitive Drunk Man, made separate from others by his advanced consciousness, who acts as Scotland's psychological barometer, not the unselfconscious masses. Exercising an intellectual irrationalism that, paradoxically, enables him the more fully to discern a transcendent reality, in his search for a metaphysical Scotland the Drunk Man claims to 'stert whaur the philosophers leave aff' (*CP1*, 87).

The Drunk Man begins his odyssey in quest of the absolute by wrestling with Presbyterianism and its cultural and political consequences in the wasteland of modern Scotland. In the process, he betrays his own Calvinist inheritance through his elect attitude to his fellow nationals and the national culture. The real Scotland has lost its spirit and has been buried underneath the dross of a fake tourist culture. Even Scotland's most famous export, whisky, has been watered down, and now 'the stuffie's no' the real Mackay' (*CP1*, 83). Whisky is a metaphor for the deplorable condition of a nation from which the essence has been stripped to benefit others, leaving Scotland 'destitute o' speerit' (*CP1*, 83). It is the Drunk Man's self-imposed task to expose this counterfeit culture in order 'To prove my saul is Scots' (*CP1*, 83). He will do so by treating of 'what's still deemed Scots and the folk expect', such as whisky and Burns, before moving on to 'heichts whereo' the fules ha'e never recked' (*CP1*, 83). For the Drunk Man searching for the essential nation and its worthy inhabitant, the metaphysical Scot, '*Sic transit gloria Scotiae*' (*CP1*, 84) – all the cultural glories of pre-Reformation Scotland have passed away to be replaced by the populist Kailyard offerings of Presbyterian ministers and the canny music-hall caricature of a Scot, 'Harry Lauder (to enthrall us)' (*CP1*, 164).

In a metaphysical poem soaked with references to Christ and Calvary, the visionary Drunk Man is clearly in thrall to his Calvinist formation. However, his elect superiority leaves him somewhat at odds with his Scottish environment and its myth of Burnsian egalitarianism. MacDiarmid's elitism signifies an attempt to dismember within himself the spiritual remnants of a Calvinist Christianity, inherited from his Langholm childhood, that bears resemblance to Burnsian socialism:

> O gin they'd stegh their guts and haud their wheesht   [*stuff*]
> I'd thole it, for 'a man's a man' I ken,
> But though the feck ha'e plenty o' 'a' that',   [*majority*]
> They're nocht but zoologically men.
>
> (*CP1*, 85)

According to David McCrone, 'In the Scottish myth, the central motif is the inherent egalitarianism of the Scots.'[21] McCrone analyses Burns's 'Is There for Honesty Poverty', arguing that the poem

> seems to strip away the differences which are essentially social constructions. In spite of these (the 'a' that'), Burns is saying, people are equal. His meaning of equality is, however, ambiguous. He is calling not for a levelling down of riches, but for a proper, that is, moral appreciation of 'the man o' independent mind'. It is 'pith o' sense and pride o' worth' which matter, not the struttings and starings of 'yon birkie ca'd a lord'. The ambiguity of his message is retained to the last stanza – 'that man to man the world o'er shall brothers be for a' that' – an appeal to the virtues of fraternity rather than equality in its strict sense.[22]

What McCrone understands to be the 'ambiguity' of Burns's poem is mirrored in the paradoxical nature of Calvinism. On the one hand, it inculcates a spirit of equality in its adherents; on the other, it predestines some to salvation while damning the rest. MacDiarmid's sense of elect superiority – in part a psychological mechanism to compensate for an inferiority complex connected to his feelings about his self-repressed nation – would leave him impatient with the concept of fraternity. As W. N. Herbert points out, 'the antisyzygy which most fiercely powered' MacDiarmid's life and writing was 'love and revulsion for himself and for his nation'.[23] If MacDiarmid is one of the elect then he is free to 'adopt a thorough antinomian attitude' towards 'all sorts of vibrantly commonplace people' (*LP*, 78), particularly the majority of post-Union Scots scorned by the Drunk Man:

> To save your souls fu' mony o' ye are fain,
> But deil a dizzen to mak' it worth the daen'.
> I widna gi'e five meenits wi' Dunbar
> For a' the millions o' ye as ye are.
>
> (*CP1*, 107)

As well as thinking it one of Burns's poorer pieces, hardly meriting its world renown, MacDiarmid deplored the 'A Man's a Man for a' That' egalitarian attitude of chummy ordinariness associated not only with the poem but more generally with Scottish identity:

Keep all your 'kindly brither Scots,'
Your little happinesses,
Your popular holiday resorts,
Your damned democracy.

('The North Face of Liathach', *CP2*, 1055)

For MacDiarmid, such 'damned democracy' retards Scotland's intellectual and artistic development by keeping genius at the same level as the merely talented in a spirit akin to the 'I kent his faither' syndrome. The cost of such egalitarianism is, however, greater than the price of mere personal put down – it implies the inability or unwillingness to produce and nurture a national intelligentsia, an elite of cultural workers. This 'determined "preference for the inferior"' ('Burns Today and Tomorrow', *A*, 207) is not specific to Burns but rather his cult:

The excessive futilities which have accompanied this cult are without parallel in the history of the world. Nations whose history has been starred with relays of men of poetic genius as great or greater than Burns have not allowed their significance to run to sand in this way – even if, at the very worst, they have had, in respect of this or that poet, a crop of antiquaries and bibliographers and biographers and marginalists of all kinds, at least all of them have had a powerful cultured class, a dominant intelligentsia, able to secure for each genius in turn his proper setting and an adequate valuation based on the essentials of his work, and thus to ensure his due influence. Their quality is not obscured and their force dissipated by hordes of mediocrities. Literature in these countries has its standards and its definite sphere and functions. It is only in Scotland where there are no cultural standards – where there is little love or appreciation of literature – that so grotesque a travesty of literary honour could have developed itself. What would Burns himself think of it all? ('The Burns Cult (I)', *CSS*, 354)

The Burns cult is the cultural detritus of a provincialised Anglo-Scotland unable to develop an intelligentsia of its own. The final question, though rhetorical, has the implicit answer: the same as MacDiarmid, advocate of the self-elected elect.

Like many modernists, such as the youthful Edwin Muir's elitist pseudonym Edward Moore in *We Moderns* (1918),[24] MacDiarmid found inspiration for his elect persona in the work of Nietzsche. According to Bruce Detwiler, the goal of humanity for Nietzsche is the production of the highest type of human being, the 'cultural aristocrat' such as himself.[25] Nietzsche opposes politically equalising, spiritually levelling forces in the form of Christianity and liberal democracy as favouring the many against the few. The elite of cultural workers who produce the future through their will to creative power can have nothing to say to those of mob mind and spirit, who require the anti-evolutionary state protection of democracy to save them from necessary extinction. When Nietzsche does tentatively approve of the democratic process it is in the hope of provoking an 'aristocratic countermovement' that will squash the interests of the masses.[26] Correspondingly, Nietzsche's fear of socialism is such that he deceptively endorses democratic reforms as a means of pacifying potentially radical workers' action. Nietzsche did not live to see the rise of National Socialism in Germany but Detwiler draws a parallel between his 'willingness to aestheticize politics' and fascism.[27] Nietzsche's appeal to modernist artists, such as D. H. Lawrence, Wyndham Lewis and MacDiarmid, lay not only in the central role given to them as the self-elected elect in his politically absolutist society, but also in his atheistic proposition that 'it is only as an aesthetic phenomenon that existence and the world are eternally justified'.[28] After the death of God, the artist is a replacement god giving life to a new system of values propounded in the religion of culture.

Many of the *New Age* Nietzscheans of the early 1920s were actually political progressives and Guild Socialists, such as the Edwin Muir of *Latitudes* (1924), who believes that Nietzsche 'brought a new atmosphere into European thought'.[29] *A Drunk Man* seeks to apply such modernist values to expressly Scottish circumstances. What John Burt Foster calls the 'polaristic thinking' of Nietzsche's Apollonian–Dionysian dualism informs MacDiarmid's version of the Caledonian antisyzygy: as Nietzsche attempts the realisation of a balanced human psyche, so MacDiarmid seeks to balance Anglo-created distortions within a provincialised Scottish polity.[30] Viewing the over-concentration in Scotland on the omnipresent figure of Burns and the cult made of his person and democratic ideals as a danger to the future health of the culture, in 'Towards a Scottish Renaissance' (1929) MacDiarmid insists that 'aristocratic standards must be re-erected. We in Scotland have been too long grotesquely over-democratised. What is wanted now is a species of Scottish Fascism' (*RT2*, 80). In Montrose, MacDiarmid wrote 'Plea for a Scottish Fascism' and 'Programme for a Scottish Fascism' for the *Scottish Nation* in 1923. In 'Plea' he argues that 'Scottish Fascism will spring naturally from the Left' (*RT1*, 84). 'Programme' synchronises socialism with a national awakening that 'sets the spiritual above the material' (*SP*, 35). This aristocratic Gaelic extremism seeks to neutralise the baneful political effect on an undemocratic Scottish polity of Labour Unionism and its cultural concomitant, the philistine Burns cult.

In much of his writing on Burns MacDiarmid adroitly employs a triune process similar to that of Nietzsche in relation to Christ: disavowal, identification, succession. Like Christianity, the Burns cult acts as a false interpreter, seeking to dilute the sheer difficulty of the ideals espoused by the individual of genius in order to allow for easy application in the lives of the mediocre many. In *A Drunk Man* Burns and Christ are linked as Nietzschean *Übermenschen*, each hailed as contributors to the spiritual evolution of humanity yet suffering from the mob mentality of their followers:

A greater Christ, a greater Burns, may come.
The maist they'll dae is to gi'e bigger pegs
To folly and conceit to hank their rubbish on.
They'll cheenge folks' talk but no' their natures, fegs!

(*CP1*, 86)

That the Drunk Man-poet dies in order that Scotland may be reborn is not only Christ-like but reminiscent of Nietzsche's *The Birth of Tragedy* (1872) in which the self-sacrifice of the Dionysian creative hero allows the collectivity to live in Apollonian order. MacDiarmid adapts Nietzsche's eternal recurrence to suggest that the lives of most newborn children are worthless since, unlike Christ, they will contribute nothing to spiritual progress or the extension of consciousness:

Millions o' wimmen bring forth in pain
Millions o' bairns that are no' worth ha'en'.

Wull ever a wumman be big again
Wi's muckle's a Christ? Yech, there's nae sayin'.

(*CP1*, 103)

Such elitism revolves around MacDiarmid's spiritual evolutionism, his desire that Scotland and humanity be better than at present, finding a goal, religious in scope yet of earthly application. Reversing Christian ethics, Nietzsche's 'commandment: *will* a self and thou shalt *become* a self', in order that 'you should become him who you are' envisages elite humans transcending the democratic commonality.[31] Far from being drunk on the applause of the crowd, the Drunk Man praises the solitary unpopularity of genius; happy to be unhappy and follow 'The road that led me past / Humanity sae fast', he is able to construct his own values since freeing himself 'frae the dominion / O' popular opinion' (*CP1*, 141). For the Drunk Man, living in the post-imperial flux of a Scotland with neither a continuing universal mission abroad nor democratic political control at home, the only hope of a *becoming* nation lies with individual self-realisation along Nietzschean lines:

> And let the lesson be – to be yersel's,
> Ye needna fash gin it's to be ocht else.   [*bother*]
> To be yersel's – and to mak' that worth bein'.
> Nae harder job to mortals has been gi'en.

> (*CP1*, 107)

Equating the Drunk Man's 'root-hewn Scottis soul' (*CP1*, 95) with the fractured soul of modernity, the metaphysical value system of the poem owes as much to the self-hating irrationalism of what Peter McCarey calls Dostoevsky's 'splintered psychology' as it does to the spiritual evolutionism of the radically aristocratic Nietzsche.[32] For Nietzsche, Dostoevsky was the great psychologist, taking brilliant estimate of the unfathomable human heart; for the Drunk Man, he is the '*Christ o' the neist thoosand years*' (*CP1*, 139). Like Nietzsche, MacDiarmid values Dostoevsky because he licenses vitally individualistic vision. Dostoevskian characters such as the irrationalist anti-hero, the 'sick' and 'angry man' of *Notes from Underground*, help create the Drunk Man as seer.[33] When the 'self-tormented spirit' (*CP1*, 105) of the Drunk Man turns 'to debauchery and dirt, / And to disease and daith' (*CP1*, 128) he mimics the loser-wins posture of Dostoevsky, that which Sartre was to apportion to the psychosomatically sick Flaubert, *l'idiot de la famille*.[34] Such a gamble entails the assumption of a mystical life-in-death faith that enables its bearer to fully experience the tragic sense of life in people and nations, to painfully see what the many, who are dead to life, can never imagine: the awaited heaven of artistic posterity.

So the Drunk Man asks, 'What are prophets and priests and kings, / What's ocht to the people o' Scotland?' (*CP1*, 108). For the seer, the ordinary see nothing but themselves; like the self-important and circumscribed talk of rural 'ploomen in a pub', the populations of Edinburgh and Glasgow 'want to hear o' naething / But their ain foul hubbub' (*CP1*, 108). Even with his extreme self-consciousness, however, the Drunk Man rationalises that 'The fules are richt; an extra thocht / Is neither here nor there' (*CP1*, 108). He comes to 'envy' the uncultured 'rude health', the limited perception of the ploughmen Cruivie and Gilsanquhar that saves them from the 'curse' of the visionary: the 'gnawin' canker' (*CP1*, 108) of an intellect diseased through the exacerbation of comprehension that yet breeds the soul that separates the self-elected elect from the mob. The irrationalist makes a virtue out of being in the wrong, that place of creative contradiction 'whaur / Extremes meet', the better to look down on the pitiful spectacle of 'the curst conceit o' bein' richt / That damns the vast majority o' men' (*CP1*, 87). On an inner voyage 'ootward boond frae Scotland', the Drunk Man 'has shipped aboord Eternity' (*CP1*, 100).

Yet in spite of the elitism of the visionary Drunk Man seeing through the void that is Scotland, he uses his powers to prophesy the spiritual evolution of humanity, believing that 'organs may develop syne / Responsive to the need divine / O' single-minded humankin' (*CP1*, 163). The task of developed consciousness is to use the visionary mysticism that has probed 'man's benmaist hert', the mystery of the inner world, in order 'To bring what lies withoot to licht' (*CP1*, 163). It is the 'function' of 'Poetry' to effect 'that unity' (*CP1*, 163) of ruptured subject and object, so constantly recreating the meaning of life. Only the poet as Christ can achieve this task, the sacrificial artist conjoined with mystic as spiritual evolutionist. As MacDiarmid states in 'Art and the Unknown': 'The ideal observer of art – as against art-at-work – is God, conscious of all that has been and *will* be achieved' (*SP*, 39). After such knowledge as the Drunk Man has reaped from his spiritual odyssey only Silence is left, and the descent of the self-elected elect to rejoin common humanity.

MacDiarmid's metaphysical Scotland, his equation of home with the winning to God's perfection, derives from his Calvinistic outrage at what he sees as a lack of spiritual growth in the majority and a concomitant feeling of elect superiority that he belongs to the few who have or can spiritually evolve:

> Aye, this is Calvary – to bear
> Your Cross wi'in you frae the seed,
> And feel it grow by slow degrees
> Until it rends your flesh apairt,
> And turn, and see your fellow-men
> In similar case but sufferin' less
> Thro' bein' mair wudden frae the stert! . . .
>
> (*CP1*, 134)

Born a Calvinist, the Drunk Man spiritually comprehends the physical agony and metaphysical torment of the crucified Christ and knows that such suffering symbolises humanity's lot. However, the elect modernist poet, infected with a double dose of elitism, believes himself to suffer more than ordinary Scots, particularly in a Calvinist culture that he considers artistically sterile. Arguably, it is not the so-called fractures of the nation's history or the philistine nullity of Calvinism that create a cultural vacuum, but an absolutist MacDiarmid in pursuit of a metaphysical Scotland. This vision, synchronous, as it can only be, with the failure of Scotland to fulfil such an impossible ideal in reality, accordingly empowers the poet to redeem the nation through his saviour-like presence. In this reading, MacDiarmid's essentialised nation is a warped fiction transgressing the bounds of historical actuality. Mirroring the schizoid colonial psyche he wishes to make whole, his insistence that modern Scottish identity is defectively divided arises from his own contradictoriness and is both a mirror of and a contributory factor to the Scottish cringe that many post-MacDiarmid Scottish intellectuals have worked so hard to dispel.

Tom Nairn describes *A Drunk Man* as 'that great national poem on the impossibility of nationalism'.[35] It is, rather, a postcolonial epic of self-hate and longing for that which cannot be imagined in a parochialised Scotland: a nation beyond the need of nationalism. With the Scottish masses evincing the aboulic soul of the colonial, MacDiarmid creates a metaphysical Scot, a Nietzschean figure, a Dionysian Calvinist if you like, who will reveal the nation's true historical destiny. His elect spiritual evolutionism, inherited from the very Calvinism that the Drunk Man repudiates, envisions an eternalised nation transcending the Unionist Scottish wasteland – this Eliotian idea being, in any case, a metropolitan malady indicative of waning cultural and political predominance. The Drunk Man's journey from the particularity of a marginalised, oppressed local culture to the healing mystical totality of the universal is later found in Aimé Césaire's postcolonial poem *Cahier d'un retour au pays natal* (*Notebook of a Return to the Native Land* – completed in 1939, but not published in full until 1947). In *A Drunk Man*, from the bones of a defunct imperial Scotland with its sick colonial soul, a metaphysical nation arises.

As he moves from the evolutionary optimism of *A Drunk Man* to the defeated Celticism of *To Circumjack Cencrastus*, MacDiarmid begins to understand that the irrationalism on which he has relied to lead Scotland from its provincialised state is a symptom of the capitalist disorder that alienates the visionary poet from the masses. Reaching creative crisis in *Cencrastus*, he glimpses the possibility that his religious conception of the evolutionary importance of culture is the ineffectual vanity of the solitary brusquely challenged by the sheer banality of life with its necessity of earning a living. The visionary poet believes the masses to be politically responsible for their own intellectual and cultural servitude, and in moments of despair at his grand evolutionary design he fears improvement to be impossible:

> It's waesome that millions s'ud be cut off
> Frae Art, like the Neanderthal brutes at large
> When Plato raised his een to Socrates

And heard his haly virtuosities.
But what's to dae? We micht as weel grieve owre
Beasts no' bein' able to read, and seek to teach,
As waste the energies that can address
Their mental betters on the mass o' men.

(CP1, 229)

The harried *Montrose Review* reporter curses all that compels him to 'pretend or feel / That life as maist folk hae't is real' (*CP1*, 236), yet admits that 'Pars aboot meetins', weddins, sermons, a' / The crude events o' life-in-the-raw' (234) are more important to the majority than 'this poetry stuff' (235). The superiority complex of his spiritual evolutionism and creator's hubris jar with the undoubted unpopularity of his elitist work: 'I canna gie the folk hokum' (*CP1*, 252). Subordinate to his materialistic boss, and 'the system that can gie / A coof like this control o' me' (*CP1*, 235), he questions the final and financial worth of his art, undauntedly deciding that '*the purpose o' poetry*' is '*to cairry us as faur as ever it can / 'Yont nature and the Common Man*' (255).

At the time of the composition of *Cencrastus*, MacDiarmid garnered strength for his socialist elitism from American historian James Harvey Robinson's bestseller *The Mind in the Making: The Relation of Intelligence to Social Reform* (1921).[36] Cofounder in 1919 of the New School for Social Research in New York and a leading proponent of 'New History', which emphasised social, scientific and intellectual rather than political progress, Robinson was critical of capitalism, particularly the impact on high culture of America's burgeoning consumer and business ethos. Robinson's book appealed to MacDiarmid for its Nietzschean attempt to bring ideological and ethical values in line with scientific discovery and material advances. As Nietzsche pilloried the nineteenth-century attachment to Christian ethics in a materialist age in which a belief in God had died, so Robinson argues in favour of 'bringing the mind up to date' (*MM*, 11) with the technological realities of modernity. Writing as A. L. for the *Scottish Educational Journal* of 19 September 1930, MacDiarmid utilises Robinson's book to confirm his evolutionary belief 'that mankind has barely begun to think yet, what is commonly regarded as thinking being almost entirely a process of rationalising very dubiously derived preconceptions' ('Literature and the Occult', *RT2*, 242).

For Robinson, paradigmatic shifts from old ways of thinking to radical new standards have been achieved in the past by a minority possessed of 'exceptional intellectual venturesomeness' (*MM*, 83). His book is a call for like-minded individuals in the present to transform the world through the power of creative thought and genius. According to

Robinson, 'the great mass of humanity', of whatever historical era, have simply sat back and accepted the intellectual fruit of 'a very small number of peculiarly restless and adventurous spirits' (*MM*, 56). In a highly MacDiarmidian passage, Robinson asserts his elitist credo: 'Creative intelligence is confined to the very few, but the many can thoughtlessly avail themselves of the more obvious achievements of those who are exceptionally highly endowed. Even an ape will fit himself into a civilized environment' (*MM*, 56). An academic exposition of the formation of an elitist creative imagination, *The Mind in the Making* would have appealed to the instinct for Romantic self-invention in MacDiarmid as the solitary, heroic artist ranged against the ignorant masses. In lines set to music by Ronald Stevenson, the poet of *Cencrastus* believes that the unacknowledged legislation of his art improves the vulgar multitude its beauty eludes:

Better a'e gowden lyric
The mob'll never ken
For this in the last resort
Mak's them less apes, mair men,
And leads their leaders albeit
They're owre blin' to see it.

(*CP1*, 266)

Robinson's book licenses the direction of the many through the ideas of the few. Like MacDiarmid, Robinson assumes that it is the cultural producers who transform the world, rather than that their creations reflect changes already happening in and through material development. As such, the argument of both poet and historian – that culture extends consciousness, which in turn creates more culture, and that this is *a priori* a good thing – is merely circular, leading, like MacDiarmid's Curly Snake of *Cencrastus*, nowhere but back to the self, the spiritual superiority of the elect cultural producer. Finding his spiritual nadir at the mid-point of the poem, MacDiarmid sees the social futility of his elect creativity:

Progress? There is nae progress; nor sall be,
The cleverest men aye find oot again
For foolish mobs that follow to forget,
As in the Past, the knowledge men ha'e haen
At stented periods frae the dawn o' Time: [*certain*]
And Sisyphus anew begins his climb.

(*CP1*, 243)

The final line signals his willingness to start afresh, be reborn to a new credo. Still refusing to discard his spiritual evolutionism, yet attempting to disentangle himself from the individualistic irrationalism of *A Drunk Man*, MacDiarmid now puts his faith in the 'Unconscious goal of history, dimly seen / In Genius whiles that kens the problem o' its age / And works at it' (*CP1*, 287). MacDiarmid's communism is born of the struggle between the alienated irrationalism bred from the forces of capitalism seeking to short-circuit consciousness and his new belief that the consummating genius of History will defeat the mental limits imposed by 'the High Treason to mankind' of capitalist instrumental reason ('Third Hymn to Lenin', *CP2*, 899). As MacDiarmid left Montrose for Depression London, then industrial Liverpool and on to the poverty of Whalsay in the 1930s, a metaphysical Scotland must have seemed more like a bourgeois fantasy than a political necessity.

Many of the ideas of the self-elected elect would seem to belong on the political right, veering towards the fascistic, despite MacDiarmid's protestation in 1923 of the leftist origins of a Scottish fascism. The cultural aristocracy of Nietzsche combined with Dostoevsky's reactionary irrationalism create a MacDiarmidian spiritual evolutionism that owes much to his Calvinist heritage and resembles extreme *laissez-faire* right-wing economics applied to spirituality – to the 'strong' go the glittering prizes, the 'weak' be damned. However, MacDiarmid's communism does not necessarily contradict the modernist irrationalism of *A Drunk Man*. Writing to William Soutar (1898–1943) from Whalsay on 2 August 1937, Grieve tells the bedridden poet – with whom he planned to write a book of lyric poems entitled *The Commons of Scotland* – that nothing in communism is undermining of the singularity of their vocation, and, like a cadre of communist leaders, poets should 'undertake the responsibility of self-electing themselves (or being elected by their exceptional faculties) as the mouthpieces of their peoples' (*L*, 162). Describing himself in *Lucky Poet* as 'the extremes of High Tory and Communist meeting' (*LP*, 4), there are certain similarities in MacDiarmid's conception of these seemingly antagonistic positions. Each is an authoritarian, highbrow project that sees the real enemy as the philistine bourgeoisie, the middle-class middlebrow. MacDiarmid the irrationalist of the self-elected elect and spiritual communist share a detestation of bourgeois values as a block on evolutionary creativity and political revolution. 'I would never care a brass farthing for what any man had, but only for what he *was*, and preserve an absolute absence of the enthusiasm of the market-place' (*LP*, 92) he writes from the austerity of Whalsay. His claim that he has 'no use for anything between genius and the working man' (*LP*, 402) shows MacDiarmid's communism resembling his earlier mysticism in its absolutist distrust of the democratic mean.

The Cadre of Spiritual Communism

If the intellectual hero of the Drunk Man is Dostoevsky, reactionary apostle of the irrational, then the 'greater Christ' (*CP1*, 86) of MacDiarmid's messianic materialism is Vladimir Ilich Ulyanov, better known as Lenin.[37] MacDiarmid's interest in Lenin stretches back to the years immediately following the revolutions of 1917, the poet's spiritual communism rooted in memories of Langholm. This long-standing concern with events in Russia helps explain MacDiarmid's dislike of what he saw as the opportunistic communism of the Auden group, assuming their metropolitan concerns to be culturally elitist and politically imperialistic. However, a fundamental tenet of the Leninism to which MacDiarmid sings three hymns is that the masses have to be led to revolutionary action through the theoretical guidance of a cadre of elite intellectuals.

First published in Stuttgart in 1902, *What is to be Done?* elucidates Lenin's idea that 'without revolutionary theory there can be no revolutionary movement'.[38] Only through theory can class consciousness be built, without which potential revolutionary activity descends to the level of mere revolt, 'a purely spontaneous movement' (*WD*, 98) with no lasting social and political efficacy. The battle between what Lenin terms the 'spontaneous' and 'conscious' working-class movement is a choice between the reformism of the former and the revolution that will follow from the latter.

> Threading with great skill the intricate shuttling path
> From 'spontaneity' to preoccupation with design,
> From the realistic 'moment' to the abstraction of essential form
> And ending with a fusion of all their elements,
> At once realistic and abstract
>
> ('Third Hymn to Lenin', *CP2*, 899)

MacDiarmid sees Lenin's revolutionary propaganda as a welding of theory and practice presaging his own synthesis of poetry and politics. Those who advise spontaneity – that is, a working-class movement purely from within the proletariat, with no guiding intellectual consciousness brought from without – condemn the workers to 'a strengthening of the influence of bourgeois ideology' (*WD*, 105) such as is evidenced in the reformism of trade unionism. Yet, paradoxically, the conscious element brought to the workers from outside their number that will advance revolutionary action is the theoretical input of a vanguard of bourgeois intellectuals, a group to which Lenin belonged but whose capacity for un-dialectical free-thinking he fiercely mistrusted:

'the intellectuals, the lackeys of capital, who think they're the brains of the nation. In fact, they're not its brains, they're its shit.'[39] Despite being sceptical of the intelligentsia, the university-educated Lenin, whose mother had inherited a landed estate, continually insists in *What is to be Done?* on the inability of the workers to develop a revolutionary consciousness for themselves.

Lenin claims 'that it is only from outside the economic struggle, from outside the sphere of relations between workers and employers' (*WD*, 143), that revolutionary consciousness can be developed. In other words, too stupefied by the alienating mechanisms of capitalism, the workers cannot advance their consciousness beyond the level of bourgeois ideology in order to dispense with the leadership of bourgeois intellectuals. This would imply that Lenin believes that bourgeois intellectuals stand outside the economic realm, objective in respect of capitalist relations in comparison with the compromised subjectivism of the proletariat. None the less, he is aware that the ideological roots of communism lie within the very class privilege that it purports to abolish:

> The teachings of socialism, however, grew out of the philosophic, historical, and economic theories elaborated by educated representatives of the propertied classes, by the intelligentsia. By their social status, the founders of modern scientific socialism, Marx and Engels, themselves belonged to the bourgeois intelligentsia. In the very same way, in Russia, the theoretical doctrine of social-democracy arose altogether independently of the spontaneous growth of the working-class movement; it arose as a natural and inevitable outcome of the development of thought among the revolutionary socialist intelligentsia. (*WD*, 98)

Just as Lenin alleges that the workers are too implicated in the capitalist process to understand it sufficiently to construct a revolutionary alternative, so the elitism that dictates that the workers must be the revolutionary tools of bourgeois intellectuals re-enacts the selfsame exploitative relations of capitalism which communism seeks to break.

Attempting to rescue a viable socialism from the violent authoritarianism of Bolshevism, Robin Blick argues that Leninism did not evolve from the tenets of Marx and Engels, but originated in the Robespierrean Terror of the French Revolution: 'Lenin was fully aware of the link between his own political doctrine and the *élitist* and manipulative precepts of Jacobinism.'[40] In 'The Course of Scottish Poetry' from the *Scottish Educational Journal*, July 1932, a less famous Grieve pseudonym, James Maclaren, notes 'the relationship of *Hymns to Lenin* today with Burns's welcome to the French Revolution' (*RT2*, 312). The poet of 'First Hymn' conflates himself and Lenin with 'the unkent Bards wha made / Sangs peerless through a' post-anonymous days' (*CP1*, 298) so aligning his communist poetry with a traditional cultural communalism. Through his Leninism, MacDiarmid wants to keep Scottish culture in touch with contemporary international revolutionism, just as Burns in the eighteenth century had done with 'The Tree of Liberty' (not published until 1838) and the revolutionary millenarianism of 'Is There for Honest Poverty'.[41]

At first glance, the equalitarianism of Burns's poetry and the democratic orality of many of the songs he collected and adapted would seem to be deeply at odds with MacDiarmid's laudation of Lenin's autocratic genius:

> Here lies your secret, O Lenin, – yours and oors,
> No' in the majority will that accepts the result
> But in the real will that bides its time and kens
> The benmaist resolve is the poo'er in which we exult   [*inmost*]
> Since naebody's willingly deprived o' the good;
>   And, least o' a', the crood!
>
>   (*CP1*, 298–9)

Referring to this stanza in 'Constricting the Dynamic Spirit: We Want Life Abundant' from *New Scotland*, 2 May 1936, Grieve explains that his communism is 'purely Platonic' as it desires 'the lifting of all suppressions and thwarting or warping agencies' in society:

> I do not believe that any one – and least of all the crowd – will willingly be deprived of the 'good', nor do I believe that my own, or anybody else's ideas of the latter are valid. I am as all poets and dynamic spirits must be – purely 'irrational'. (The emphasis is on the 'purely'.) (*RT2*, 549)

Still an adherent of the self-elected elect, the poet approves of communism as the political manifestation of an '*inward necessity*' ('Second Hymn to Lenin', *CP1*, 327) or spiritual power, similar to the Will of Nietzsche, that is coincident with his art.

Even in his communist poems MacDiarmid assumes the cultural to be more important than the political. Revolution is needed primarily in order to free the workers from the economic forces that block their access to high culture. Lenin's materialism is 'richt', but only as far as it goes; the poet is 'Aimin' at mair than you aimed at / Tho' yours comes first, I know it' ('Second Hymn to Lenin', *CP1*, 323). Having established himself in a previous incarnation as a modernist poet of the irrational with *A Drunk Man*, scorning the intellectual and spiritual abilities of the many to understand the metaphysics of the self-elected elect, MacDiarmid now wishes to '*win through to the man in the street*':

> *Are my poems spoken in the factories and fields,*
>   *In the streets o' the toon?*

> *Gin they're no', then I'm failin' to dae*
> *What I ocht to ha' dune.*

('Second Hymn to Lenin', *CP1*, 323)

This does not seem to square with the elitist who in 'Burns Today and Tomorrow' (1959) declares himself 'an unrepentant and militant high-brow', but even in his desire to reach the supposedly uncultured mass MacDiarmid does 'not believe that the great body of the public needs nothing but "pap"' (*A*, 232). Rather, this proponent of what is difficult – 'Nae simple rhymes for silly folk / But the haill art' – equates the challenging intellectuality of modernist poetry with the rigours of the Marxist dialectic: 'as Lenin gied / Nae Marx-without-tears to workin' men / But the fu' course insteed' ('Second Hymn to Lenin', *CP1*, 325). As 'the greatest turnin'-point' in history since Christ ('First Hymn to Lenin', *CP1*, 297) Lenin is the 'Barbarian saviour o' civilization' ('Second Hymn to Lenin', *CP1*, 324), his communism that which can ensure the continuance of high culture in the face of capitalist mass culture. MacDiarmid repeatedly cites with significant approval Lenin's insistence that 'it would be a very serious mistake to suppose that one can become a Communist without making one's own the treasures of human knowledge' (*LP*, 153). Communism cannot ignore 'more than two thousand years of development of human thought' (*LP*, 153), dismissing it as a ghastly Christian error, but must assimilate the cultural glories of the past, ensuring that they inform the revolutionary future. Communism is, in fact, 'the final outcome' (*LP*, 153) of the accumulation of knowledge to date, the spiritual synthesis of twenty centuries of material progress.

MacDiarmid makes much of Lenin in the 1930s, the revolutionist becoming one of the poet's great men of genius. However, the Russian died in 1924 when the poet was in Montrose imagining a metaphysical Scotland. John Maclean, who in 1917 became Lenin's Bolshevik consul in Scotland, inspires the conception of a revolutionary Red Scotland that MacDiarmid constructed while living in Shetland. Born in Langholm, MacDiarmid's international communism develops from a Scottish source and 'Glasgow Invokes the Spirit of Lenin' (*CP2*, 893), the 'alternative title' of 'Third Hymn to Lenin', shows a continuing national resonance. Despite the social unrest in Glasgow that lead to a riot in George Square on 31 January 1919, the image of a revolutionary Red Clydeside has been disputed. According to David Howell, 'any characterisation of Glasgow as a potential "Red Base" must come to terms with the fact that less than one in five of the Glasgow electorate [in 1918] met even the undemanding requirement of a vote for Labour'.[42] Glasgow and Scotland remained staunchly Unionist and mainly conservative. For all his new-found materialism, MacDiarmid's Red Scotland is an essential-ist idea of the nation similar to the metaphysical model elaborated by the irrationalist poet of the self-elected elect, but now requiring the theoret-ical reinforcement of an elite cadre of communist intellectuals.

Despite the elite authoritarianism of his Leninism, with its belief in revolution from above, henceforth MacDiarmid claimed to be 'organi-cally welded with the manual workers / As with no other class in the social system' ('Manual Labour', CP1, 656). In Lucky Poet he insists on a 'vigilant determination to see that I allowed nothing to come between me and my class' and is 'determined to strengthen and develop my organic relationship to the Commons of Scotland' (LP, 232). MacDiarmid's assertion that he finds a place for his radical republican politics in organic connection to the Scottish workers suggests Antonio Gramsci's idea of the need for the proletariat to develop organic intel-lectuals from within its own class. MacDiarmid was introduced to Gramsci's work by Hamish Henderson (1919–2002), who mentions in a letter to 'Chris' from Milan in 1950 that he is 'working hard' on a trans-lation of Gramsci's 'Letters from Prison'.[43] Five years later, with the pub-lication of In Memoriam James Joyce, MacDiarmid calls Gramsci 'that heroic genius' for his disinterested study of 'comparative linguistics in prison', quoting from 'his Lettere dal Carcere' (CP2, 745).[44]

For Gramsci 'all men are intellectuals', but only a minority 'have in society the function of intellectuals'.[45] The 'new stratum of intellectuals', the organic intellectuals of the working class, must adapt their know-ledge to the conditions of modern life; as such, 'technical education, closely bound to industrial labour even at the most primitive and unqual-ified level, must form the basis of the new type of intellectual' (PN, 9). Gramsci's new intellectual is acquainted with subjects marginal to the humanity-bound discourse of the traditional, 'vulgarised type of the intellectual' of the ruling order – 'the man of letters, the philosopher, the artist' (PN, 9). MacDiarmid certainly wanted a Scottish intelligentsia that would raise the nation's cultural standards in line with the inter-nationalist critical dicta of the Scottish Renaissance movement, but he was suspicious of the professionalisation of literature and the bourgeois 'culture class' thrown up by capitalism, calling them in 'To the Younger Scottish Writers' a 'Middle-class vanguard' possessed of an 'intellectual poverty thinly coated / By a veneer of artistic sophistication' (CP1, 636).

Like MacDiarmid, Gramsci understood the importance of education as a root to societal change; both knew that in a capitalist society education is a class issue, hegemony being necessarily pedagogical. Luciano Pellicani explains that 'every hegemony is founded on a historical bloc, in other words, on an organic system of social alliances held together by a common ideology and a common culture'.[46] The 'educatit classes' (*CP1*, 361) may celebrate the centenaries of Goethe and Scott in order to conserve their present political dominance, but the workers will never know the big names recycled from the past of bourgeois culture, their access blocked by the class interests of a stratified education system and a bourgeois interpreting class 'wha find / The present owre muckle for their nerve' ('The Oon Olympian', *CP1*, 355). The workers must develop their own culture, one that goes far beyond 'Framed pictures of the grocer's calendar type' ('Art and the Workers', *CP2*, 1304), if they are to challenge the capitalist order. MacDiarmid insists on an *engagé* poetry that questions the innate acquisitiveness of the traditional intellectual's cultural values:

Art must be related to the central issues of life,
Not serve a sub-artistic purpose that could as well
Be served by the possession of a new motor-car
Or a holiday on the Continent perhaps.
('To the Younger Scottish Writers', *CP1*, 634)

His Gramscian emphasis on the importance of culture to the class struggle underlines the spirituality of the poet's communism and his understanding of the importance of the spiritual to the maintenance of the present social order. In this, MacDiarmid remains true to Lenin's exhortation that the communist should assimilate bourgeois Christian culture as a means to transform the capitalist social order from which it originates and through which it prolongs its hegemony. Born just a year before MacDiarmid in peasant rural Sardinia, Gramsci shared with the poet an early enthusiasm for Mussolini. Both fascism and communism were mass movements that yet relied on the theoretical formulations of an elite cadre of intellectuals for their effective function. Gramsci considered the masses and the intellectuals to be indissolubly linked and that any understanding of mass consciousness could only come through an examination of the intellectual classes. This suggests that the masses are controlled, indeed created as such, through the dominance of the ruling intelligentsia. The appeal of authoritarian political movements to the cultural intelligentsia of modernism becomes clearer: artists and intellectuals, marginalised by the secularising process of industrialisation, seek to compensate by a reassertion of their former priestly power through leadership of absolutist political organisations. The 'clerks', in Julien Benda's disapproving words, become 'the spiritual militia of the material'.[47]

Notwithstanding his insistence that they are not true intellectuals and belong to a decadent class, the cultural intelligentsia is interested in Gramsci due to his theory that modern capitalist hegemony is actuated at the superstructural level. Political society, or the state, effects power as force through government agencies such as the army and police; civil society – a sociological concept first elaborated by Adam Ferguson (1723–1816) in *Essay on the History of Civil Society* (1767) – engineers social and cultural relationships through education, law and religion, establishing power through consent. In order to wrestle political authority from a ruling order an emergent group must first gain hegemonic control through a war of position within civil society before it can dominate the state functions of the nation – hence the importance for the working class of developing an organic intellectual elite able to challenge the cultural authority of traditional intellectuals.

Christopher Harvie explains that there is a 'two-part model' of institutionalism in Scotland, a split between political and civil society emerging from the Union and the British focus of the Scottish Enlightenment, and points out that Scottish civil society is administered with a 'small-n-nationalism'.[48] MacDiarmid distrusted the 'middlebrows' of the national ' "interpreting class" – ministers, bankers, school-teachers, business men, and what not' ('Burns Today and Tomorrow', *A*, 232), believing Scotland's reputedly independent Three Estates, the ruling faction of Scottish civil society, to be little more than an anglicised fifth column facilitating English state rule of Scotland.

The Interpreting Class

MacDiarmid took his concept of the interpreting class from John Buchan (1875–1940). Buchan's autobiography *Memory Hold-the-Door*, published in the year of his death, describes the 'intellectual atmosphere' of the immediate aftermath of World War One and contrasts the search for peace and privacy of 'plain folk everywhere', who were attempting 'sturdily to rebuild their world', with the ideological emptiness of the intellectuals:

> The interpreting class, which Coleridge called the 'clerisy', the people who should have influenced opinion, ran round their cages in vigorous pursuit of their tails. If they were futile they were also arrogant, and it was an odd kind of arrogance, for they had no creed to preach. The same type before the War had prostrated themselves in gaping admiration of the advance of physical science and the improvements in the material apparatus of life. There was little of that left. The War had shown that our mastery over physical forces might end in a nightmare, that mankind was becoming like an overgrown child armed with deadly weapons, a child with immense limbs and a tiny head. But this belated enlightenment seemed to drain their vitality. Just as many of the boys

then leaving school, who had escaped war service, suffered from a kind of *accidie* and were inclined to look for 'soft options' in life, so the interpreting class plumed themselves wearily on being hollow men living in a waste land.[49]

Scathing of 'those who called themselves intellectuals' at this period of incipient modernism, Buchan denounces the cultural elite for having 'no absolute values' and 'being by profession atomisers, engaged in reducing the laborious structure of civilised life to a whirling nebula'.[50] Buchan expresses distaste for the postwar intelligentsia because of their solipsistic lack of leadership. Instead of pointing the majority in the direction of civilisation's regeneration, the hollow men of the twenties were busy examining the ruins of their own intellectual value system. Unwilling to incriminate themselves in the desecration of civilised values – as the proprietors of culture, this would be to burn down their own house – the intelligentsia look for an Other to accuse: perhaps the Jews, certainly the mob. A statesman *manqué*, Buchan the literary intellectual is censuring his own type, albeit of a new generation, with a dereliction of intellectual duty in failing to lead the masses.

MacDiarmid's objection to the interpreting class lies not in their lack of intellectual leadership, as Buchan would have it, but that they have too much influence on the shaping of culture, particularly that doled out to the workers. MacDiarmid agrees with T. S. Eliot in his preference for an unlettered audience for his poetry rather than a literate middle-class readership as 'it would be easier to enlist the interest of the former, they would follow the exposition far more patiently and with a genuine desire to learn and without the interposition of intractable prejudices of all kinds' (*LP*, 350). From the perspective of being open to new cultural developments, 'the professional classes in Scotland to-day are utterly hopeless compared with the working class' (*LP*, 350). MacDiarmid argues that the 'educated classes' are incapable of understanding and welcoming fresh ideas, having already reached an intellectual 'saturation level' (*LP*, 349) that is detrimental to themselves and the masses they profess to culturally enlighten:

> Alas! The thought of ninety-nine per cent of our people
> Is still ruled by Plato and Aristotle
> Read in an historical vacuum by the few
> From whom the masses receive
> A minimum of it but along with that
> A maximum incapacity for anything else.
>
> ('The Gaelic Muse', *CP1*, 662)

The circumscribed vision of the interpreting class is due to the 'planned indoctrination to which they have been subjected' (*LP*, 349), trained by a capitalist education for their supervisory, middle-management role in the economy – an idea finding contemporary resonance in Noam Chomsky's contention that 'the intellectual elite is the most heavily indoctrinated sector' of society.[51] According to MacDiarmid, being the intellectuals entrusted with the smooth running of capitalist civil society 'has practically insulated them from any mental activity altogether', other than the exercising of 'their conceit as "educated persons"' and 'their professional jealousy' (*LP*, 349–50).

The indoctrinated interpreting class is what Chomsky calls the 'secular priesthood' of the capitalist social order and their job is to indoctrinate others in the faith.[52] MacDiarmid opposed what he perceived as the commercial and anglicised agenda of the Scottish teaching profession, believing it to be the prime means through which the interpreting class actuated its rule of civil society in a stateless nation. But he also recognised popular communication outlets as being integral to the capitalist propaganda process, not just schools and universities, and these include 'the majority of public platforms (especially the religious and political ones), the radio, TV, the cinema, and of course the press' ('To Hell with Culture', *RT3*, 301). By undermining autonomous thinking such 'public platforms' allow the interpreting class to propagate a capitalist culture that 'does most harm to the broad masses of the people' (*RT3*, 301) by stultifying their ability to challenge a hierarchical social order that is ubiquitously presented as natural. This culture of the educated that is so deleterious to the masses is exclusively concerned with getting on in the world rather than acquiring the spiritual wisdom that could break such a cycle of sordid materialism. MacDiarmid wishes such culture to hell.

MacDiarmid's speech, 'To Hell with Culture', in which he presented these thoughts to Edinburgh's Porch Philosophical Club in 1953, was also published in the *National Weekly*. The title and many of the ideas are borrowed from Herbert Read's essay of the same name. (MacDiarmid dedicated 'Riding in a Fog' to Read and 'Durchseelte' to Read's wife.) Read's *To Hell with Culture*, essays on the complex interactions between the artist and capitalist society, appeared in 1963, but the article to which MacDiarmid owes a debt was written under pressure of war in 1941. Read's socialistic thesis is that culture should be integral to the business of living rather than being itself a business. In a natural political order culture is inextricably bound up with the fabric of existence; in a decadent social system culture becomes a commodity that acts as a spiritual palliative, an escape from life. 'The cultured Greeks', he claims, 'had no word for culture'; for them 'culture was a way of life itself.'[53] It was the Romans, 'the first large-scale capitalists in Europe' (*HC*, 10), who commodified and hence invented 'culture'. Read wants to do away with the 'immense veneer' of capitalist culture that attempts to hide 'the cheapness and shoddiness at the heart of things' (*HC*, 30). A 'democratic revolution' (*HC*, 30) would eradicate 'the fake culture of our present civilization' (26), making the interpreting class a thing of the past, and so ensuring that 'the future will not be conscious of its culture' (13).

MacDiarmid likewise believes that 'culture and civilisation are all lies, and museums and furniture just dustcatchers' (*RT3*, 300). Whilst agreeing with Read's disapproval of capitalist culture, MacDiarmid's Romantic conception of authorship would reject the correlative dictum to Read's title: 'To hell with the artist.' (*HC*, 23). For MacDiarmid, it is only artists of genius who can transcend a capitalist culture that seeks to stifle their transformational vision while promoting mere talent at their expense: 'It isn't culture that is needed now. It is something very different – to which culture is generally implacably opposed, just as "the good is the enemy of the best". I mean genius' (*RT3*, 303). Culture is a decorative guise of the middle class, a group approving of the self-possessed professionalism of the talented. In a capitalist era awash with the businesslike proficiency of the interpreting class it is genius that is required to speak to all humanity, not merely to a narrow class culture. In the binary of art and industry, spirit and matter, culture becomes what Alan Sinfield calls the bourgeois 'conscience of capitalism',[54] with the interpreting class as cultural schizophrenes divided between the prophet and the professional. For MacDiarmid, the damaging duality of Scottish culture has produced an interpreting class that, 'when they are not just out and out Quislings, are exactly of the same kind as the ministers, professors, and other *literati* who imagined themselves so much more important than Burns' (*RT3*, 298–9).

MacDiarmid's scathing analysis of the interpreting class arises from his loathing of an anglicised Scottish middle class that has provincialised the nation. His most concerted critical effort to remould national opinion, to create a place for his cultural politics, came through the pages of the teachers' *Scottish Educational Journal*, collected in *Contemporary Scottish Studies*. This was to take the battle directly into the enemy camp, the philistine home of Scotland's most influential body of the interpreting class. *Contemporary Scottish Studies* is as conspicuous an example of canon formation as that conducted by Eliot, but one that goes deeper than the assertion of a particular set of literary values to a preference for a specific national type. In 'R. B. Cunninghame Graham' (24 July 1925), MacDiarmid contrasts the 'Men', those of unique artistic individualism, such as novelist Norman Douglas (1868–1952), composer F. G. Scott and Scottish Colourists J. D. Fergusson (1874–1961) and Samuel J. Peploe

(1871–1935), with the 'Mob', populists who lack artistic and intellectual worth, like the hugely successful novelist Annie S. Swan (1859–1943) and the vernacular poet Gilbert Rae (b.1875). According to 'the nature of things' in the market system, the 'Mob' type will 'always immensely out-number' the 'Men' (CSS, 36). However, 'due to the cultural consequences of the existing political relationship between Scotland and England' (CSS, 37), the triumph of the populists over the true artist is greatly exacer-bated. Rather than reformulating a separate Scottish cultural tradition through which their work could find its canonical place, the populists write for a larger, more lucrative mass market. MacDiarmid's idea of the authentic Scottish artist is the highbrow male who sees art as central to his mission to internationalise Scotland – someone, in fact, very like MacDiarmid. Without this national type he believes that 'Scottish life is deprived of its natural self-corrective' (CSS, 37). The highly illuminating final phrase suggests that MacDiarmid sees the Scottish artist's role as involving the teacherly amendment of errors of political judgement and cultural taste committed by the Scottish public. He wishes the 'Men' to save the masses from themselves, the 'Mob'.

MacDiarmid extends his personalised scrutiny of the Scottish psyche in Scottish Eccentrics, a rejoinder to Edith Sitwell's English Eccentrics (1933), amongst whom she includes Carlyle. Writing from the margin-ality of Whalsay, a place eccentric to the cultural and political concerns of metropolitan Britain, MacDiarmid's biographical sketches suggest a Scottish identity wildly different from the contemporary stereotype of the dour Scot. He chooses his eccentrics from all classes of the nation, but through them illustrates his disdain for the middle-class mediocrity that finds its comfortable home in the neuk of Anglo-Scottishness. With their utter disregard for the rules of provincial normalcy, MacDiarmid's eccentrics confound the expectations of the purse-proud, canny Scots of bourgeois Scottish Unionism. They are not too feart to be fools in the face of the disapproval of popular opinion and so they gull a public wrapped in the confines of monetary reason. As he says of the stylistic 'extravagances' (SE, 27) of Sir Thomas Urquhart (c.1611–1660) – amongst many talents that would interest an author in search of eccentrics, the translator of Rabelais – 'this is not the sort of thing that appeals to the man in the street, and in these democratic days Urquhart is an insult to common sense' (28). MacDiarmid claims that their own literature and history are as 'unintelligible' as contemporary science and modernist art to the majority of Scots because 'their constant appeal is to common sense in the lowest sense of the term' (SE, 303).

With their superfluity of eccentric creativeness MacDiarmid's eccentric Scots tauntingly expose the anti-creative, materialist common sense of contemporary, middle-class Anglo-Scots. With an ill-noted wicked sense of humour, the poet fancifully writes 'of the Rev. Robert Kirk, M.A., who was kidnapped by elves for betraying the secrets of the polity of their commonwealth' (*SE*, 313), so introducing the extremes of the imagination to a national scene stifled by the philistine mediocrity of the interpreting class of religion and education. In his insightful essay on William McGonagall (c.1830–1902), MacDiarmid lambasts the lowering democratic spirit pervading Scottish life that allowed for the 'brutal baiting' (*SE*, 70) of a man whose mental faculties were very probably impaired. McGonagall is the bastard twin of true creativity whose doggerel enables the masses to laugh at poetry as a mere fancy of the mad while they display the same 'incurable illiteracy, the inaccessibility to the least enlightenment' (*SE*, 70) that is reflected in the face of the deranged poet.

For MacDiarmid, neither McGonagall nor his mocking public are to blame for their lamentable ignorance, but rather the social and political order that ensures that 'the attentions of the people are carefully kept in certain directions' (*SE*, 265). Social control of the potentially revolutionary masses is the root of the interpreting class's power in capitalist cultural politics: 'A nation of football spectators and picture-house fans is far more easily controlled than would be one with a like passion for being *au fait* with science and speculative ideas' (*SE*, 265). With elect irony, a futuristic MacDiarmid imagines Ibrox Park, home of Glasgow Rangers Football Club, 'packed tight' to listen to

a debate on 'la loi de l'effort converti'
Between Professor MacFadyen and a Spainish pairty.

('Glasgow, 1960', *CP2*, 1039)

However, with capitalist entertainment to sap their mental energy after a day spent working to make others wealthy, the majority have little encouragement to interest themselves in the intellectual revolutions of modern science that MacDiarmid believes will free them from servitude. 'The consequence is that the twentieth century is still populated (save for an infinitesimal minority) by Neolithic Man.' (*SE*, 265). Ascribing his own spiritual communism to another of his eccentrics, the peripatetic philosopher Thomas Davidson (1840–1900), MacDiarmid argues that 'he stood for the highest culture for the breadwinners, for the people who have to "go to work" early' (*SE*, 145). Enculturation of the working class will 'give them an intelligent view of the world' (*SE*, 145), while also disempowering the interpreting class of its retarding influence.

MacDiarmid understands that it is in the interests of their continued class rule that the bourgeois interpreting class should mediate between the workers and high culture. In line with the stratification of the capitalist division of labour, it is the managerialist cultural brokers who professionally create the artificial, academic divisions between the high culture of the educated few and the mass culture suitable for the ignorant many – a discourse of distinction characterised by Andreas Huyssen as the 'Great Divide'.[55] In 'The Present Position of Scottish Music' (1927), MacDiarmid argues that ' "public opinion" is manipulated to respond to the professional interest' of musicians and critics (A, 52). The role of the interpreting class in the 'commercialism of our age, accentuated in Scotland by our denationalization and provincialization' (A, 51), sabotages public receptivity to the quirky progressiveness of modernist music:

> The Man in the Street is 'disinterested'. He has 'no axe to grind'. He would respond to the new work if he was given the chance of hearing it – before the middlemen, the parasites, had imbued him with the prejudices necessary to their business. (A, 52)

What MacDiarmid gives with one hand, however, he takes away with the other, his radical desire that the masses should be able to freely access high culture somewhat undermined by the elitism of the modernist creator who believes that 'the arts are not democratic. There is no equality in them. If democracy and creative art are incompatible, democracy will go' (A, 51).

Such contradictions characterise modernism under capitalism, ensuring for Lawrence Rainey that it is 'neither a straightforward resistance nor an outright capitulation to commodification but a momentary equivocation that incorporates elements of both in a brief, necessarily unstable synthesis'.[56] This same 'unstable synthesis' of radicalism and reaction is evident in an academic project that is informed by modernism. The linguistic difficulty of much modernist writing in the early twentieth century, its literary allusiveness and appeal to the educated few, is reminiscent of professional academic studies at the dawn of a new century.[57] Thomas Strychacz argues that modernism 'was shaped profoundly by a convergence of professional discourse and the rise of mass culture'.[58] Both modernism and academia tangle confusedly with mass society, the growth of which accentuates the perception of their elitist specialism, yet neither truly understands or connects with this shadowy Other. If the creator of high culture requires the legitimising power of the professional critic to ensure canonical stature, then both the intellectual and artist need the university as an institutional barrier defending their cultural authority from the uneducated masses. Rooted in what Joyce Piell Wexler describes as the 'ideological contradiction between art and money' pervading the high culture industry,[59] this dichotomy enables many professional artists and intellectuals to live comfortably inside the power system created by a knowledge that their specialised hegemony prioritises, whilst also allowing them to believe they stand rebelliously opposed to the economic relations of capitalism through the apparently marginal nature of their vocation.

The congenital contradictions of capitalism are evident in the history of the intellectual class. For Karl Mannheim, 'The crux and turning point in Western history is the gradual dissolution of the compact caste-like strata. The scholar was the first to be affected by this shift.'[60] The once feudalistic priestly caste of the intellectual elect has been declassed and is now forced to sell its ideological wares in the marketplace of modern capitalism alongside the products of mass culture. This generates a conflict between the transcendental, universalistic ('generic') mission of the intellectual and the political and social ('genetic') ends that seek to circumscribe this; a clash between timeless spirit and historical matter that, according to George Konrád and Ivan Szelényi, is fundamental to the artist and intellectual of capitalist culture:

> Often the schizophrenia inherent in the intellectual's role is apparent in one and the same individual. The greatest of them incorporate the contradictions between their generic and genetic roles into the antinomies of their thought – which does not by any means prove that their thinking is inconsistent.[61]

This is an apposite description of the difficulties of reconciliation at the heart of MacDiarmid's politics: his elitism cleaves to a modernist conception of high culture that the Marxist poet wishes to be directly available to the workers by excising the bourgeois intermediation of the interpreting class; yet he also derides the intellectual level of the masses, local and universal, believing in the necessity of an authoritarian leadership by a highbrow cadre. 'I am consumed with love for the people I detest' ('Glasgow', *CP2*, 1337), says the communist MacDiarmid of the Glasgow 'keelies' (1333). Such individual contradictions illustrate MacDiarmid's dialectical struggle with the consuming forces, the 'short circuiters o' consciousness' of capitalism ('Ode to All Rebels', *CP1*, 508).

The Short-Circuiters of Consciousness

MacDiarmid's disdain for the cultural interpreting class of capitalism derives from his belief in the power of knowledge to effect social change. It is the task of the artist-intellectual to stimulate the process of spiritual evolution, not to stand in the way of material emancipation by serving

the class interests of capitalist culture. Explaining his apparently contradictory position as communist and modernist elitist, MacDiarmid argues

> that all that seeks to evade the stereotyped and to prevent the short-circuiting
> of human consciousness is in the interests of the people, and safeguards their
> inheritance, while all that 'keeps people in their place', that prophesies easy
> things for them, life without tears, all that simplifies for their dull wits, all that
> talks down to them, all that assumes that the heights are not for them, but
> only for such-and-such, are the shibboleths of their enemies (*LP*, 236–7).

MacDiarmid dismisses capitalist democracy as sham, believing the
marketing of mass culture to be a means of politically disenfranchising
potentially revolutionary and creative individuals. His anti-liberalism
denounces capitalism's ability to 'legitimize conflicts of interest' (as
Konrád and Szelényi put it),[62] neutering dissent by absorbing it into the
body politic, even rewarding those of the intellectual interpreting class
who analyse its inner workings with professional promotion. In 'Ode for
the 350th Anniversary of Edinburgh University' MacDiarmid claims that
the university not only 'can't produce / A creative artist worth a damn'
(*CP2*, 1285), but that

> It's equally true none of the big noises
> In science, etc., in the world to-day –
> And least of all in Finance – belong here;
> But of second-rates we've a rich array –
> The men who do the super-donkey work,
> The slave-drivers, the factors for the rulers, –
> And hordes of expert parasites,
> Sinecure-holders and mob-befoolers.
>
> (*CP2*, 1286)

Disdainful of the educational interpreting class of Scotland, the self-
taught MacDiarmid will direct the Scottish masses to a new order.
MacDiarmid states in 1931 that the 'Scottish Renaissance Movement
wants to produce entirely different kinds of people to those turned out
by our schools as they are' in the capitalist economy of a denationalised
Scotland. In order for this new national type to appear an elect 'disbelief
in the value of popular discussion, a repudiation of democratic principle,
and the conviction that an "adequate minority" can "seize power" ' are
essential requirements ('Whither Scotland?', *RT2*, 278).

The authoritarianism of MacDiarmid's Dr Stockmann-like belief in an
intellectual minority that is always right has a basis in his perception that
the majority under capitalist education and culture are so ill-served by
what he calls the 'parasitical "interpreting class" ' (*RT2*, 485) as to be
rendered almost incapable of decision. Evoking Ibsen's 1882 play, in

'Problems of Poetry Today', from the *New English Weekly* for September 1933, he identifies the popularising proponents of mass entertainment as being 'the enemies of the people' (*RT2*, 486) whom it pays, both financially and in cultural and political power, to pander to the mass market – a market they fashion in order to sell created wants to a now homogenised, captive bloc. It is in the interests of the interpreting class to strip the masses of their individuality so that by 'stereotyping their stupidity' (*RT2*, 486) through mass culture they can be better fitted to the mechanised role of a working class. For MacDiarmid, genuine culture is only produced by individuals and its effect is spiritually and intellectually individualising and, potentially, politically liberating: 'The interests of poetry are diametrically opposed to whatever may be making for any robotisation or standardisation of humanity or any short-circuiting of the human consciousness' (*RT2*, 486).

MacDiarmid's conception of high art as a bulwark against the homogenising forces of consumer capitalism is suggestive of the critical theory of the Frankfurt School, in particular Theodor Adorno's work on the culture industry. In his Preface to the *Collected Poems* (1970) of Burns Singer (1928–64), MacDiarmid cites Adorno, alongside Lukács, Benjamin and Gramsci, as theoretically informing his own Marxism (*RT3*, 505). For Adorno, the mass culture created by capitalism is totalitarian in essence and action, designed and controlled from above to regulate the leisure time of the masses just as completely as the division of labour governs their working day. Only high art can sneak through the small gaps in the oppressive capitalist whole created by the instrumental rationality of the Enlightenment. The very autonomy of such art from ideology or system, the modernist elitism that renders it inexplicable to the masses and keeps it the cultural capital of the educated few, is precisely wherein lies its revolutionary potential. Under capitalist conditions, however, the revolutionary promise of a united working class is ignominiously simulated in their alienated mass participation in the lure of the culture industry: 'They become a collective through the adaptation to an over-mastering arbitrary power.'[63] Unlike much postmodern theory, which allows the consumer a measure of self-conscious and ironical independence from the machinations of the market, Adorno's totalising Marxian modernism proposes that the 'customer is not king', the masses being no more to the culture industry than 'an object of calculation; an appendage of the machinery'.[64]

Under the dominion of the culture industry Everyman loses individuality through capitalism's 'integration of opposites', thus assuming Marcuse's one-dimensionality: 'At the most advanced stage of capitalism, this society is a system of subdued pluralism, in which the competing institutions concur in solidifying the power of the whole over the individual.'[65] Writing in 1968, high watermark of postmodern pop art – 'or, as I call it, anti-art' (*Company*, 78) – and student protest, MacDiarmid exhibits his Marxist elitism:

> As Professor Herbert Marcuse of California has said recently the reason for the student revolt is that it is impossible to get through the barrier constituted by the vast majority of mankind hopelessly brain-washed and manipulated by the great mass media and unable to think for themselves. This throws a greater responsibility than ever on the educated few. The problem, as Antonio Gramsci the great Italian Marxist theoretician said, is a problem of consciousness.[66]

Opposing the dumbing-down basic to capitalist mass culture, MacDiarmid believes consciousness can be expanded, not with the counter-culture drugs of the 1960s, but through 'A learned poetry wholly free / From the brutal love of ignorance' ('The Kind of Poetry I Want', *CP2*, 1030). Alan Swingewood argues that, 'as part of the legitimising ideology of capitalist domination, the concept of mass culture has been transposed directly into literary and theoretical forms'.[67] He finds parallels in the cultural Marxism of Adorno and Marcuse and the conservative elitism of T. S. Eliot and F. R. Leavis, who frankly admits that 'culture has always been in minority keeping'.[68] Despite their divergent politics, the self-elected elect of theory and criticism unite in the belief that high culture is under threat from the entertainment industry and media.

MacDiarmid's only concerted period of paid employment was his decade as a journalist in Montrose. Observing the interpreting class from the inside, he had difficulties believing in the 'freedom of the press', claiming that under capitalism 'that only means permitting a group of newspaper owners to undo public education and debauch the popular taste'. His belief that in the interests of increased standards 'an authoritarian position must be (and will be, since the preservation, let alone the furtherance, of civilisation depends upon it) re-established' ('Problems of Poetry Today', *RT2*, 487) evokes a Leninist stance. In 'Scotland and the Banking System', which appeared in the *New Age* in 1927, Grieve, then editor–reporter of the *Montrose Review*, focuses on the 'vested interests' of the Scottish press, exposing the anti-nationalist bias of Scottish newspapers:

> All the Scottish papers aver that the demand for Scottish nationalism is made by a 'handful of fanatics', and has no real weight of 'public opinion' behind it – but what is 'public opinion', and how far is it reflected by a Press which, in a country which has always been overwhelmingly radical and republican,

and where today a third of the entire electorate vote Socialist, is solidly anti-
Socialist. (*RT2*, 14–15)

MacDiarmid maintains that the symbiosis of the money monopoly and
Unionism precludes the possibility of a free Scottish Press. Instead of
fighting Scotland's corner, newspaper owners and editors neglect Scottish
opinion for greater economic gain:

> There were twa Robert Bruces.
> Ane edited 'The Glasgow Herald.'
> The ither focht for Scotland
> When it was *less* imperilled.
>
> (*To Circumjack Cencrastus, CP1*, 264)

Writing 'Mr Pooh Bah' for the *Free Man* in 1932, Grieve is no less
scathing of the 'Philistine dictatorship' at the BBC, particularly under the
Scottish Director-Generalship of Sir John Reith (1889–1971) – 'the last
man in the world to be entrusted with anything cultural' (*RT2*, 400).
'Whither Scotland?' from 1931 had bemoaned the 'absence of competent
and responsible control' (*RT2*, 281) of Scottish media by Scots. A year
later, MacDiarmid realises that the root of the problem goes deeper than
individuals such as Reith. Control of mass communications, such as daily
newspapers and the BBC, by a self-interested interpreting class is fundamental not only to the continuance of bourgeois culture and the British
class system but is actually the ideological glue binding the United
Kingdom; one only has to consider 'the BBC personnel – a snobbish set
of young English Public School or University people, or Anglo-Scots of
the same kidney, thoroughly unrepresentative of the great sections of BBC
patrons' (*RT2*, 400) – to understand how this coalescent domination of
class and nation is implemented. In Jean Baudrillard's postmodernity,
'The media are not *co-efficients*, but *effectors* of ideology.'[69] Disaffected
by the deliberate short-circuiting of consciousness that passes for democracy in capitalist public communication mediums, MacDiarmid enacts a
revolutionary intellectual dictatorship of his own.

With *In Memoriam James Joyce* (1955) MacDiarmid institutes the
kind of poetry he wants. Lengthy, highbrow, materialist, this is a nationalist poem committed to 'difficult knowledge' ('The Kind of Poetry I
Want', *CP2*, 1013) and an internationalist's poetic paean to the diversity
of national cultures and languages. Praising a variety of specificities, it is,
none the less, elitist in its sheer length, being impossible to assimilate in
anything like one reading. MacDiarmid was drawn to the writing of epic
poems in part because they would be 'far too long / To be practicable
for any existing medium' (*LP*, 130). If capitalist communication
mediums are corrupt and corrupting then in eschewing such outlets an

oppositional poetry, whilst seemingly elitist, actually presages a radical new order. As MacDiarmid writes in 'Charles Doughty and the Need for Heroic Poetry', 'It is epic – and no lesser form – that equates with the classless society' (*SP*, 126).[70] Such ambitions, however, summon the poem's failures: while it insists on the importance of knowledge to spiritual and political emancipation, the facts that it catalogues are so abstruse as to render their liberatory possibilities negligible to all but the educated few; although it aims to break the imperialist hegemony of English, its 'Vision of a World Language' (written almost entirely in English) is imperiously anti-imperial and necessarily abridged. Perhaps this is saying no more than that the poem is caught on a pin between two eras, that of elitist modernism and a postmodern cultural politics. *In Memoriam James Joyce* uses the tools of an older metaphysical Scotland to propose a post-imperial future. In the tradition of the democratic intellect, the poem's generalist knowledge rejects the capitalistic specialism represented most cruelly in the division of labour – which promotes the parasitical professionalism of the interpreting class – in favour of an autodidactic merging of media. Although the poem is only partly addressed to Joyce, MacDiarmid's use of him as a marker of artistic and ideological valour none the less indicates his own position: the elitism of modernist high art uneasily converging with the revolutionary socialism of a postcolonial politics of place.

'How much knowledge of imaginative literature / Does it need to make a proper man?' asks this self-taught, self-appointed literary expert at the beginning of 'England is Our Enemy' (*CP2*, 858). MacDiarmid's answer combines the elitist claim 'that in each 100,000 souls / Five are reasonably civilised' with the contention that 'literature in Anglo-Saxondom / Has, after growing / More and more provincial, died' (*CP2*, 862) – the class-based culture of the English having torn art from organic connection with the masses. As Alan Riach points out, 'the English ethos' for MacDiarmid 'represents a refusal to engage actively in the inheritance of a people's property'.[71] For this autodidact, to be ignorant of the abundant wealth of world literature is not to be fully human, just as to lack appreciation of the national culture is to be a denationalised provincial – 'that abominable thing, British' ('Backward *Forward*' (1928), *RT2*, 52). True internationalism is that which understands 'the separate glories' of individual nations but recognises equally the cultural indivisibility of 'works going together to make one whole, / And each work being one stone / In a gigantic and imperishable fabric' (*CP2*, 870).

This poem of 'difficult intellectual pleasure' (*CP2*, 751) exemplifies MacDiarmid's belief in the inseparable relationship between nationalism and internationalism. Like Joyce he is committed to a linguistically uncommon literature of complex generalist knowledge, confuting the notion that imperial rule is founded on the cultural superiority of an Anglo-Saxondom purportedly 'More civilised, more virtuous than the rest!' (CP2, 789). Seeking to combat the monopoly wielded by English, the Scot somewhat fancifully claims 'There is no language in the world / That has not yielded me delight' (CP2, 818). Such elitist assertions, however fictitious in actuality, display MacDiarmid's concomitant allegiance to the linguistic diversity of international culture and national political sovereignty: 'A language is / A form of life; but there are many forms of life' (CP2, 799). For such nationalist multiplicity to flourish, however, the false internationalism of monoglot global capitalism that flattens cultural difference through its geographic and economic omnipresence – the McDonaldisation of culture – must be challenged. In this competitive mass culture humans are 'cheaper than safety' (CP2, 840), the dignity of individual difference lost in a world 'Unconcerned about values, / Indifferent to human quality / Or jealous and implacably hostile to it' (840–1).

For MacDiarmid, capitalism is no promise of variety and individual self-realisation; rather, it acts imperialistically to short-circuit the consciousness of individual and national difference. He opposes a capitalist society in which 'Mechanical authoritarianism' has almost extinguished individuality and there is 'everywhere the worship of "efficiency", / Of whatever "works" no matter to what ends' (CP2, 841). In the face of such denial of difference he asserts a 'particularity of vision':

Look! Here and there a pinguicula eloquent of the Alps
Still keeps a purple-blue flower
On the top of its straight and slender stem.
Bog-asphodel, deep-gold, and comely in form,
The queer, almost diabolical, sundew,
And when you leave the bog for the stag moors and the rocks
The parsley fern – a lovelier plant
Than even the proud Osmunda Regalis –
Flourishes in abundance
Showing off oddly contrasted fronds
From the cracks of the lichened stones.
It is pleasant to find the books
Describing it as 'very local.'
Here is a change indeed!
The universal *is* the particular.

(CP2, 845)

The visionary invocation to 'Look!' and see the incalculable and splendid variety of local nature is sharply distinguished from the 'speed-up, the "church work", the lead poisoning / The strain that drives men nuts' (CP2, 840) of a specialised industrial economy where 'Culture is slowly declining' (842) and individuals and nations are blinded to their own singularity by global capitalism.

In this ideological scheme of things 'It is unlikely that man will develop into anything higher' (*CP2*, 842). Just as certain animals that were unable to evolve have vanished for good, so too humans, already 'returning to barbarism', will also 'finally become extinct' (*CP2*, 842) unless they can develop a society that prioritises creativity and knowledge. We are living in 'a world that is barely within / The limits of present human comprehension' (*CP2*, 836) to our short-circuited consciousness and what is needed is a creative evolution merging the materialist findings of science with sparks of spiritual insight in a generalist poetry confronting the contradictions of capitalism with 'the power of conscious reflection' (837). MacDiarmid seeks a 'new species' of humans who are 'intensely organized' and 'In proper balance with a society / Itself in proper ecological balance' (*CP2*, 837). The environmentalism of 'My Songs are Kandym in the Waste Land' will 'curse and strive to combat / The leper pearl of Capitalist culture' (*CP2*, 1142) that renders barren all that it consumes. Such holistic care for the earth indicates the global nature of MacDiarmid's politics, his internationalisation of Scotland through universal concerns: 'Our ideal ethnological method / May be fairly called the ecological one' (*CP2*, 788). MacDiarmid's later work, particularly *In Memoriam*, prefaces a postmodern world in which industrialism not only threatens humanity's relation with itself, as troubled the nineteenth century, but with natural creation.

MacDiarmid's poetry of generalist knowledge resembles Walter Benjamin's almost necessarily incomplete *magnum opus*, *The Arcades Project*. Benjamin's *Illuminations*, first published in Germany in 1955, the same year as *In Memoriam James Joyce*, sheds theoretical light on the modernism and mass culture of late capitalism. *The Arcades Project* is his Herculean attempt to grapple with almost every aspect of 'the Capital of the Nineteenth Century', Paris. For Benjamin, Paris was the centre of nineteenth-century civilisation, the metropolis where material development and cultural excellence collided in an imperial drama of poetry and progress, the city's arcades symbolising the optimism of capitalist invention and the ugly underside of bourgeois aspirations.

A modernist Marxist with mystical inclinations and an unconventional historiographical methodology, Benjamin vastly outdoes even MacDiarmid in his magpie-like propensity for the collection of unattributed quotations: 'This work has to develop to the highest degree the art of citing without quotation marks.'[72] Combining this with the power of personal insight, he builds a 'literary montage' (*AP*, 460) that sheds a piercing sidelight on the cultural history of one of the great imperial powers of the nineteenth century. Similarly to MacDiarmid in *In Memoriam*, Benjamin lets these modernistic fragments speak cryptically for themselves: 'I needn't *say* anything. Merely show' (*AP*, 460). As a Marxist concerned 'to demonstrate a historical materialism which has annihilated within itself the idea of progress' (*AP*, 460) Benjamin understands that the difficulty and fitfulness of such 'knowledge comes only in lightning flashes' (456) that are essentially spiritual in nature. This is reflected in the unfinished, fragmentary nature of a composition dialectically struggling to unearth the cultural history of an era. Benjamin's method of composition finds affinity with that of *In Memoriam*, a generalist poem with a gargantuan, absolutist appetite for 'a vast panoply of knowledge' (*CP2*, 825). For Benjamin 'everything one is thinking at a specific moment in time must at all costs be incorporated into the project then at hand' (*AP*, 456). MacDiarmid mirrors this in his dictionary dredging and newspaper scouring, picking up information wherever he can find it. On the run from the evolutionary end game that is 'intellectual apathy' ('The Kind of Poetry I Want', *CP2*, 1013), he wants

A poetry fully alive to all the implications
Of the fact that one of the great triumphs
Of poetic insight was the way in which
It prepared the minds of many
For the conception of evolution

(CP2, 1027)

As the neglected remnants found in *The Arcades Project* exhume the buried cultural history of a nineteenth century on the capitalist cusp of modernity, so the amassed generalist knowledge of *In Memoriam James Joyce* preludes the paradigmatic shift to a postmodern era just opening as MacDiarmid began the poem in Whalsay. Rejecting Benjamin's metropolitan obsession with Paris, MacDiarmid's global vision is of a world politically and imaginatively decentred through the loss of European imperial control. Benjamin and MacDiarmid were born in the same year, just eight years from the end of a nineteenth century whose fascination for the German as he looked back on it was mingled with foreboding for the future. Dying at his own hands in 1940 before the full horror of the nightmare of history could engulf him, Benjamin did not live to witness global capital's new imperialism, which overruns ancient national barriers and renders obsolete the Marxian dogmas of the 1930s. *In Memoriam James Joyce* is MacDiarmid's endeavour to deal with this change and optimistically oppose the short-circuiting of consciousness that the imperialism of a capitalist new world order brings in its wake.

From the nationalist irrationalism of *A Drunk Man,* through the spiritual communism of the 'Hymns to Lenin' to *In Memoriam James Joyce* the political evolution of MacDiarmid's poetry marks the shift from elitist modernism (indicative of the waning of British imperial control) to the ideal of a postcolonial society. He adjures Scotland to evolve politically as he has done:

> What the Scottish people need above all to-day to realize is that (in keeping with all that is really valuable in their past) static adherence to any particular methodology marks the decline of civilization, for the temporal character of the universe decrees that the only alternative to advance is decay (*LP,* 154).

MacDiarmid wants contemporary Scots to find the dynamic diversity and internationalism of their pre-Union traditions in order to radically free the nation from the cultural and political stagnation of adherence to English metropolitanism and international capital. MacDiarmid's elitism remains pronounced throughout his artistic development. Yet, despite his exasperation at the intellectual level of the universal majority, and a very particular scorn for the national indifferentism of his own folk, MacDiarmid stays true to his elect faith in the evolutionary potential of creative generalist thought and high art to transcend a capitalist order that spiritually enfeebles and politically disenfranchises the masses.

> Clear thought is the quintessence of human life.
> In the end its acid power will disintegrate
> All the force and flummery of current passions and pretences,
> Eat the life out of every false loyalty and craven creed
> And bite its way through to a world of light and truth.
>   ('The Terrible Crystal', *CP2,* 1094)

Notes

1. James Joyce, *A Portrait of the Artist as a Young Man* (London: Paladin, 1990), p. 257.
2. James Joyce, *Letters, vol. II,* ed. Richard Ellmann (London: Faber & Faber, 1966), p. 109.
3. T. S. Eliot, *The Waste Land, Collected Poems 1909–1962* (London: Faber & Faber, 1974), p. 77.
4. Ezra Pound, 'Canto LIII', *Selected Cantos* (Faber & Faber, 1987), p. 67.
5. Christopher Schedler, *Border Modernism: Intercultural Readings in American Literary Modernism* (London & New York: Routledge, 2002), p. xi. Schedler's work belongs to a critical paradigm disputing the metropolitan axis of modernism; see, for instance, Robert Crawford, *Devolving English Literature,* 2nd edn (Edinburgh: Edinburgh University Press, 2000) and Alex Davis and Lee M. Jenkins (eds), *Locations of Literary Modernism:*

Region and Nation in British and American Modernist Poetry (Cambridge: Cambridge University Press, 2000). For a refiguring of modernism from its metropolitan male model see, for instance, Jane Dowson, *Women, Modernism and British Poetry, 1910–1939: Resisting Femininity* (Aldershot: Ashgate, 2002); Bonnie Kime Scott (ed.), *The Gender of Modernism* (Indianapolis: Indiana University Press, 1990).

6. John Carey, *The Intellectuals and the Masses: Pride and Prejudice among the Literary Intelligentsia, 1880–1939* (London: Faber & Faber, 1992), p. 5.
7. Ibid., p. 21.
8. Matthew Arnold, *Culture and Anarchy: An Essay in Political and Social Criticism* (London: Smith, Elder, 1882), pp. 44, 36.
9. Ibid., pp. 81, 80.
10. See Jed Esty, *A Shrinking Island: Modernism and National Culture in England* (Princeton & Oxford: Princeton University Press, 2004), pp. 108–62 for Eliot's attempt to culturally reorient a declining imperial England towards an organic, Tory nationalism.
11. T. S. Eliot, *Notes towards the Definition of Culture* (London: Faber & Faber, 1949), p. 27.
12. Ibid., p. 42.
13. Eliot, *The Waste Land, Collected Poems 1909–1962*, p. 65.
14. Michael Tratner, *Modernism and Mass Politics: Joyce, Woolf, Eliot, Yeats* (Stanford: Stanford University Press, 1995), p. 3.
15. See Peter Ackroyd, *T. S. Eliot* (Harmondsworth: Penguin, 1993), pp. 109–130.
16. Palinurus [Cyril Connolly], *The Unquiet Grave* (London: Hamish Hamilton, 1945), p. 17.
17. Ibid., p. 17.
18. W. H. Auden, 'Psychology and Art To-day', *The English Auden: Poems, Essays and Dramatic Writings 1927–1939*, ed. Edward Mendelson (London: Faber & Faber, 1986), p. 334.
19. Ibid., p. 334.
20. Hamish Henderson's phrase 'Self-elected Elect' has been borrowed from his letter to *The Scotsman*, 21 February 1968 (part of his '1320 Club Flyting' with MacDiarmid), in Alec Finlay (ed.), *The Armstrong Nose: Selected Letters of Hamish Henderson* (Edinburgh: Polygon, 1996), p. 164.
21. David McCrone, *Understanding Scotland: The Sociology of a Stateless Nation* (London & New York: Routledge, 1998), p. 90.
22. Ibid., p. 91.
23. W. N. Herbert, *To Circumjack MacDiarmid: The Poetry and Prose of Hugh MacDiarmid* (Oxford: Clarendon Press, 1992), pp. 224–5.
24. Edward Moore, *We Moderns: Enigmas and Guesses* (London: George Allen & Unwin, 1918).
25. Bruce Detwiler, *Nietzsche and the Politics of Aristocratic Radicalism* (Chicago & London: University of Chicago Press, 1990), p. 171.
26. Ibid., p. 174.
27. Ibid., p. 113.
28. Nietzsche, cited in Detwiler, p. 104.
29. Edwin Muir, 'A Note on Friedrich Nietzsche', *Latitudes* (New York: B. W. Huebsch, 1924), p. 86.

30. John Burt Foster, Jr., *Heirs to Dionysus: A Nietzschean Current in Literary Modernism* (Princeton, NJ, & Guildford, Surrey: Princeton University Press, 1981), p. 42.
31. Friedrich Nietzsche, *A Nietzsche Reader*, trans. R. J. Hollingdale (Harmondsworth: Penguin, 1977), pp. 232, 235.
32. Peter McCarey, *Hugh MacDiarmid and the Russians* (Edinburgh: Scottish Academic Press, 1987), p. 31.
33. Fyodor Dostoyevsky, *Notes from Underground / The Double*, trans. Jessie Coulson ([1864 / 1846] Harmondsworth: Penguin, 1972), p. 16.
34. See Jean-Paul Sartre, *The Family Idiot: Gustave Flaubert*, 4 vols., trans. Carol Cosman (Chicago: University of Chicago, 1991). Sartre accuses Flaubert of reneging on the revolutionary principles of his Romantic youth to become the ultimate bourgeois; once an advocate of peasant uprising, on return from Siberian exile Dostoevsky became a conservative nationalist.
35. Tom Nairn, *The Break-Up of Britain: Crisis and Neo-Nationalism* (London: New Left Books, 1977), p. 169.
36. James Harvey Robinson, *The Mind in the Making: The Relation of Intelligence to Social Reform* (London: Watts, 1934); all further references in the text as *MM*.
37. According to Robert Service, after the October Revolution 'Lenin appeared as a Soviet Christ: superhuman powers were attributed to him', *Lenin: A Biography* (London: Macmillan, 2000), p. 394.
38. V. I. Lenin, *What is to be Done?* trans Joe Finesberg and George Hanna, ed. Robert Service (London: Penguin, 1989), p. 91; all further references in the text as *WD*.
39. Lenin, cited in Jonathan Glover, *Humanity: A Moral History of the Twentieth Century* (London: Pimlico, 2001), p. 278.
40. Robin Blick, *The Seeds of Evil: Lenin and the Origins of Bolshevik Élitism* (London: Steyne, 1995), p. 50.
41. See Liam McIlvanney, *Burns the Radical: Poetry and Politics in Late Eighteenth-Century Scotland* (East Linton: Tuckwell, 2002), pp. 189–219 for Burns's reaction to the French Revolution.
42. David Howell, *A Lost Left: Three Studies in Socialism and Nationalism* (Manchester: Manchester University Press, 1986), p. 193.
43. Henderson, *The Armstrong Nose*, p. 42.
44. Henderson claims that MacDiarmid is here 'quoting an unsigned article in the TLS', *The Armstrong Nose*, p. 166.
45. Antonio Gramsci, *Selections from the Prison Notebooks*, eds and trans. Quintin Hoare and Geoffrey Nowell Smith (London: Lawrence and Wishart, 1998), p. 9; all further references in the text as *PN*.
46. Luciano Pellicani, *Gramsci: An Alternative Communism?* (Stanford: Hoover Institution Press, 1976), p. 32.
47. Julien Benda, *The Treason of the Intellectuals*, trans. Richard Aldington ([1928] New York & London: Norton, 1969), p. 75.
48. Christopher Harvie, *Scotland: A Short History* (Oxford: Oxford University Press, 2002), pp. 228, 188.
49. John Buchan, *Memory Hold-the-Door* (London: Hodder & Stoughton, 1940), pp. 183–4.
50. Ibid., p. 184.

51. James Peck (ed.), *The Chomsky Reader* (London: Serpent's Tail, 1995), p. 35.
52. Ibid., p. 35.
53. Herbert Read, *To Hell with Culture, and Other Essays on Art and Society* (London: Routledge & Kegan Paul, 1963), p. 10; all further references in the text as *HC*.
54. Alan Sinfield, *Literature, Politics and Culture in Postwar Britain* (London & Atlantic Highlands, NJ: Athlone Press, 1997), pp. 28–9.
55. Andreas Huyssen, *After the Great Divide: Modernism, Mass Culture, Postmodernism* (London: Macmillan, 1988).
56. Lawrence Rainey, *Institutions of Modernism: Literary Elites and Public Culture* (New Haven & London: Yale University Press, 1998), p. 3.
57. See Alan Bloom, *The Closing of the American Mind: How Higher Education Has Failed and Impoverished the Souls of Today's Students* (New York: Simon & Schuster, 1987); also, Roger Kimball, *Tenured Radicals: How Politics Has Corrupted Our Higher Education* (New York: Harper Row, 1990).
58. Thomas Strychacz, *Modernism, Mass Culture and Professionalism* (Cambridge: Cambridge University Press, 1993), p. 5.
59. Joyce Piell Wexler, *Who Paid for Modernism? Art, Money, and the Fiction of Conrad, Joyce, and Lawrence* (Fayetteville: University of Arkansas Press, 1997), p. xii.
60. Karl Mannheim, *Essays on the Sociology of Culture* ([1956] London: Routledge, 1992), p. 117.
61. George Konrád and Ivan Szelényi, *The Intellectuals on the Road to Class Power*, trans. Andrew Arato and Richard E. Allen (Brighton: Harvester Press, 1979), pp. 22–3.
62. Ibid., p. 33.
63. T. W. Adorno, *The Culture Industry: Selected Essays on Mass Culture*, ed. J. M. Bernstein (London & New York: Routledge, 2001), p. 95.
64. Ibid., pp. 99.
65. Herbert Marcuse, *One-Dimensional Man: Studies in the Ideology of Advanced Industrial Society* (London: Routledge & Kegan Paul, 1964), pp. xii, 50.
66. Hugh MacDiarmid, 'Introduction' to Oliver Brown, *Witdom: Essaygrams – An Extension of 'The Extended Tongue'* ([1953] Glasgow: Piper Books, 1969), pp. 7–8.
67. Alan Swingewood, *The Myth of Mass Culture* (London: Macmillan, 1977), p. 119.
68. F. R. Leavis, *Mass Civilisation and Minority Culture* (St John's College, Cambridge: The Minority Press, 1930), p. 3.
69. Jean Baudrillard, *For a Critique of the Political Economy of the Sign*, trans. Charles Levin (St Louis: Telos Press, 1981), p. 169.
70. See Alan Riach, *Hugh MacDiarmid's Epic Poetry* (Edinburgh: Edinburgh University Press, 1991) for an extended discussion of this point.
71. Ibid., p. 123.
72. Walter Benjamin, *The Arcades Project*, trans Howard Eiland and Kevin McLaughlin (London & Cambridge, MA: The Belknap Press of Harvard University Press, 2002), p. 458; all further references in the text as *AP*.

Index